COGNITIVE BEHAVIORAL THERAPY FOR PERINATAL DISTRESS

Countless studies have established the efficacy of cognitive behavioral therapy (CBT) for many manifestations of depression and anxiety. In *Cognitive Behavioral Therapy for Perinatal Distress*, Wenzel and Kleiman discuss the benefits of CBT for pregnant and postpartum women who suffer from anxiety and depression. The myths of CBT as rigid and intrusive are shattered as the authors describe its flexible application for perinatal women. This text teaches practitioners how to successfully integrate CBT structure and strategy into a supportive approach in working with this population. The examples used in the book will be familiar to postpartum specialists, making this an easily comprehensive and useful resource.

Amy Wenzel, PhD, ABPP, is author and editor of fifteen books, many of which are on perinatal psychology or cognitive behavioral therapy. She lectures internationally on issues relevant to mental health and psychotherapy and provides ongoing supervision to clinical psychologists, social workers, and psychiatric nurses.

Karen Kleiman, MSW, LCSW, is a well-known international expert on postpartum depression. She is founder of The Postpartum Stress Center, a premier treatment and professional training center for prenatal and postpartum depression and anxiety. She has written several books on perinatal distress.

COGNITIVE BEHAVIORAL THERAPY FOR PERINATAL DISTRESS

Amy Wenzel
with
Karen Kleiman

NEW YORK AND LONDON

First published 2015
by Routledge
711 Third Avenue, New York, NY 10017

and by Routledge
27 Church Road, Hove, East Sussex BN3 2FA

Routledge is an imprint of the Taylor & Francis Group, an informa business

Library of Congress Cataloging-in-Publication Data
Wenzel, Amy.
Cognitive behavioral therapy for perinatal distress / Amy Wenzel, Karen Kleiman.
    pages cm
  1. Postpartum psychiatric disorders—Treatment. 2. Puerperium—Psychological aspects. 3. Pregnancy—Psychological aspects. 4. Postnatal care—Psychological aspects. 5. Cognitive therapy. I. Kleiman, Karen R. II. Title.
RG850.W46   2014
618.7'6075—dc23   2014008841

ISBN: 978-0-415-50804-9 (hbk)
ISBN: 978-0-415-50805-6 (pbk)
ISBN: 978-1-315-76910-3 (ebk)

Typeset in Sabon
by Apex CoVantage, LLC

CONTENTS

FIGURES

FOREWORD

Amy Wenzel and I were first introduced at the University of Pennsylvania, where we met with two colleagues to join forces on behalf of postpartum women. The four of us convened to contribute to what developed into a new screening tool for postpartum women. I confess I was simultaneously impressed and intimidated by the level of academic prowess surrounding me. I can usually hold my ground by maintaining eye contact and listening with fierce determination, but frankly, every time Amy spoke, I was struck by how little I thought I knew. It was then I first realized how differently our brains worked. When she asked me to join her for coffee after the meeting, I promptly donned my grown-up hat so as not to reveal my hesitation about engaging in a private dialogue with her. After all, being twenty years her senior, how dare she already have published fourteen books and authored 100 peer-reviewed journal articles? Really? How could I possibly expect to hold a respectable conversation with her? That's when I pulled out my Oprah card. *"You were on the Oprah Show?!"* she gasped, with amazement, like a school girl. Now, we could talk.

While individually, we claimed success and integrity in our accomplishments, we each wanted a taste of what the other had developed so well. She hoped to break into the self-help book market and move her scholarly work toward a more general audience, while I sought greater authority within the academic community.

Amy can rattle off statistics from current research like I can recite my shopping list in my head while I'm going down the grocery aisles. The obvious difference is that I'm thinking about eggs and broccoli; she is thinking about randomized clinical trials, pragmatic clusters, and the regulation of GABA receptors in affective disorders. Sometimes I pretend to know what she's talking about lest I give myself away and she regrets ever deciding to work with me! But truth be told, we each possess strengths that complement the other and when we combine our areas of expertise, we realize we have a great deal to learn from each other.

One thing is indisputable. Amy's proficiency in the field of cognitive behavioral therapy (CBT) is unmatched. She is a master scholar, a frequently-sought-out expert in the field, trained by the father of CBT, Dr Aaron Beck, and when she isn't helping clients change their lives for the better, she is teaching therapists how to apply these skills to their clinical work. I loved the idea of incorporating Amy's expert knowledge and utilization of CBT as a treatment option at The Postpartum Stress Center. To my delight, she affiliated with us, which afforded us the perfect place to send our pregnant and postpartum moms when we determined that CBT would be the best treatment choice.

But there was one problem. I was not convinced that CBT was a great option for the majority of women in our practice who suffered significant levels of distress. Amy had some work to do to convince me that a pregnant or postpartum woman would appreciate and benefit from the CBT model. I was concerned it was too structured, too didactic, too rigid, with too much talking and way too much homework. Perhaps most important to me, I truly believed it went against the grain of my fundamental premise that "holding" (Kleiman, 2009) postpartum women is the key to healing. The therapeutic relationship is paramount and that CBT would be too much work could interfere with that somehow. I worried that CBT would feel intrusive and counterintuitive both to me, and to the women I treat, at least at the height of their suffering.

Amy immediately refuted my apprehension and claimed I simply didn't have all the information. She explained that CBT is flexible and the construction of CBT interventions accommodates beautifully to the specific needs of the client and absolutely embraced the therapeutic relationship as a vital component. Even so, when Routledge asked us to write a book for their CBT series, Amy jumped at the idea and I thought, well, here's a challenge, how do we really make this work for the perinatal population? How do we modify the strategies and tweak the interventions on behalf of pregnant and postpartum women? Can we preserve the psychodynamic and supportive perspective that drives much of my work? I felt like we were attempting to put a square block into a round hole. This is when I basically sat back and watched Amy do her magic. In *Cognitive Behavioral Therapy for Perinatal Distress*, Amy brilliantly teaches practitioners how to successfully integrate CBT skills into their practice, always taking into account the unique needs of pregnant and postpartum women. She was right, I didn't have all the information.

Cognitive Behavioral Therapy for Perinatal Distress did two things for me. First, it validated what I suspected all along—I was already practicing aspects of CBT with my clients, I just wasn't calling it that. Like so many other interventions that I think I'm making up or grabbing from my bag of good instincts, I have been helping women reframe their negative thinking for decades. It is precisely what needs to be done when a pregnant or postpartum woman surrenders to the overwhelming and misguided negative bias that permeates her thoughts. CBT is a hands-on, practical approach to problem solving, which is both appealing to, and essential for, recovery from any postpartum emotional illness. In this book, Amy provides the tools and exquisite vignettes that help the clinician see exactly what needs to be said in response to the faulty thinking that is so pervasive in the perinatal population. She offers specific treatment strategies and a script to go along with them so the reader can experience first hand how the interactions might take place. In this way, Amy superbly brings these theoretical constructs to life. The women she follows throughout the pages of this book will seem familiar to any postpartum specialist, making it an incredibly useful resource.

The second valuable lesson I learned from *Cognitive Behavioral Therapy for Perinatal Distress* is that CBT works. Pregnant and postpartum women respond well to the proactive style, the structured, time-limited commitment to treatment, and the tangible focus of CBT. Whereas I previously believed that CBT would be too much work for a tired mom encumbered by symptoms, I am now certain that moms who struggle with problematic beliefs and faulty thinking will be relieved by the collaborative effort to reduce the distress associated with those thoughts. The reader will see how carefully and purposively Amy pays attention to the distinct nature of perinatal symptoms and adapts the expectations and coping strategies accordingly.

With greater emphasis being placed on non-pharmacologic interventions for perinatal depression and anxiety, women and their treating practitioners are seeking good, effective approaches that they can count on for symptom relief. *Cognitive Behavioral Therapy for Perinatal Distress* provides the evidence, the tools, and the techniques to accomplish this. Amy has succeeded in blending her years of CBT research with her clinical work and offers it as a practical and effective protocol for the treatment of perinatal depression and anxiety. She has rounded off the corners and shown me that the block does indeed fit into the round hole. You just have to know what you are doing. Thank you, Amy. Now I know.

Karen Kleiman
Founder, The Postpartum Stress Center, LLC
Author, *Therapy and the Postpartum Woman*

1

PERINATAL DISTRESS

An Overview

It is increasingly being recognized that the transition to parenthood is difficult and is associated with significant stress that can put women at risk of mental health problems. Although a newborn can bring much joy and fulfillment to one's life, there is no getting around the fact that, for many women, pregnancy is fraught with discomfort and excruciating uncertainty, and that the postpartum period brings overwhelming sleep deprivation, fatigue, and emotional ups and downs. Moreover, perhaps like no other event in one's life, the process of becoming a mother makes one critically examine core values and beliefs and can change her sense of self. When the transition to parenthood is difficult, this shift can feel unwanted and scary. Common sentiments expressed by women who seek treatment for distress during the perinatal period are, "I don't feel like myself" and "I can't imagine ever feeling normal again."

Although postpartum depression has received a great deal of attention for many years in research literature and in the media, more recently, it has been recognized that anxiety is a significant manifestation of postpartum distress in its own right (Wenzel, 2011). There is increasing awareness that clinically significant expressions of depression and anxiety are not limited to the postpartum period. Many women experience depression and anxiety during pregnancy, which has the potential to affect self-care and care of the developing fetus (e.g., attendance at prenatal visits, use of alcohol or drugs; Lobel, Dunkel-Schetter, & Scrimshaw, 1992). This recognition led the developers of the *Diagnostic and Statistical Manual, 5th Edition* (DSM-5) (American Psychiatric Association, 2013) to change the "with postpartum onset" specifier associated with the diagnosis of major depressive disorder to "with perinatal onset," defined as the onset of depression during pregnancy or in the first four weeks following childbirth.

Although the DSM-5 recognizes the onset of postpartum depression only within the first four weeks following childbirth, many perinatal experts define postpartum depression as occurring at any time during the first year following childbirth (e.g., C. T. Beck & Driscoll, 2006).

1

For example, women may experience an increase in distress when they return to work, which often occurs 8 to 12 weeks following childbirth. Moreover, some researchers have indicated that breastfeeding protects against some manifestations of emotional distress, as some hormones remain elevated in order to stimulate milk production (Klein, Skrobala, & Garfinkel, 1995). Because many women choose to nurse their infants for at least six months, according to the guidelines put forth by the World Health Organisation (WHO, 2003), it follows that some women may exhibit signs of emotional distress several months after the birth of their child when they discontinue breastfeeding. This is particularly true if they wean abruptly.

This book describes the application of a well-established psychotherapeutic approach to the treatment of *perinatal distress*, defined as the experience of depression and/or anxiety during pregnancy or within the first postpartum year. Depression is a fairly circumscribed construct; the symptoms that contribute to a diagnosis of major depressive disorder are: (a) depressed mood more of the time than not; (b) anhedonia, or the loss of interest in previously enjoyable activities; (c) appetite disturbance; (d) sleep disturbance; (e) psychomotor disturbance; (f) fatigue; (g) a sense of worthlessness or inappropriate guilt; (h) concentration difficulties or indecisiveness; and (i) suicidal ideation (APA, 2013). Diagnosing depression in perinatal women can be difficult, as many of the symptoms (e.g., sleep disturbance, fatigue) can also be attributable to being pregnant or to having a newborn. The key feature in establishing a diagnosis of major depressive disorder in a perinatal woman is that the symptoms must be in excess of that which are expected by her life circumstances (Wenzel, 2011).

In contrast, perinatal anxiety is more diffuse and can have many manifestations, defined as follows:

- *Generalized anxiety*: Generalized anxiety is excessive, uncontrollable worry associated with the following symptoms: (a) restlessness; (b) fatigue; (c) concentration difficulties; (d) irritability; (e) muscle tension; and (f) sleep disturbance. In order to meet the criteria for a diagnosis of generalized anxiety disorder (GAD), a person must report these symptoms more days than not for a period of at least six months (APA, 2013). Perinatal women who report a shorter duration of worry are diagnosed with adjustment disorder with anxious mood (Matthey, Barnett, Howie, & Kavanagh, 2003).
- *Panic attacks*: A panic attack is a sudden onset of intense fear or discomfort that peaks within several minutes. Characteristic symptoms of panic attacks include: (a) heart palpitations; (b) sweating; (c) trembling; (d) shortness of breath; (e) a sensation of choking; (f) chest pain or tightness; (g) gastrointestinal distress; (h) dizziness

or lightheadedness; (i) chills or hot flashes; (j) tingling or numbness; (k) derealization or depersonalization; (l) a fear of losing control or going crazy; and (m) a fear of dying during the episode. A person is diagnosed with panic disorder when she has recurrent panic attacks accompanied by persistent worry about having the attacks or a change in behavior because of the attacks (e.g., avoiding circumstances that are perceived as prompting the attacks; APA, 2013).

- *Social anxiety*: Social anxiety is excessive fear of negative evaluation by others or embarrassment in front of others. A diagnosis of social anxiety disorder is made when the person goes to great lengths to avoid social or evaluative situations, or endures them with great distress, and when the social anxiety causes significant life interference or subjective distress (APA, 2013).
- *Obsessions and compulsions*: Obsessions are unwanted, intrusive thoughts, often of a disturbing nature. Compulsions are mental or behavioral rituals that a person performs, often to neutralize the anxiety associated with obsessions. In order to be diagnosed with obsessive compulsive disorder (OCD), the obsessions or compulsions must be time consuming (i.e., take up at least one hour per day), cause life interference, or cause clinically significant distress (APA, 2013).
- *Posttraumatic stress*: Posttraumatic stress is emotional distress resulting from exposure to actual or threatened death, serious injury, or sexual violence. Many women perceive childbirth to be traumatic, as they fear that they or their child will die during childbirth. A person is diagnosed with posttraumatic stress disorder when he or she has had exposure to a traumatic event, as defined above, and experiences symptoms in the realms of: (a) re-experiencing the trauma (e.g., through intrusive memories); (b) avoidance of memories or reminders of the trauma; (c) negative effects on mood or cognition (e.g., lack of interest in meaningful activities, detachment from others); and (d) increase in arousal and reactivity (e.g., irritability, hypervigilance) for at least one month (APA, 2013). If a person experiences these symptoms immediately after the trauma, but they have not yet persisted for one month, then he or she is diagnosed with acute stress disorder.

Many mental health practitioners question when to make a diagnosis of one of these mental health disorders. After all, the transition to parenthood is one of substantial adjustment, and surely most new mothers experience some emotional lability as their hormone levels drop to their pre-pregnancy levels. Research does, indeed, support this observation. The *postpartum blues* is a transient mood disturbance experienced by 40–80% of new mothers, characterized by a few days of tearfulness, mood swings, and insomnia (Buttner, O'Hara, & Watson, 2012). The key in this definition is the word "transient"; if these symptoms persist for at least two weeks out of a month then a diagnosis of major depressive disorder should be considered. In addition to the duration of symptoms, a diagnosis of a depressive, anxiety, obsessive compulsive-related, or trauma or stressor-related disorder should be considered if the woman is experiencing life interference or substantial emotional distress. The most salient example of life interference in perinatal women is difficulty caring for the newborn or for older children in the household. This does not mean that asking for help is diagnostic of perinatal distress, as cognitive behavioral therapists encourage perinatal women to seek assistance with child care in order to maintain optimal self-care during the transition to parenthood. However, when a woman is having trouble providing consistent care, avoiding providing child care, or letting essential duties slip, she meets the criteria for life interference associated with her emotional distress.

Features of Perinatal Distress

Women who experience perinatal distress are usually quite concerned about their emotional state. They want to know whether what they are experiencing is normal, whether they are going crazy, and whether their children would be better off being raised by somebody else. Although entire books can be written about the features of perinatal distress, this section describes some highlights from the empirical literature about the prevalence, risk factors for, and consequences and cost of perinatal emotional distress. The important message is that perinatal distress is common and understandable in light of many vulnerability factors that put women at risk of emotional distress in times of stress, such as the transition to parenthood (see also Chapter 2). It is a significant public health problem, as untreated emotional distress is associated with adverse effects in children and lost work days.

Prevalence

The majority of studies examining the prevalence of perinatal emotional distress have focused on postpartum depression. When postpartum depression is defined as major and minor depression, the prevalence has been estimated at 19.2%; when only cases of major depression are considered, then the prevalence has been estimated at 7.2% (Gavin et al., 2005). Even though the rates are high, there is only weak evidence that the perinatal period represents a time of increased risk for depression, relative to other times in women's lives (O'Hara & McCabe, 2013), although a small body of literature suggests that there is a subset of women who are particularly vulnerable to develop postpartum depression, relative to depression at other times in their lives (e.g., Bloch et al., 2000; Forty et al., 2006).

Studies have also investigated the prevalence of various manifestations of perinatal anxiety. Those rates are as follows:

- *GAD*: Results from some studies suggest that the rates of GAD are elevated in pregnant (10.5%; Adewuya, Ola, Aloba, & Mapayi, 2006) and postpartum (8.2% at 8 weeks, 7.7% at 6 months, 7.0% at 12 months; Wenzel, Haugen, Jackson, & Brendle, 2005) women, relative to rates between 1% and 3% in women representative of the general population (Jacobi et al., 2004). However, it must be acknowledged that other studies have reported low rates of GAD in perinatal samples (e.g., 0.6%; Navarro et al., 2008).
- *Panic disorder*: Research shows that the prevalence of panic disorder during pregnancy is elevated (5.2%; Adewuya et al., 2006; 2.5%; Guler et al., 2008) relative to the rate of panic disorder in women representative of the general population (1.3%; Jacobi et al., 2004). In contrast, the rate of panic disorder in the postpartum period is similar (1.4%; Wenzel et al., 2005) to that observed in women representative of the general population (Jacobi et al., 2004).
- *Social anxiety disorder*: There is a paucity of research that has examined the prevalence of social anxiety disorder in perinatal women. In one exception, Adewuya et al. (2006) reported that 6.4% of women in their third trimester of pregnancy met criteria for social anxiety disorder, relative to 1.7% of non-pregnant women. Wenzel et al. (2005) found prevalence of 4.1%, not appreciably different from rates of up to 5.2% in women representative of the general population (Magee, Eaton, Wittchen, McGonagle, & Kessler, 1996). Although these results might suggest that social anxiety is not particularly problematic for perinatal women, particularly those who are postpartum, Wenzel (2011) noted cases of women who reported a postpartum onset of social anxiety that was associated with isolation from friends (especially friends without children) and marital dissatisfaction that was beyond the typical dissatisfaction that accompanies the transition to parenthood.
- *OCD*: A recent meta-analysis found that the risk for OCD during pregnancy (2.07%) and the postpartum period (2.43%) was elevated relative to the risk at other times in a woman's life (1.08%; Russell, Fawcett, & Mazmanian, 2013). Moreover, research by Jonathan Abramowitz and his colleagues suggests that at least two-thirds of new mothers, if not more, experience upsetting intrusive thoughts about harm coming to their infants (e.g., Abramowitz, Schwartz, & Moore, 2003).

5

- *PTSD*: Approximately one-third of women report that they had a stressful childbirth experience (Creedy, Shochet, & Horsfall, 2000), and 10–15% of women describe having fear that they or their baby will die during delivery (Lyons, 1998). Studies using responses to PTSD checklists to diagnose PTSD have reported that between 3% (Czarnocka & Slade, 2000) and almost 6% (Creedy et al., 2000) report clinically significant symptoms of posttraumatic stress.

Taken together, the implications of these rates are staggering. We cannot simply add the rates to obtain an overall estimate of the prevalence of perinatal distress, as these manifestations of emotional distress often co-occur. Nevertheless, we can make a conservative estimate that 10–15% of perinatal women meet diagnostic criteria for one or more depressive, anxiety, obsessive compulsive-related, or trauma- or stressor-related disorder. Each year, there are approximately 4 million births in the United States (*www.susps.org/overview/birthrates.html*; M. Martin et al., 2009). This means that approximately 400,000 to 600,000 women meet diagnostic criteria for one of these disorders each year. This number does not account for the significant numbers of women who report sub-syndromal symptoms of these disorders, or symptoms that do not reach the threshold for a diagnosis, but are concerning to women and noticeable to their significant others (cf. Wenzel, 2011). It also does not account for emotional distress in women who experience pregnancy loss or infertility. Thus, there is a clear need for healthcare services that detect perinatal distress, can effectively treat it in women who experience it, and prevent it in women who are at risk of it. A foundation for treatment and prevention packages is described in this book.

Risk Factors

Investigation of the factors that put women at risk of perinatal anxiety are still in their infancy, but many studies have been conducted that identify factors that put women at risk of postpartum depression. Results from these studies have been aggregated into several meta-analyses (C. T. Beck, 2001; O'Hara & Swain, 1996; Robertson, Grace, Wallington, & Stewart, 2004). The most significant risk factors for postpartum depression that emerged from these meta-analyses include a history of depression, depression and anxiety during pregnancy, a neurotic personality style, low self-esteem, life stress, a poor partner relationship, and a low level of social support. A history of depression, an episode of emotional distress that is already in place, a neurotic personality style, and low self-esteem can function as vulnerabilities to emotional distress during major life transitions. Additional life stress, a poor partner relationship, and a low level of social support could exacerbate the stress associated with the transition to parenthood all the more. Other risk factors identified by these meta-analyses include low socioeconomic status (SES), which is often associated with financial difficulties and pressures, being single, having an unwanted pregnancy, obstetric complications, and a difficult infant temperament. It is not difficult to imagine how these factors would present challenges during the transition to parenthood.

One life stressor that has received increasing attention by researchers is the effect of intimate partner violence (IPV) on postpartum adjustment. IPV is defined as "physical violence, sexual violence, threats of physical/sexual violence, and psychological/emotional abuse perpetrated by a current or former spouse, common-law spouse, non-marital dating partners, or boyfriends/girlfriends of the same of opposite sex" (Chang et al., 2005). According to a systematic review by Beydoun, Beydoun, Kaufman, Lo, and Zonderman (2012), studies have found that between 4% and 44% of women have experienced physical, sexual, and/or emotional abuse in the past year. When they pooled results from 37 studies into a meta-analysis (see more about meta-analysis in Chapter 3), they determined that the risk of postpartum depression was 1.81 times greater in women who were exposed to IPV, compared to women who were not exposed to IPV. Clearly, IPV is a significant stressor that not only has the potential to disrupt the transition to parenthood, but also put the woman and fetus or infant at risk of harm. IPV is receiving an increasing amount of attention in both the research literature and in clinical practice, and we strongly encourage therapists to assess for its presence as they begin work with perinatal clients.

Consequences

Although emotional distress is associated with impaired functioning and personal suffering at any time in a person's life, it is particularly concerning in the perinatal period, when women have an infant (and possibly other young children) for whom they care. Research shows that postpartum depression is associated with a host of negative infant and child outcomes, such as poor cognitive functioning, insecure attachment, and emotional and social maladjustment (see Murray & Cooper, 2003, for a comprehensive review). For example, studies have demonstrated that postpartum depression is associated with impaired ability in child care practices such as putting infants down to sleep, using car seats correctly, and attending well-child visits (Field, 2010; Zajicek-Farber, 2009), as well as diminished responsiveness to infants (e.g., Beebe et al., 2008; Stanley, Murray, & Stein, 2004). Postpartum depression has been linked with behavioral problems that span from early childhood through to adolescence (Avan, Richter, Ramchandani, Norris, & Stein, 2010; Murray et al., 2011), as well as cognitive impairment (e.g., poorer language and IQ development; Grace, Evindar, & Stewart, 2003). These findings would understandably be alarming to any new mother who is experiencing emotional distress.

However, it is important to acknowledge that some scholars have concluded the chronicity of depression is more significant in explaining these results than the timing of depression (Sohr-Preston & Scaramella, 2006). Thus, early intervention for perinatal distress has the potential to shorten the length of the episode and reduce the likelihood of future episodes, thereby limiting the child's exposure to maternal emotional distress. In other words, although these findings should be taken seriously, they do not guarantee that children will be affected by a woman's episode of perinatal distress.

Treatment of Perinatal Distress

This cursory overview of the literature suggests that perinatal distress is widespread and that it has the potential to be associated with adverse consequences to the mother and child alike. Thus, it is the duty of healthcare professionals to develop and refine treatment approaches that can reduce the devastation that it causes to women, children, and families. Research shows that most perinatal women prefer psychotherapy over pharmacotherapy (Battle, & Salisbury, Schofield, & Ortiz-Hernandez, 2013; Pearlstein et al., 2006), as it is logical that they would have concerns about the effects of taking medication during pregnancy or while breastfeeding. Fortunately, there are well-established psychotherapies with demonstrated efficacy in treating depression and anxiety.

Let us start with consideration of perhaps the most well-established psychotherapy for perinatal depression—Interpersonal Psychotherapy (IPT; Weissman, Markowitz, & Klerman, 2000). IPT is a short-term (e.g., 16 sessions), time-limited approach to psychotherapy that is rooted in psychodynamic theory but focuses on interpersonal distress in the present. Therapists work with their patients on current interpersonal distress in one or more of the following domains: (a) role transitions; (b) role disputes; and (c) unresolved grief. Clients begin to understand their psychiatric distress in the context of their interpersonal relationships and make tangible gains in approaching their relationships with increased balance, formulating reasonable expectations of their relationships as well as for their own role in their relationships, and communicating effectively. IPT has been embraced wholeheartedly by the community of scholars who research treatments for perinatal distress, who reasoned that IPT would have particularly strong face validity for perinatal women who are facing the transition to parenthood, and hence, a major transition in their roles that has the potential to be associated with conflict in their close relationships. In a landmark study of a community sample of women with postpartum depression, O'Hara, Stuart, Gorman, and Wenzel (2000) found that IPT was associated with significantly greater reductions in interviewer-rated and self-reported symptoms of depression and significantly greater improvements in social functioning relative to a waiting list control condition. Spinelli and Endicott (2003) extended IPT for postpartum depression to antenatal depression and found that it was more efficacious than a parenting education program in reducing interviewer-rated and self-reported symptoms of depression. Moreover, IPT has been adapted into a culturally sensitive brief format for inner-city, low-income women with impressive results (Grote, Bledsoe, Swartz, & Frank, 2004).

There is no question that IPT is a sound option in treating women with perinatal depression, as its evidence base is impressive. It is important to acknowledge that there is another short-term, time-sensitive approach to therapy that has an even greater evidence base supporting its efficacy in treating a wide range of manifestations of emotional distress in treatment seeking adults. This therapy is called *cognitive behavioral therapy* (CBT). CBT is an active, problem-focused approach to treatment that has its roots in the basic theory that cognition, the way in which people think about their life circumstances, plays a large role in their emotional state and their subsequent behavioral choices (see more extensive information about cognitive behavioral theory in Chapter 2). CBT is a *collaborative* enterprise, such that the therapist and client are regarded as equal members of a team, and the client takes substantial ownership over the direction of the course of treatment. CBT uses Socratic questions to create an environment of *guided discovery*, whereby the therapist uses guided questioning to stimulate critical thinking so that the client draws her own conclusions and devises her own solutions, rather than being told what to do by the therapist. Using guided discovery, cognitive behavioral therapists help clients to: (a) see the relation between their thinking, mood, and behavior; (b) develop skills to evaluate their thinking in order to view their life circumstances as accurately and helpfully as possible; (c) engage in healthy behaviors that promote optimum mental health; and (d) develop the ability to tolerate uncertainty, discomfort, and adversity that people invariably experience in life. It is hoped that clients develop a sound understanding of principles of cognitive and behavioral change, as well as skill in applying strategies that achieve these principles, so that they no longer need therapy and can manage emotional distress on their own.

CBT has the potential to be another good match for perinatal women who are seeking treatment for emotional distress. It is a time-sensitive therapy, meaning that clients enter treatment with the understanding that there will be an endpoint and that, eventually, they will have acquired the ability to cope with emotional distress without the help of a professional. Many courses of CBT that have been reviewed in the empirical literature are 12 or 16 sessions long, and one study found that many clients showed substantial improvement in as few as four sessions (Hirsch, Jolley, & Williams, 2000). A time-sensitive course of treatment is desirable for clients, like perinatal women, who are juggling multiple demands in their lives and who often have difficulty scheduling and attending appointments. Cognitive behavioral therapists hope that their clients will take home something tangible from each session, whether that something tangible is a skill, a new way of viewing their life circumstances, or a solution to a problem. In other words, its problem focus in the here-and-now has the potential to help perinatal women to feel better immediately by coaching them to use tangible tools and strategies to manage emotional distress and solve life problems.

There are two potential advantages that CBT has over IPT. First, as is described in Chapter 3, there is a vast literature that establishes CBT's efficacy for anxiety, obsessive compulsive-related, and trauma- and stressor-related disorders. IPT was developed to treat depression, and it has since been adapted to treat other manifestations of emotional distress, such as panic disorder, social anxiety disorder, and PTSD (for a summary, see Wenzel, 2014a). Nevertheless, there is a much greater evidence base for the use of CBT for anxiety-based manifestations of emotional distress, and experts have carefully developed and evaluated many specific strategic interventions that would be relevant to perinatal women with these clinical presentations. Second, the CBT community, as a whole, is directing much attention to *dissemination*, or the exporting of empirically supported CBT approaches to community agencies and the therapists who are employed by these agencies. There has been a burgeoning of programs that are designed to train and supervise therapists as they acquire skill in demonstrating competency in CBT (e.g., Stirman, Buchhofer, McLaulin, Evans, & Beck, 2009; Wenzel, Brown, & Karlin, 2011). Moreover, countless workshops, webinars and other training resources are devoted to instruction in the practice of CBT. Although there are resources and training devoted to the practice of IPT, they are more limited than those available for training in CBT. Thus, perinatal women in need will likely have an easier time finding a therapist in their community who has received training and supervision in CBT than they would in finding a therapist in their community who has received training or supervision in IPT.

One point about terminology deserves note. CBT was developed in the 1960s by Dr. Aaron T. Beck, who originally labeled the treatment *cognitive therapy*. Although the word "cognitive" was emphasized in this title, behavioral strategies were incorporated into even the earliest versions of the treatment. As the field progressed, numerous CBTs were developed which all retained cognitive therapy's basic premise that our thinking plays an important role in our emotional state and behavior, as well as other important features, such as its structure and problem focus. Today, the terms cognitive therapy and CBT are used synonymously (J. S. Beck, 2011; Greenberg, McWilliams, & Wenzel, 2014). The term "CBT" is used primarily in this book, although references to "cognitive therapy" are made when describing studies that used that precise terminology. The book also describes CBT that reflects the core features of cognitive therapy that were developed and tested in Dr. Beck's original approach to treatment. The *Beckian approach* to CBT has at its heart a cognitive case conceptualization of the individual client's clinical presentation, or the understanding of the client's symptoms and life circumstances in light of cognitive behavioral theory. This conceptualization influences the strategic interventions that the cognitive behavioral therapist delivers (see Chapter 2), which means treatment is flexible, and interventions are delivered on the basis of what is appropriate for the client's clinical presentation. In other words, every course of Beckian CBT is different because each client is different, which differs from other CBT protocols that mandate certain tasks to be addressed in particular sessions.

Overview of the Book

This book describes a Beckian approach to the treatment of perinatal distress, including depression and the various manifestations of anxiety described in this chapter. It provides a general framework for using cognitive case conceptualization and collaboration with the client to translate into strategic intervention to treat salient aspects of perinatal clients' clinical presentations. It is not a substitute for established treatment manuals on the market. Indeed, if a client presents with a pure manifestation of a condition for which there are established treatment manuals (e.g., panic disorder; Barlow & Craske, 2007), those manuals should be used to guide treatment, as they have the greatest amount of empirical support for their efficacy. However, most clients will have mixed depression-anxiety clinical presentations, with a "flavor" of several manifestations of emotional distress, and with the focus of their concerns being targeted to the unique experience of childbirth, the transition to parenthood, and caring for a newborn. The cognitive behavioral approach described in this book describes well-established cognitive and behavioral strategies that are incorporated into empirically supported treatment protocols for depression, anxiety, obsessive compulsive-related, and trauma- and stressor-related disorders. The glue that holds them together for mixed depression-anxiety clinical presentations is the cognitive case conceptualization.

The first chapters in the book provide background that will help readers understanding the theoretical basis of, and rationale for, the use of CBT with perinatal clients. Chapter 2 presents a biopsychosocial model of perinatal anxiety, as well as the cognitive model that underlies CBT. We reconcile the two models and describe how they facilitate cognitive case conceptualization. We end the chapter with descriptions and conceptualizations of four cases that we follow throughout the book. In Chapter 3, we describe the efficacy of CBT for treatment seeking adults with the manifestations of perinatal distress that we defined in this chapter, and we evaluate the smaller literature that has evaluated CBT for perinatal depression and anxiety. We comment on how the treatment described in this book is both similar to, and different from, the cognitive behavioral approaches that have been studied by researchers. Chapter 4 emphasizes the importance of the therapeutic relationship, describing aspects of the therapeutic relationship that are important for cognitive behavioral therapists to cultivate, and describing highlights from the empirical literature on the association between aspects of the therapeutic relationship and outcome.

Chapters 5–11 can be viewed as a treatment manual that will orient the reader to standard CBT strategies for depression and anxiety and discuss their adaptation to perinatal women. Chapter 5 presents an overview of the early, middle, and late phases of treatment, describing the general structure of sessions, and linking the cognitive case conceptualization process to treatment planning. Chapter 6 provides a template for conducting cognitive restructuring of situational thoughts and underlying beliefs with perinatal women, describing ways to identify, evaluate, and modify these cognitions so that they minimize mood disturbance. Chapter 7 describes behavioral interventions for perinatal depression, with a focus on behavioral activation, or active engagement in one's environment, and self-care. Chapter 8 describes two types of behavioral interventions for anxiety: (a) affective coping skills, or tools for managing high affect and agitation; and (b) exposure, or the process of having systematic contact with a feared stimulus or situation in order to overcome fear-based avoidance. Chapter 9 presents steps for helping clients to acquire effective problem-solving skills and to modify unhelpful attitudes toward problems or their own problem-solving abilities. Chapter 10 illustrates steps for communication skills training, as well as tips for addressing relation issues that often emerge during the perinatal period. Chapter 11 describes the activities that occur in the late phase of treatment, which occur when clients are moving toward the completion of treatment.

Chapter 12 serves as a conclusion to the book, in which we summarize the main tenets of CBT that are important for mental health professionals who work with perinatal women to be mindful of, describe special circumstances that perinatal mental health experts often encounter, and make a call for future research. After reading Chapter 12, it will be clear to the reader that this book is the first step in advancing a Beckian approach to the cognitive behavioral treatment of women with perinatal distress. The pace of research in this area is accelerating rapidly, and we hope that the cognitive behavioral approach described in this book will serve as a foundation to address many of the clinical questions that are of yet unanswered for the treatment of perinatal distress.

2

A COGNITIVE BEHAVIORAL CONCEPTUALIZATION OF PERINATAL DISTRESS

Theoretical models of psychopathology provide a rich template for clinicians to understand the factors that contribute to their clients' clinical presentations. They allow clinicians to quickly assimilate seemingly disparate pieces of information into a coherent and comprehensive portrait of their clients' presenting problems, and they point to promising avenues for intervention. They also allow researchers to conduct targeted research that clarifies the specific mechanisms at work in the etiology and treatment of mental health disorders. There are two theoretical models that advance the understanding of cognitive behavioral therapy (CBT) for perinatal distress. The first model, described by Wenzel (2011), captures factors that explain the etiology of perinatal distress. Many perinatal women present for treatment with despair, desperately wanting to know the answer to the question: "Why is this happening?" Wenzel's (2011) biopsychosocial model of perinatal distress can help these women to make sense of their current situation.

In addition, CBT has its basis in a rich model that incorporates cognitive, emotional, and behavioral factors to gain a comprehensive understanding of the factors that contribute to the etiology, maintenance, and exacerbation of emotional distress. Cognitive behavioral therapists are mindful of this model as they develop a *cognitive case conceptualization* of their clients' clinical presentations, or as they apply cognitive behavioral theory to the understanding of their clients' experiences, emotional state, stressors, challenges, and strengths. Communication of the cognitive case conceptualization to clients gives them a sense that their therapist understands their current and historical life circumstances. It also instills hope and optimism because clients see that their current emotional distress is understandable in light of cognitive and behavioral patterns that developed as a result of their vulnerabilities and formative experiences. When therapists deliver an intervention in a strategic manner, they can use the cognitive behavioral model as a template to understand and explain to the client the mechanism by which it is expected to exert its effects.

In this chapter, we first present Wenzel's (2011) biopsychosocial model of perinatal distress. Next, we describe the salient cognitive and behavioral components of the cognitive behavioral model. We then consider the ways in which these two models can be used jointly in advancing CBT for perinatal clients. Finally, we describe the process of cognitive case conceptualization, taking care to illustrate how the theory is translated to the individualized understanding of perinatal clients' clinical presentations. During this discussion, we present case descriptions of four women with perinatal distress who we follow throughout the book, demonstrating how therapists apply the biopsychosocial model of perinatal distress and cognitive behavioral theory to their cognitive case conceptualizations.

A Biopsychosocial Model of Perinatal Distress

Wenzel (2011) advanced a biopsychosocial model of perinatal distress (see Figure 2.1) by using the groundbreaking theoretical work of Milgrom,

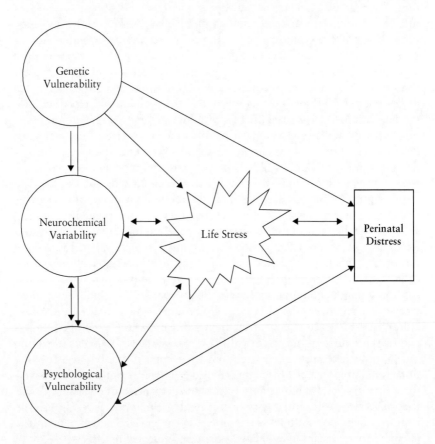

Figure 2.1 The Biopsychosocial Model of Perinatal Distress.

Source: Adapted with permission from Wenzel (2011).

Martin, and Negri (1999) and empirical work of Ross, Sellers, Gilbert Evans, and Romach (2004) and incorporating the larger literature on vulnerabilities to emotional distress. The term "biopsychosocial" implies that multiple factors are hypothesized to contribute to the development of perinatal distress. Those factors are designated in the circles on the left hand side of the figure and are regarded as *vulnerabilities*. The presence of a vulnerability does not guarantee that a person will experience perinatal distress, but it indeed increases the likelihood that a person will experience perinatal distress under circumstances that activate it.

Three domains of vulnerability have relevance in understanding the etiology of perinatal distress. *Genetic vulnerability* refers to the extent to which a woman has a genetic predisposition for depression, anxiety, and other expressions of emotional distress. Although there is no precise test to determine genetic vulnerability, most mental health professionals infer genetic vulnerability from a client's personal and family history of mental health disorders. The more episodes of clinically significant emotional distress that a woman has had, and the more family members who have struggled with mental health disorders, the higher her loading is on the factor of genetic vulnerability. Ross et al.'s (2004) empirical research indeed determined that a personal and family history of mental health disorders predicted symptoms of perinatal distress.

Like genetic vulnerability, *neurochemical variability* is a biological factor. Whereas genetic vulnerability is a distal factor that remains constant, neurochemical variability is a proximal factor that can vary as a function of time and circumstances (e.g., second trimester of pregnancy, six weeks postpartum). It is well known that childbirth is associated with dramatic fluctuations in hormones, and that some of these fluctuations can affect neurotransmitters associated with mood (e.g., catecholomines, serotonin). Research has not consistently identified any particular level of any particular hormone that can explain the onset of perinatal distress. Thus, researchers now advance the notion that some women who are vulnerable to perinatal distress might be particularly sensitive to rapid shifts in hormone levels (Altemus, 2001; Glover & Kammerer, 2004; Nonacs, 2005). It is this sensitivity that is captured in our conceptualization of neurochemical variability.

Psychological vulnerability refers to psychological styles that have the potential to increase the likelihood that perinatal women will have difficulty adjusting to the transition to parenthood. The empirical literature is rich with descriptions of psychological vulnerabilities associated with depression, anxiety, obsessive compulsive-related, and trauma- or stressor-related disorders. For example, Michel Dugas and his colleagues have identified several psychological variables that contribute to the experience of generalized anxiety, or excessive, uncontrollable worry. These variables include the *intolerance of uncertainty, inaccurate positive beliefs about worry* (e.g., that worry prevents problems from occurring), a *poor problem orientation* (i.e., an unhelpful cognitive style that interferes with problem solving; see Chapter 9), and *cognitive avoidance* (Dugas, Freeston, & Ladoceur, 1997; Dugas, Gagnon, Ladouceur, & Freeston, 1998; Ladouceur, Talbot, & Dugas, 1997). *Anxiety sensitivity* is a fear of anxiety-related sensations due to the belief that they are indicative of harm (McNally, 1989; Reiss, Peterson, Gursky, & McNally, 1986). Although anxiety sensitivity is elevated in people with many types of anxiety, it is particularly sensitive in identifying clients who are vulnerable to develop panic disorder and posttraumatic stress disorder (Olatunji & Wolitzky-Taylor, 2009). A related variable, the *catastrophic misinterpretations of bodily sensations* (D. M. Clark et al., 1997), has also been used to explain the onset and maintenance of panic disorder. Moreover, *rumination*, or the tendency to focus excessively on how badly one feels, predicts a host of expressions of emotional distress, especially depression (Nolen-Hoeksema, Wisco, & Lyubomirsky, 2008).

All of the psychological vulnerabilities described in the previous paragraph have been identified in samples of research participants who were representative of adults in the general population, not only perinatal women. However, there is nothing that precludes these constructs from having relevance to perinatal women. Perhaps the most discourse and research on psychological vulnerabilities associated specifically with perinatal distress is in the area of intrusive thoughts, most commonly associated with obsessive compulsive disorder (OCD). According to Jonathan Abramowitz and his colleagues (e.g., Abramowitz, Moore, Carmin, Wiegartz, & Purdon, 2001; Abramowitz, Schwartz, Moore, & Luenzmann, 2003; Fairbrother & Abramowitz, 2007), most people experience odd and intrusive thoughts on occasion, but people who experience associated emotional distress tend to do so because they interpret the thoughts as threatening or significant and then go to great lengths to avoid activation of the thoughts. Although avoidance reduces emotional distress in the short term, it increases obsessional anxiety in the long term, as it prevents the person from learning that the thoughts are not harmful. Thus, the tendency to attach great significance to random intrusive thoughts and a pattern of avoidance behavior are also psychological vulnerabilities that could predispose women to emotional distress.

Elsewhere, we have labeled intrusive thoughts experienced by perinatal women as *scary thoughts* (Kleiman & Wenzel, 2011). Examples of scary thoughts include concerns about dropping the baby down the stairs, images of stabbing the baby with a kitchen knife, and urges to touch the baby's genitals while bathing him. Perinatal women report being repulsed by these thoughts, viewing them as wholly inconsistent with who they view themselves to be (i.e., ego-dystonic). Their emotional distress comes from grave concerns about the consequences of the thoughts, or the significance that they attach to them. For instance, some women believe that just thinking the thought increases the likelihood that they will actually act on the thought, which is indicative of a cognitive bias called a *probability bias* (cf. Abramowitz et al., 2003). Other women equate thinking a thought with actually committing a bad behavior and conclude that they are a bad person, which is indicative of a bias called a *morality bias* (cf. Abramowitz et al., 2003). Research by Abramowitz and his colleagues has identified related psychological variables that predict emotional distress associated with intrusive thoughts in perinatal women, including high moral standards, an overestimation of threat, an inflated sense of responsibility, unhelpful beliefs about the importance of and need to control thoughts, perfectionism, and intolerance of uncertainty (Abramowitz, Schwartz, & Moore, 2003; Abramowitz, Khandker, Nelson, Deacon, & Rygwall, 2006; Abramowitz, Nelson, Rygwall, & Khandker, 2007).

Note that these three areas of vulnerability—genetic, neurochemical, and psychological—do not exist in isolation; it is hypothesized that they influence one another. The arrows that lead from genetic vulnerability to neurochemical variability and to psychological vulnerability suggest that genetic vulnerability influences these other two vulnerability domains. In addition, there is a bidirectional arrow between neurochemical variability and psychological vulnerability because it is hypothesized that they exert reciprocal influences on one another. In other words, when a perinatal woman experiences abrupt changes in hormone levels, it is likely that some of her psychological vulnerabilities (e.g., anxiety sensitivity) are activated or exacerbated; conversely, it is likely that psychological vulnerabilities make the experience of neurochemical variability more difficult to tolerate than they would be in the absence of these psychological vulnerabilities.

According to Milgrom et al.'s (1999) theoretical model of perinatal distress and Ross et al.'s (2004) empirical model of perinatal distress, vulnerability factors were directly associated with perinatal distress, and they were also mediated by *life stress*. Life stress can mean many things. Ross et al. reasoned that low socioeconomic status (SES) could be a marker for life stress, in that people of low SES backgrounds often have financial pressures and worries about money. Another source of life stress that they identified was a lack of social support. Although these are two important sources of life stress, it is important to be mindful of the fact that there are infinite ways in which people can experience life stress, including behavior problems in older children, work demands, and even daily hassles such as a difficult commute. Stressors that are specific to the perinatal period include pregnancy complications, difficult-to-schedule doctor's appointments, pressure to complete the nursery before the baby is born, and making a decision about child care (cf. Milgrom et al., 1999).

This biopsychosocial model represents a *diathesis-stress* approach to understanding emotional distress. According to diathesis-stress models, people who struggle with emotional distress are characterized by unique diatheses, or vulnerabilities, that translate into emotional distress and unhelpful thinking especially in periods of their lives in which they experience stress, disappointment, and challenges (cf. O'Hara, Rehm, & Campbell, 1982). In this particular diathesis-stress model of perinatal distress, there are bidirectional arrows between perinatal distress and life stress, and between perinatal distress and two of the vulnerability factors. These arrows signify that perinatal distress could exacerbate life stress, as well as exacerbate sensitivity to neurochemical variability and the psychological vulnerabilities.

The Cognitive Behavioral Model

The cognitive behavioral model was developed by Dr. Aaron T. Beck (A. T. Beck, Rush, Shaw, & Emery, 1979) and refined by his daughter Dr. Judith S. Beck at the Beck Institute for Cognitive Behavior Therapy (cf. J. S. Beck, 2011). It is a model that conceptualizes psychological (especially cognitive) variables that contribute to general emotional distress, thus also characterizing the etiology of emotional distress, like the biopsychosocial model described previously. However, it also provides a heuristic for understanding how CBT can work in treating emotional distress.

Figure 2.2 displays the basic cognitive behavioral model. According to cognitive behavioral theory, cognition plays a central role in understanding our emotional, behavioral, and physiological reactions that are experienced in specific situations. In other words, it is not so much that

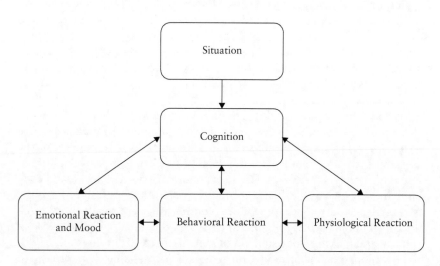

Figure 2.2 Basic Cognitive Behavioral Model of Emotional Distress.

Source: Adapted with permission from Greenberg, McWilliams, & Wenzel (2014).

certain situations, stressors, or triggers *make* us feel a specific way, but instead it is the *meaning* that we make of those situations, stressors, or triggers. We call these situation-specific cognitions *automatic thoughts* because they often arise so quickly that we do not always know that we are making some sort of judgment or interpretation. We just know that we feel a certain way.

Imagine two women in their third trimester who hope to feel their baby kicking or moving one afternoon, only to find that they cannot feel movement. Woman #1 has the automatic thought, "Oh no! Something is wrong with my baby" whereas woman #2 has the automatic thought, "She's probably just sleeping right now. I'll check again later." Not surprisingly, woman #1 feels panicked, her heart pounding, and her rate of breathing escalating. She immediately puts in a frantic call to the nurse at her obstetrics practice. Woman #2, in contrast, does not feel much emotion at all. She continues with what she was doing, smiling to herself as she imagines her baby sleeping in the womb. Both women found themselves in identical situations—they were hoping to feel their baby moving, and they could not detect movement. However, they had very different interpretations of the experience (i.e., different automatic thoughts), and as a result, they had very different emotional, physiological, and behavioral reactions.

Notice the bidirectional arrows among the constructs of cognition, emotional reaction and mood, behavioral reaction, and physiological reaction. These bidirectional arrows are included because the constructs often influence one another. For example, woman #1 was already experiencing emotional upset after having to discipline her 3-year-old child. This emotional upset increased the likelihood that she would experience a catastrophic automatic thought, such as "Something is wrong with my baby." Thus, it is simplistic to posit that cognition unilaterally causes people to have certain emotional, physiological, and behavioral reactions. A more accurate description is that cognition plays an important role in increasing the likelihood of experiencing certain emotional, physiological, and behavioral reactions.

The automatic thoughts that we experience in particular situations are not random. Rather, they are predictable on the basis of underlying beliefs that have developed across the course of our lives. Figure 2.2 is an expanded cognitive behavioral model that depicts this in more detail. According to this model, key features of our background make it more or less likely that we will be characterized by certain underlying beliefs. In other words, these background factors are vulnerabilities that predispose us to having certain cognitive and behavioral patterns. These background factors can take on many forms. *Environmental* background factors capture factors external to the person that could play a role in developing emotional distress and a vulnerability to certain underlying beliefs. They can reflect ongoing adversity (e.g., domestic violence in the household while growing up; living in poverty), ongoing interpersonal experiences (e.g., being teased or bullied; being verbally abused by a spouse or partner), and single events that make a profound impact on a person (e.g., being in a serious car accident; being humiliated in front of others). *Biological* background factors capture factors that serve as a biological predisposition to the current emotional distress that a client is reporting. Similar to that which was described in the previous section regarding the biopsychosocial model, if a person has a family history of depression and anxiety, then it is likely that she has a genetic predisposing for these manifestations of emotional distress and could be vulnerable to develop underlying beliefs consistent with these types of emotional distress. *Psychological* background factors capture psychological styles and tendencies that could increase a person's vulnerability to develop certain

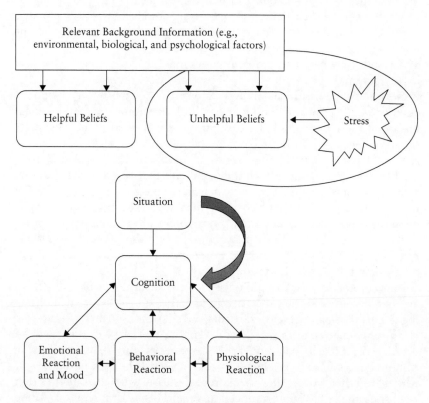

Figure 2.3 Expanded Cognitive Behavioral Model of Emotional Distress.

Source: Adapted with permission from Greenberg, McWilliams, & Wenzel (2014).

underlying beliefs and are the same types of factors as described in the previous section on the biopsychosocial model of perinatal distress.

Most people, even people who have a history of chronic emotional distress, are characterized by both adaptive and helpful and maladaptive and unhelpful underlying beliefs. For example, consider a woman who has had great academic success but who also experienced physical abuse at the hands of her father during childhood. Her academic success might contribute to a healthy sense of self, such as "I'm competent" or "I'm a worthwhile person." However, the physical abuse that she experienced might contribute to an unhealthy sense of self, such as "I deserve to be punished" or "I'm worthless." In times of relative calm, this woman might operate according to the adaptive and helpful beliefs. It is likely that she would not meet diagnostic criteria for a mental health disorder during such times. In contrast, in times of stress (see Figure 2.3), her maladaptive and unhelpful beliefs are activated, and she operates primarily according to these beliefs, rather than her healthier beliefs. It is likely, then, that she would indeed meet diagnostic criteria for a mental health disorder during such times. Thus, the cognitive behavioral model described here is another example of a diathesis-stress model, in that it is hypothesized that the most unhelpful beliefs and behavioral patterns are enacted in times of transition, challenge, and disappointment.

Reconciliation of the Two Models

Figure 2.4 depicts a reconciliation of these models, which captures relevant constructs to explain perinatal clients' emotional distress. There are many similarities between the biopsychosocial model of perinatal distress and the cognitive behavioral model of emotional distress. Assumptions inherent in both models are that: (a) people are characterized by biological and psychological vulnerabilities that predispose them to experience emotional distress; and (b) these vulnerabilities are most likely to be activated or expressed in times of life stress. In many ways, the cognitive behavioral model takes the biopsychosocial model of perinatal distress two steps further by: (a) capturing the underlying beliefs that emerge from the vulnerability factors and that also contribute to emotional distress; and (b) outlining how vulnerabilities, life stress, and underlying beliefs are manifest, in particular situations in clients' lives. Thus, one could regard the basic cognitive behavioral model depicted in Figure 2.2 as a specific expression of the interplay between the vulnerabilities, life stress, and underlying beliefs, which is displayed in the bottom section of Figure 2.4.

Cognitive behavioral therapists use these conceptual models as a way to identify modifiable factors that can be targeted in treatment. The

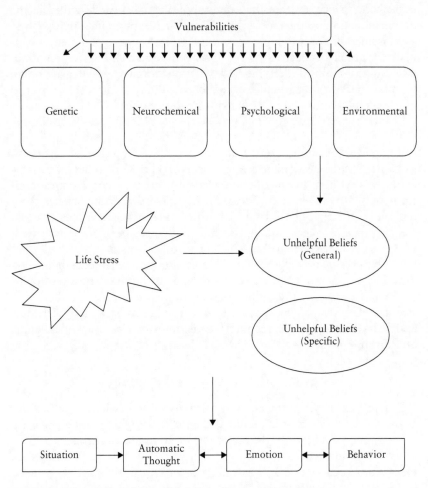

Figure 2.4 Cognitive Behavioral Model of Perinatal Distress.

modifiable risk factors common to both models are the psychological vulnerabilities. In addition, the cognitive behavioral model points to underlying beliefs, situation-specific automatic thoughts, and resulting behavioral patterns that are modifiable and serve as targets of treatment. Therapists who work with perinatal women find that two types of beliefs require attention. The first type of belief is common to most clients who seek treatment for emotional distress and are characterized by global judgments of the self (e.g., "I'm a failure"), others (e.g., "Others will reject me"), the world (e.g., "The world is dangerous"), and the future (e.g., "Things will not get better"). However, the second type of belief is somewhat specific to the perinatal population and includes judgments about one's competence as a parent, what it means to be a mother, and what a family "should" look like. Although the more general beliefs typically are in the "background" for many perinatal women, the parenting- and family-specific beliefs usually assume primary importance when women seek treatment at this time in their lives.

Cognitive Case Conceptualization

As stated previously, cognitive case conceptualization is the process by which therapists apply theory to understanding the etiology, maintenance, and exacerbation of their clients' clinical presentations (cf. J. S. Beck, 2011; Kuyken, Padesky, & Dudley, 2009; Persons, 2008). Although it considers many factors that contribute to the client's emotional distress, it focuses specifically on the modifiable psychological factors that will, in turn, be targets of treatment. Cognitive case conceptualization is a continuous and evolving process. From the first time a therapist meets a client he or she will be eliciting information to form hypotheses about the client's genetic, neurochemical, and psychological vulnerabilities; the historical and current environmental conditions that might have reinforced certain ways of viewing the self or the world; and the way in which the psychological vulnerabilities manifest themselves in everyday situations in which the client notices emotional upset. The therapist often assimilates relevant information into an organized form, such as the one depicted in Figure 2.5. However, this is not merely an intellectual exercise. Therapists develop the conceptualization in a collaborative manner, taking care to verify their assumptions with the client and modify the conceptualization as new information is collected.

Note that, in Figure 2.5, there are spaces for therapists to record helpful beliefs, both those that are general in nature as well as those that are specific to parenthood and family, as well as psychological strengths, environmental strengths, and buffers against life stress. It is important to be just as cognizant of our clients' strengths as we are to their challenges (Kuyken et al., 2009), as attending to strengths communicates respect for clients' resilience and identifies resources that can be harnessed in overcoming emotional distress.

In the following sections, we introduce four perinatal women whom we follow throughout the book. They represent real clients that we have treated, with identifying information and specific circumstances altered. In these sections, we demonstrate how relevant pieces of their clinical presentation and psychosocial history are integrated into their cognitive case conceptualization.

VULNERABILITIES
Genetic Vulnerability:
Neurochemical Variability:
Psychological Vulnerability:
Psychological Strengths:
Environmental Adversity:
Environmental Strengths:
UNDERLYING BELIEFS
General Unhelpful Beliefs:
General Helpful Beliefs:
Specific Unhelpful Beliefs about Parenting and Family:
Specific Helpful Beliefs about Parenting and Family:

Figure 2.5 Cognitive Case Conceptualization Diagram for Perinatal Clients.

Life Stress:
Buffers Against Life Stress:
SITUATIONAL EXAMPLE
Situation:
Automatic Thought:
Emotional Reaction:
Behavioral Reaction:

Figure 2.5 Continued.

Tara

Tara is a 32-year-old Asian woman who presented for treatment when her first-born child, Thomas, was 3-weeks-old. Her husband worked long hours as he was finishing his post-doctoral fellowship. Although he had a lucrative job opportunity that was scheduled to start in six months, when Tara presented for treatment, the family was struggling financially. Tara reported a great deal of generalized anxiety and frequent panic attacks. She indicated that most of the panic attacks were triggered by "being in her head," when she was questioning her competence and wondering whether her son and husband would be better off with a more competent mother and wife. She described having many existential worries, such as "What is the purpose of my life?" "What's the point of life if there is only pain and suffering?" She met criteria for major depressive disorder with postpartum onset. Her therapist also noted a significant anxiety component to her clinical presentation, as Tara reported excessive worry and rumination, accompanied by occasional panic attacks.

Tara indicated that her parents and siblings were psychologically healthy; she viewed her mother as the "paragon of all mothers" and believed that she could not possibly be as good as her mother. Tara described a history filled with many successes, such as graduating in the top 5% of her high school class, holding leadership roles in many extracurricular activities in high school and college, having a close circle of friends, and completing a master's degree with honors, although she admitted that she received treatment for bulimia when she was in college and that, during that time, she had a poor body image and engaged in promiscuous sexual activity as a way of feeling good about her body. Although the struggles with bulimia were significant enough that she took a semester off from school, she reported that she used the time traveling abroad and hiking through the Swiss Alps, where she achieved a great deal of personal growth and clarity. Tara also recalled that she had difficulty coping with the uncertainty of graduate school applications, as she was restless and agitated as she waited to see which programs accepted her, and she ruminated over whether she was going to make a wrong decision.

Tara stated that during pregnancy she had relatively positive views of herself as a mother and of the family unit into which she expected to bring her son. She was close to her parents and her in-laws, and she viewed her relationship with her husband as loving and mutually respectful. The pregnancy was planned, and she and her husband were excited about the timing of the pregnancy, as their child would still be an infant when they relocated for her husband's new job. She worked until a few days before she had her son, with the understanding that she would not resume work because she would move six months later. Tara had gone into her final weeks of pregnancy with a sense of confidence and optimism. Thus, she was particularly taken aback when she began to experience debilitating anxiety soon after her son was born, causing her to question many of the positive ways she had been viewing herself until that time.

In her cognitive case conceptualization, Tara's therapist regarded her as having a modest genetic vulnerability to emotional distress. Tara had a history of bulimia, low self-esteem, and situational anxiety, but she did not have a family history of mental health disorders. Her therapist hypothesized that neurochemical variability could be playing a role in her current emotional distress, as she had given birth only three weeks before her first visit. Her therapist was certain that Tara was characterized by an intolerance of uncertainty, on the basis of Tara's difficulty coping with graduate school applications, and she also hypothesized that Tara was characterized by perfectionistic tendencies. However, her experience in the Swiss Alps also suggested that Tara is characterized by psychological resilience and psychological mindedness. Tara had few environmental adversities and many environmental strengths, such as loving parents with whom she had a close relationship, a stable childhood in which she felt safe, and continued close relationships with her family-of-origin and in-laws. These close familial relationships were also conceptualized as buffers against the life stress of preparing for a relocation for her husband's job.

Tara's therapist hypothesized that Tara experienced diametrically opposed underlying beliefs depending on the stress that she was experiencing in her life. Tara had a history of many impressive accomplishments, so her therapist reasoned that when things were going well, Tara viewed herself as competent. However, her therapist also suspected that when faced with uncertainty about performing at the level that she expected of herself, beliefs of failure and incompetence predominated. Although childbirth and parenting a newborn would be considered life stressors for any new mothers, Tara's therapist suspected that an even more relevant source of life stress was the experience of anxiety itself, which likely came on as another form of situational anxiety, but then "took on a life of its own" after Tara began to ruminate on its underlying meaning (e.g., incompetence as a parent). Because Tara viewed her mother in such a positive light, her therapist suspected that she held many unrealistic expectations of her performance as a mother and as a wife.

Lyla

Lyla is a 35-year-old Caucasian woman who presented for treatment when her first-born child, Jack, was 3 months old. She had been in a relationship with her husband for fifteen years and married for ten, and she regarded him as her sole source of social support. Lyla indicated that she was the middle child of a family with nine children, but that she perceived that she was singled out as the "black sheep." At the time she presented for treatment, Lyla described having uncomfortable relationships with her mother and siblings and dreaded the frequent family gatherings to which she believed she was expected to attend. She reported that she had been depressed throughout her entire adult life and had been in therapy "on and off" for many years. Lyla presented for this course of treatment when she wondered whether she was providing adequate care to her son because she was sleeping so much. Her therapist diagnosed her with major depressive disorder, recurrent, as well as social anxiety disorder.

Lyla suspected that her mother and many of her siblings struggled with mental health issues, although she did not know whether any of them had received a diagnosis or sought treatment because "those things weren't talked about in my house." She recalled her father, who was recently deceased, as a bitter and angry person who drank too much beer and had a difficult time showing affection toward his children. She indicated that she was often ostracized by her peers while growing up, which she attributed to the belief that her older siblings often "egged on" other kids in their school and neighborhood to tease her. Lyla indicated that she eventually "just gave up" on peer relationships, as every friend she had eventually turned on her. Despite these interpersonal difficulties, Lyla reported that she got good grades, although she attributed her academic success to the fact that she was afraid of being reprimanded by the nuns at her Catholic school, rather than to positive attributes like intelligence or perseverance.

Lyla indicated that she and her husband waited many years to have children because she was afraid that she would "pass her genes on" to a child and that the child would be "as messed up as I am." Moreover, she was unsure whether she would be a good mother, as she believed that she did not have a good role model in her mother and was unsure what being a good mother would be like. Although the pregnancy was not planned specifically, three months before she conceived, she and her husband decided to discontinue birth control to "see what would happen." Lyla reported being very nauseous and "emotional" during pregnancy, to the point where she would cry uncontrollably in front of clients. These circumstances prompted her to take temporary disability from her position as an office clerk.

In her cognitive case conceptualization, Lyla's therapist regarded her as having significant genetic vulnerability to emotional distress on the basis of Lyla's personal history of mental health problems and Lyla's description of the members of her family-of-origin. Because Lyla experienced significant episodes of acute, and often inappropriate, emotional expression during pregnancy, her therapist hypothesized that Lyla was particularly sensitive to neurochemical variability. Her therapist regarded Lyla's psychological vulnerability as a pessimistic cognitive style, on the basis of Lyla's self-reported formative experiences and the way in which she presented during the psychological assessment, and her psychological strength as a sharp intellect, on the basis of Lyla's report that she got good grades as well as the questions that she asked of her therapist during the initial visit. Although Lyla described a great deal of environmental adversity, such as tense relationships with the members of her family-of-origin, the recent loss of her father, and social isolation, her therapist identified a strong relationship with her husband as an environmental strength.

Lyla's therapist hypothesized that Lyla was characterized by a number of self-deprecating beliefs, such as those falling in the domains of unlovability, failure, and worthlessness that developed from the messages that she took away from early interactions with her parents, siblings, and peers. In contrast, Lyla revealed very little, if any, positive views of herself. Lyla did not describe rigid expectations of parenting and her family, stating only that she wanted her own family and her relationship with her child to be very different from what she had experienced. However, she admitted that she expected herself to be a poor mother. Lyla's therapist identified current life stress as consisting of financial pressures, as money was tight because she was no longer bringing home a salary, and the holidays, in which Lyla said that she would be expected to attend several gatherings with family members that she desperately wanted to avoid.

Donna

Donna is a 25-year-old Caucasian woman who resumed treatment with her cognitive behavioral therapist when her daughter, Ellie, was 8-weeks-old. She was seen three years previously for the treatment of obsessive compulsive disorder (OCD). Donna described a long history of various manifestations of OCD, such that she fixated near-constantly on intrusive thoughts of some sort of harm coming to herself or others. For example, when she was a teenager, she was convinced that she was HIV+ and was spreading the virus to others, despite the fact that she was in a monogamous relationship with the only person with whom she had had sexual intercourse. During that time, she compulsively scoured the internet looking for evidence to confirm that she was spreading the virus through nonsexual contact. When she presented for treatment three years ago, she described intrusive thoughts about running someone over while driving and associated checking behavior to make sure that there were no bodies on the road. Her checking behavior was time consuming, often making her late for work. Donna's current intrusive thought was that she had postpartum psychosis and was a danger to her infant. Although she did not avoid caring for her daughter, she described herself as feeling detached from her and feeling as though her daughter was someone else's child.

Donna grew up in a lower-middle-class family in a blue-collar town. Her father committed suicide when she was 5-years-old. She indicated that she was extremely close to her mother and two sisters ever since that time. She recalled being anxious that she would lose another one of her family members. Despite these life circumstances, she had a typical school experience, getting above-average grades, having a small but close group of girlfriends, playing in the school band, and running Varsity track. After she graduated from high school, Donna moved to a metropolitan area for junior college. She met the man who became her husband at a party when she was in her second year of college. They had been married for approximately one year when she presented for this most recent course of treatment.

Donna's therapist was able to use much of the information that she had developed into her previous cognitive case conceptualization in order to conceptualize the contributing and maintaining factors to this current episode of OCD. Donna had a significant genetic vulnerability to emotional distress, as her father struggled with chronic depression and later took his own life, and her mother had been diagnosed with an anxiety disorder. Her therapist reasoned that sensitivity to neurochemical variability might be exacerbating her emotional distress, as Donna had always been sensitive to psychotropic medications and experienced many side effects. On the basis of her previous work with Donna, her therapist knew that Donna was characterized by the psychological vulnerabilities of an intolerance of uncertainty, a reassurance seeking behavioral style, and the overattribution of significance to random mental events. However, Donna also had a number of psychological strengths, including a strong motivation to embrace CBT and learn about her OCD, as well as an openmindedness to trying new things. She had caught on quickly to CBT when she worked with her therapist in the past, and she had already been reviewing her CBT resources before her first appointment for this current episode of emotional distress. An obvious source of environmental adversity was growing up without her father after he committed suicide, but a source of environmental strength was the substantial emotional support that she received from her mother and sisters.

Through their previous work together, Donna's therapist identified the underlying belief of "Bad things randomly happen." In addition, when her OCD clinical presentation was at its worst, Donna often expressed the belief "I'm a bad person" because she was convinced she was somehow causing harm to others. However, her therapist also acknowledged that Donna perceived herself as a survivor and saw herself as being resilient in light of her father's suicide. Donna did not report having any specific unhelpful beliefs about parenting or motherhood during pregnancy, although she now wondered whether her emotional distress made her an unfit mother and was putting her daughter in danger. Donna's therapist reasoned that these concerns were exacerbated in light of two life stressors—the fact that Donna and her husband did not have family in the area to provide tangible support (e.g., help with child care), and the fact that Donna's husband worked long, grueling hours in construction, leaving her home alone for most of her waking hours and solely responsible for the care of their newborn.

Wendy

Wendy is a 38-year-old woman of Puerto Rican descent who presented for treatment soon after there was a school shooting that received national attention in the media. She had two children, ages 4 and 2½, and she was pregnant with her third child. After she learned of the school shooting, she became consumed with worry that a gunman would enter into her son's preschool. She had kept him out of school for the two weeks before she had her first visit with her therapist, which she knew she could not do forever because he continually asked to go back to school and expressed that he missed his friends. During the psychological assessment, Wendy admitted that she worried more of the time than not about whether her husband, children, or parents would experience illness or injury. For example, she viewed her husband as overweight and unhealthy, and she worried that he would die from a heart attack. She admitted to being overprotective with her children, worrying that they would be injured while playing on playground equipment or riding on rides at the fair. Before having children, Wendy indicated that she experienced a similar intensity of worry on getting good grades and saving for the future. Wendy's therapist concluded that she had a lifelong pattern of chronic worry and that she met criteria for generalized anxiety disorder (GAD).

Wendy and her three siblings were raised by her mother and father in a traditional Catholic household. Although she regarded the family as close, she perceived that her mother often gave her the message that she could not do certain things as well as her brothers because she was female. She was gifted academically and received admission invitations to many elite liberal arts colleges. However, her two older brothers attended large Ivy League universities, so she viewed her academic accomplishments as pale in comparison. After college, Wendy attended law school, but she had trouble passing the bar exam. She married her husband, also an attorney, and she decided to stay home with her children.

Wendy's therapist hypothesized that she had a moderate generic vulnerability; although she had a long history of excessive worry consistent with GAD, Wendy did not know of anyone else in her family-of-origin who was diagnosed with a mental health disorder. Her therapist also did not view her as being particularly susceptible to neurochemical variability, as she described all three of her pregnancies as being among the more calm times in her life, and the exacerbation of her excessive worry clearly was induced by the recent school shooting. Wendy's therapist viewed her psychological vulnerabilities as having positive beliefs about worry (as she believed that her worry protected others from experiencing harm), a cognitive style in which she overestimated the probability of catastrophes, and suggestibility when she learned of disasters that others had experienced (hence, concluding that she was at risk of similar disasters). However, she was characterized by a number of strengths, including intelligence, a good problem-solving ability, and insight.

Wendy was forthcoming about the belief associated with her anxiety—that harm was going to come to people she loved. This belief manifested in specific ways when she was faced with situations in which she perceived that there was a possibility that her children could be harmed. Her therapist hypothesized that she believed that she was the only adult who could adequately supervise her children, that she must protect her children from any adversity that they might face, and that her worth was measured by her ability to be a good mother. At the same time, Wendy's therapist also identified some helpful beliefs about parenting and family.

Because her family was so close, Wendy believed in the saying, "It takes a village to raise a child." Thus, she was open to having her mother and her in-laws help with child rearing, and they played a large role in her children's lives. When she presented for treatment, Wendy was experiencing the stress that most mothers of young children experience, in that she constantly felt as if she were "on the run" taking care of them, and she had little time for herself. She often stayed up late at night to have a little time for herself, resulting in mild sleep deprivation. Her therapist regarded this chronic stress as making her more vulnerable to overinterpret the acute trigger of the school shooting, thereby exacerbating her predisposition toward excessive worry.

Conclusion

The biopsychosocial model of perinatal distress provides a heuristic for understanding the pathway by which clinical presentations of perinatal distress develop. The cognitive behavioral model of emotional distress adds awareness of the underlying beliefs that develop from clients' formative experiences and how those beliefs influence the cognitive, emotional, and behavioral responses that they have in specific situations that are upsetting to them. Cognitive behavioral therapists integrate these factors, as well as sources of personal and environmental strengths, into their cognitive case conceptualizations.

The choice to use the interventions described later in this book is made on the basis of the cognitive case conceptualization. Using the cognitive case conceptualization, cognitive behavioral therapists identify psychological factors that explain, maintain, and exacerbate emotional distress that can be modified in treatment. These psychological factors might represent a vulnerability (e.g., poor problem-solving skills), they might represent a general belief that a client has developed on the basis of her formative experiences (e.g., "I'm unlovable"), or they might represent a specific belief about motherhood, parenting, or family. Cognitive behavioral therapists work with their clients to modify situation-specific cognitive, emotional, and behavioral responses that are associated with emotional upset, and they also work with their clients to identify and modify these underlying cognitive orientations. Moreover, cognitive behavioral therapists work with clients to develop adaptive coping skills for a genetic vulnerability to emotional distress and sensitivity to neurochemical variability, and they also help clients to recognize and acknowledge their strengths, as well as maximize the use of their strengths to help them weather times of adversity and disappointment. Thus, CBT is an approach to psychotherapy in which theory plays a central role in organizing information and driving strategic interventions.

3

EFFICACY OF CBT FOR PERINATAL DISTRESS

Evidence-based practice is the practice of making clinical decisions on the basis of the best available research data (Sackett & Rosenberg, 1995). It is not merely the delivery of treatments that have been demonstrated to have empirical support (i.e., empirically supported treatments; Chambless & Ollendick, 2001), although it is true that evidence-based practitioners value treatments that have been demonstrated to work in the empirical literature. Instead, evidence-based practice can be viewed as a "three-legged stool" that consists of: (a) research evidence demonstrating whether and why a treatment works; (b) clinical expertise, which combines clinical judgment and clinical experience; and (c) client preferences and values (Lilienfeld, Ritschel, Lynn, Cautin, & Latzman, 2013; Spring, 2007). This definition is especially applicable for perinatal women who seek treatment for emotional distress, as it has been observed that they respond particularly well to therapists who have expertise in working with this population (Kleiman, 2009), and they often have distinct preferences for the type of treatment that they hope to receive.

Of all of the various approaches to psychotherapy, CBT has perhaps the largest research literature supporting its efficacy. *Efficacy* is defined as the degree to which the treatment under consideration, like CBT, outperforms one or more alternative conditions in rigorously designed and implemented randomized controlled trials (RCTs). "Randomized" means that participants in the research study have an equal chance of being assigned to the treatment condition or the alternative condition(s). Randomization helps to ensure that participants in all conditions are equivalent in terms of their demographic characteristics, severity of their clinical presentation, and so on. "Controlled" means that the treatment under consideration is compared to a control condition so that there is a benchmark for interpreting the treatment's performance. RCTs are designed to test the hypothesis that the treatment under consideration outperforms the control condition in improving myriad aspects of clients' clinical presentations.

There are many types of control conditions that have been incorporated into CBT efficacy studies. Some control conditions are *no treatment* controls, such that participants in these conditions do not receive any treatment but are monitored at the same frequency as participants who receive the active treatment. When people who receive an active treatment, like CBT, report a greater degree of improvement than people who did not receive treatment, it shows that the active treatment is more efficacious than no treatment at all and demonstrates that its effects extend beyond the mere passage of time. Other control conditions are *placebo controls*, such that participants in these conditions receive a nonspecific treatment that does not contain the most important ingredients in the active treatment. A sugar pill is typically used as a control condition in studies examining the efficacy of psychotropic medications. The concept of the placebo is a bit more complicated in psychotherapy research, but it usually involves an intervention that includes only characteristics shared by all psychotherapeutic approaches, such as contact with a supportive professional or the provision of psychoeducation. When people who receive an active treatment, like CBT, report a greater degree of improvement than people who received a psychotherapy placebo, it shows that the active treatment is more efficacious than a nonspecific approach and demonstrates that its effects extend beyond time spent with a supportive mental health professional with whom the client has developed a relationship. Finally, another type of control condition is *usual care*, such that participants in these conditions are referred for whichever treatments are available in their community. When people who receive an active treatment, like CBT, report a greater degree of improvement than people who received usual care, it shows that the active treatment is more efficacious than the treatments that are typically available and demonstrates that its effects are unique and extend beyond the standard level of care.

In this chapter, we discuss the evidence that speaks to the efficacy of CBT for perinatal distress. First, we provide a broad overview of the literature that examines the efficacy of CBT for many manifestations of emotional distress in treatment-seeking adults. It is this literature that establishes the rationale for the investigation of CBT for perinatal distress, as it clearly indicates that CBT outperforms control conditions for a host of types of emotional distress. We also extend the discussion of CBT's efficacy to CBT's effectiveness in "real world" settings. Next, we describe the state of the research evaluating specific CBT approaches for perinatal distress. We conclude the chapter with considerations of ways to reconcile the two literatures and to deliver CBT to perinatal women on the basis of evidence-based principles.

Evaluation of General Literature

There are hundreds of published outcome studies on cognitive behavioral treatments that target a wide range of mental health disorders (Butler,

Chapman, Forman, & Beck, 2006). In order to make sense of the larger literature and identify trends that cut across results of individual studies, researchers have increasingly been turning to meta-analysis. *Meta-analysis* is the aggregation of data from individual studies into an effect size (ES), or a quantitative indication of the strength of an effect using a standard unit of measurement, such as a standard deviation or a correlation coefficient. This standardization allows results from studies using different outcome measures to be compared and combined using a common metric. A standard categorization used to interpret ES is as follows: no effect (ES below 0.2), small effect (ES between 0.2 and 0.5), medium effect (ES between 0.5 and 0.8), and large effect (ES 0.8 or higher) (J. Cohen, 1988). These values can be used to evaluate the magnitude of effects described in this chapter. Thus, in characterizing the state of the literature on CBT's efficacy, we rely primarily on results from meta-analytic studies, although we also describe results from single studies that are notable. In this section, we use the term "cognitive therapy" as well as the term "CBT" to reflect the terminology used by the authors of the particular clinical trial or meta-analysis.

The largest number of RCTs evaluating CBT's efficacy are focused on depression. The most notable RCT from the past ten years established that cognitive therapy is just as efficacious as antidepressant medication in the treatment of moderate to severe depression, which represented a significant shift from the attitude that psychotherapy alone was indicated for only mild cases of emotional distress (Hollon, 2011). De-Rubeis et al. (2005) randomly assigned clients with moderate to severe depression to receive antidepressant medication (paroxetine, with the possibility of augmentation with lithium or desipramine in cases in which clients did not meet established response criteria by week 8), cognitive therapy, or pill placebo. At the 8-week assessment, both the medication (50%) and cognitive therapy (43%) groups had higher response rates than placebo (25%), and at post-treatment, both the medication and cognitive therapy groups had achieved response rates of 58%. Even more compelling are the results from their 12-month follow-up period, in which the authors followed the clients who had completed cognitive therapy, the clients who had completed their medication trial, and a subset of clients who continued with their medication trial (Hollon et al., 2005). Clients who had completed cognitive therapy had much lower relapse rates than clients who had completed their medication trial (31% and 71%, respectively), and they were no more likely to relapse than patients who were continuing to take medications (47%). These results suggest that cognitive therapy is indeed efficacious for moderate to severe depression and that their effects are much more enduring than the effects of taking medications (cf. Hollon, Stewart, & Strunk, 2006).

Results from meta-analyses confirm that cognitive therapy outperforms an array of control conditions. Perhaps the most highly cited meta-analysis is an evaluation that was conducted by Gloaguen, Cotraumx, Cucherat, and Blackburn (1998). Although this meta-analysis is over fifteen years old, it is still relevant today because of its methodological rigor and comprehensiveness, as the majority of trials examining CBT purely for depression, rather than for other clinical presentations, were conducted in the 1980s and 1990s. Gloaguen et al. found that, at post-treatment, cognitive therapy was associated with greater reductions in depression than no treatment or placebo conditions (ES = –0.82), antidepressant medication (ES = –0.38), and other psychotherapies (ES = –0.24), the latter of which consisting of a diverse array of treatment approaches including psychodynamic, interpersonal, relaxation, and bibliotherapy. It was later argued that some treatments that were included in this comparison were not bona fide treatments for depression (e.g., relaxation; Wampold, Minami, Baskin, & Tierney, 2002). When those non-bona fide treatments were excluded from analyses, the ES for the comparison of cognitive therapy with other therapies dropped to –0.16, indicating that cognitive therapy was marginally superior to these other treatments.

Much empirical research also supports the efficacy of broad CBT approaches for anxiety, obsessive compulsive-related, and trauma- and stressor-related disorders. For example, Hofmann and Smits (2008) determined that CBT is associated with greater reductions in anxiety (ES = 0.73) and depression (ES = 0.65) than placebo control conditions in clients with a wide range of anxiety, obsessive compulsive, and traumatic stress disorders. Meta-analytic findings for specific anxiety, obsessive compulsive-related, and trauma- and stressor-related disorders are as follows:

- *Generalized Anxiety Disorder (GAD)*: Hanrahan, Field, Jones, and Davey (2013) found that CBT was associated with a greater reduction in worry than no treatment control and non-CBT treatment conditions, such as relaxation (ESs = 1.81 and 0.63, respectively). In addition, they estimated that at 12 months post-treatment, 57% of GAD clients receiving CBT were classified as recovered, relative to 26% of clients receiving other treatments and 15% of clients who received no treatment at all.
- *Panic Disorder*: Mitte (2005) reported that CBT was associated with greater reductions in anxiety than no treatment and placebo control conditions (ES = 0.87 and 0.51, respectively). In addition, she observed ESs of 0.72 and 0.62 for the post-treatment reduction of depression and 0.85 and 0.42 for the post-treatment improvement in quality of life, as well as a higher drop-out rate for pharmacotherapy (i.e., 20.4%) than CBT (i.e., 15.1%). A subsequent meta-analysis found that CBT was particularly efficacious when it included homework, as well as a systematic follow-up program following

the completion of treatment (Sánchez-Meca, Rosa-Alcázar, Marín-Martínez, & Gómez-Conesa, 2010).

- *Social Anxiety Disorder*: Powers, Sigmarsson, and Emmelkamp (2008) found that CBT was associated with greater reductions in social anxiety symptoms, relative to no treatment control conditions (ES = 0.86) and placebo conditions (ES = 0.38). The magnitude of ESs was similar for measures of other symptoms, including cognitive measures, behavioral measures, and general subjective distress measures, as well as for comparisons with control conditions during follow-up periods.
- *Obsessive Compulsive Disorder (OCD)*: Olatunji, Davis, Powers, and Smits (2013) found that CBT outperformed an amalgam of control conditions in the reduction of obsessive compulsive symptoms post-treatment in clients with OCD (ES = 1.39), as well as in the reduction of secondary symptoms, such as depression (ES = 0.51).
- *Posttraumatic Stress Disorder (PTSD)*: Bisson et al. (2007) compared trauma-focused CBT to no treatment/usual care control conditions for patients with PTSD and calculated the posttreatment ES for the following groups of symptoms: (a) clinician-rated PTSD symptoms (ES = –1.40); (b) self-reported PTSD symptoms (ES = –1.70); (c) anxiety symptoms (ES = –0.99); and (d) depressive symptoms (ES = –1.26), indicating that CBT outperformed control conditions in multiple aspects of these clients' clinical presentations.

It is important to understand that many RCTs are delivered under tightly controlled circumstances. For example, the therapists might be highly trained postdoctoral fellows under the supervision of the principal investigator or another psychotherapy expert. The clients might meet criteria for only one mental health condition, without complicating factors such as suicidal ideation or medical problems. There might be numerous support staff who closely monitor participants, remind them to attend therapy sessions, and help them overcome obstacles to attending therapy sessions. Although these study designs help to ensure that any significant results observed from the study can be attributed to the active treatment itself, rather than other factors (e.g., the number of sessions that participants attend), clearly they create circumstances that are different from those in which clients seek psychotherapy in "real life." Thus, there is a movement toward the conduct of *effectiveness* studies, which are studies that evaluate the degree to which active treatments outperform control conditions in "real life" circumstances. Often in these studies, therapists are employees of a particular organization or agency who received specific training in the active treatment. The clients might present with a host of concerns and symptoms, not only the one that is the target of treatment. There might be fewer, if any, mechanisms in place to ensure that the course of treatment runs smoothly and as expected. Although effectiveness studies are "messier" in their experimental designs, they often more closely approximate the way in which psychotherapy is delivered in the "real world."

CBT has been demonstrated to be effective in the treatment of depression and anxiety in effectiveness studies. In their examination of the effectiveness of CBT for depression, Hans and Hiller (2013a) calculated large reductions in depressive symptoms from pre- to post-treatment in both intent-to-treat (ES = 1.06) and completer (ES = 1.13) analyses. They also reported moderate to large ESs (range = 0.67–0.88) in post-treatment reductions in secondary outcomes, such as dysfunctional cognitions, anxiety, psychological distress, and functional impairment. Although these results are encouraging and demonstrate that CBT is effective when delivered in "real world" settings, the authors cautioned that the ES they calculated were lower than those obtained in "benchmark" RCTs examining CBT for depression.

In a companion manuscript, Hans and Hiller (2013b) calculated moderate to large ES reflecting improvement in disorder-specific symptoms from pretreatment to post-treatment in OCD (ES = 1.45), panic disorder (ES = 0.81), and social anxiety disorder (ES = 0.67). ESs were even larger when analyses were limited to clients who were considered treatment completers, rather than those who entered the studies with an intention to be treated. This meta-analysis also determined that symptoms that were not disorder-specific, such as depression, improved nearly as much post-treatment as those that were disorder-specific. A similar, slightly older meta-analysis determined that ESs in effectiveness studies examining CBT for anxiety disorders are in the range of those obtained by benchmark RCTs (Stewart & Chambless, 2009).

Although the studies and meta-analyses described in this section were not focused on perinatal distress, the results nevertheless have implications for the treatment of this population. The strategies incorporated into the CBT intervention strategies that were evaluated in these clinical trials are those that have their foundation in basic cognitive and behavioral theory and that can apply to any emotional distress, regardless of its content. Thus, there is no reason to believe that these intervention strategies would be irrelevant to the concerns of perinatal women. Therapists who deliver CBT to *any* type of client will tailor it to the client's individual needs and life circumstances. The transition to parenthood is but one of many special life circumstances that has the potential to be disruptive, thereby causing emotional distress. Moreover, CBT has been shown to be effective in addition to being efficacious, which is relevant to treating perinatal distress, as, often, treatment is delivered by paraprofessionals or nurses, rather than licensed mental health professionals, and it is delivered in settings outside of clinics and hospitals, such as in women's homes. In all, as can be seen from this cursory review of the efficacy literature, CBT has a proven "track record" for reducing symptoms of emotional distress. From an evidence-based standpoint, CBT is a logical choice of treatment for many clients, including women with perinatal distress, given the preponderance of data supporting its efficacy in treating adults with emotional distress.

One can only truly state that CBT is efficacious for perinatal distress when empirical research is conducted with this population. Many efficacy trials actively exclude women who are pregnant, especially so when psychotherapy is being compared to pharmacotherapy. Although in clinical practice psychotropic medication is indicated for some women on the basis of the risks/benefit ratio of taking the medication (Wenzel & Stuart, 2011), this decision is made only after careful consideration, including the client's preferences. Randomly assigning pregnant women to receive psychotropic medication that is not clearly without adverse effects to the fetus would be of questionable ethics. Even when efficacy trials do not include a psychotropic medication condition, there are still instances in which pregnant women are excluded for practical reasons, as a pregnancy during the course of treatment guarantees a disruption in consistent attendance, introducing variability into the data. Thus, now that there is a firm rationale for the use of CBT in the treatment of many manifestations of emotional distress, it is time to evaluate its efficacy for perinatal distress in clinical trials.

Evaluation of Perinatal Literature

The past ten to fifteen years have witnessed a significant increase in outcome studies designed to evaluate the efficacy and effectiveness of CBT for perinatal distress. The majority of the studies evaluate treatment for diagnosed postpartum depression or the prevention of postpartum depression in women who endorse risk factors (e.g., elevated scores on self-report measures of depression during pregnancy, a history of depression). We evaluate this literature and describe the main conclusions that can be drawn from it. In addition, researchers have recently begun to evaluate cognitive behavioral approaches to the treatment of perinatal anxiety. Results from two notable studies that significantly advance the literature are described, as well as a cognitive behavioral approach to prevent postpartum posttraumatic stress that is in the process of being developed and evaluated.

Perinatal Depression

One of the earliest examinations of CBT for postpartum depression was published almost twenty years ago (Applby, Warner, Whitton, & Faragher, 1997). Women ($n = 87$) who were 6–8 weeks postpartum and who scored a 12 or higher on the Edinburgh Postnatal Depression Scale

(EPDS; Cox, Holden, & Sagovsky, 1987) and were subsequently diagnosed with major or minor depression were randomly assigned to one of four conditions—fluoxetine or pill placebo coupled with either one or six sessions of cognitive behaviorally-based counseling. Results indicated that fluoxetine was more efficacious than placebo in reducing depressive symptoms and that six counseling sessions were more efficacious than one counseling session. Because there was no statistically significant interaction between pharmacotherapy and counseling, the authors concluded that they were equally as efficacious and that postpartum women can choose either on the basis of their preferences. A subsequent study confirmed that the combination of antidepressant medication (i.e., paroxetine) and CBT was efficacious in reducing symptoms of depression and anxiety from pre- to post-treatment, but that the combination of the two performed similarly as antidepressant medication alone (Misri, Reebye, Corral, & Milis, 2004).

Another highly cited study was conducted by Charbol et al. (2002) and consisted of two phases. In the prevention phase, they identified women at risk of postpartum depression, defined as scoring a 9 or higher on the EPDS, then randomly assigned them to one cognitive behaviorally-based prevention session in the hospital ($n = 97$) or no treatment ($n = 114$). At 4–6 weeks postpartum, fewer women in the prevention group (30.2%) scored in the range of probable depression on the EPDS, relative to women who received no treatment (48.2%). Women in both groups who were identified during this time period to meet criteria for major depression continued in the study, with women from the prevention condition receiving an additional 5–8 weekly one-hour cognitive behaviorally-based home visits ($n = 18$), and the women from the control condition continuing not to receive treatment ($n = 30$). Results from this phase indicated that women in the treatment group scored significantly lower on all symptom inventories and had greater recovery rates, relative to women who received no treatment. The authors concluded that a dual prevention and home-based intervention approach may be the solution to factors that have historically hampered efforts to treat perinatal women—low detection and compliance rates. A subsequent study obtained similar results favoring individual CBT over no treatment in the prevention of postpartum depression in at-risk women (Cho, Kwon, & Lee, 2008).

A particularly comprehensive examination of individual therapy for postpartum depression compared routine non-directive counselling, CBT, psychodynamic treatment, and routine primary care (i.e., control condition) in 193 women who scored 12 or above on the EPDS (Cooper, Murray, & Romaniuk, 2003). Women in the three active treatments had weekly visits with a mental health professional between 8 and 18 weeks postpartum. Results indicated that all three active treatments were associated with a significant reduction in EPDS scores, relative to routine primary care.

However, by 9 months postpartum, there were no differences in depression between the women who received the active treatments and the women who received routine primary care. Moreover, receiving an active treatment did not decrease the rate of subsequent episodes of postpartum depression, nor did it affect maternal management of early infant behaviors, security of attachment, or infant cognitive development (Murray, Cooper, Wilson, & Romaniuk, 2003). Several other studies found no differences in the reduction of perinatal depressive symptoms between individual CBT and usual care (El-Mohandes et al., 2008; Hagan, Evans, & Pope, 2004; Milgrom et al., 2011; Prendergast & Austin, 2001; Zayas, McKee, & Jankowski, 2004); others found that it outperformed usual care, but not supportive psychotherapy (Hayden et al., 2012; Morrell et al., 2009).

Group CBT approaches have also been evaluated in the literature and have the potential to be particularly attractive because: (a) they are cost-effective, treating many women in need simultaneously; and (b) they provide a forum for women going through similar experiences to provide support to one another. These CBT protocols generally had a prescribed topic for each session, such as education about postpartum depression and anxiety, education about infant behavior, pleasant events scheduling, goal setting, problem solving, cognitive restructuring, assertiveness skills, and strategies for developing a social support network. In one uncontrolled trial, Griffiths and Barker-Collo (2008) found that post-treatment, women with postpartum adjustment difficulties who participated in group CBT reported less depression, less anxiety, and more positive attitudes towards being a mother than they reported pre-treatment. However, results from studies comparing cognitive behaviorally-based group treatment to control conditions have yielded mixed results. One study found that the intervention reduced symptoms of perinatal distress relative to usual care (Honey, Bennett, & Morgan, 2002). In contrast, others found that CBT group treatment was not associated with a reduction in perinatal distress symptoms post-treatment or at follow-up assessments beyond that found in a control condition (Austin et al., 2008) or in a supportive counseling condition (Milgrom, Negri, Gemmill, McNeil, & Martin, 2005).

CBT packages have also been tailored to the needs of particular cultural and ethnic groups. The Mothers and Babies (Mamás y Bebés) course is a CBT group (called a "course" to emphasize its psychoeducational nature) for low-income women that is conducted in both English and Spanish for women at risk of developing postpartum depression (Muñoz et al., 2001). It includes topics such as fostering the mother-baby relationship, coping with stressors that could affect the mother-baby relationship, and transmitting healthy thinking to the child, using cognitive and behavioral strategies to achieve these aims. Muñoz et al. (2007) reported that the postpartum incidence of major depression was 14% in women who participated in the course, relative to 25% of those who participated in usual care. Although this difference did not reach statistical significance, it represents a small ES of 0.28. Subsequently, Le, Perry, and Stuart (2011) found that depressive symptoms were decreased in women who completed the course, relative to women who received usual care one week after the last intervention session. Tandon, Perry, Mendelson, Kemp, and Leis (2011) reported the most robust results supporting the effectiveness of this program, indicating that three months after the intervention, 9% of the women who received the course reported clinically significant depression, relative to 33% who received usual care.

Other culturally-sensitive CBT packages have been evaluated within the United States as well as internationally. For example, Jesse et al. (2010) evaluated "Insight-Plus," an intervention for African American and Caucasian rural low-income women in the United States who were at risk of developing depression during pregnancy, in 17 women who completed the full six-session protocol. The intervention targeted many themes that had been identified by focus groups as being important, such as reducing stigma, facilitating trust, and overcoming barriers, and its interventions was designed to have a low reading level and include attractive graphics. Recovery rates, defined as EPDS scores of 10 or lower, were 65% at the end of treatment, 81% at 1 month post-treatment, 91% at 4 weeks postpartum, and 75% at 8 weeks postpartum. Although results from this study are impressive, it must be noted that there is no control group, as only 4 women indicated that they would be willing to be randomized to this condition. Rahman, Malik, Sikander, Roberts, and Creed (2008) examined CBT (n = 463) compared with "general visits" delivered by village-based home health workers in rural Pakistan (n = 440). At six months following treatment, 23% of the women who received CBT met criteria for major depression, relative to 53% of women who received the general visits. The enduring effects of CBT were sustained at the 12-month follow-up assessments, with rates of major depression of 27% and 59% in the CBT and general visit conditions, respectively. Results from this study are especially notable in light of the large sample size, the impressive effects, and the fact that treatment was delivered by paraprofessionals in women's homes.

A recent evaluation of CBT for antenatal depression was described by A. Burns et al. (2013), who conducted a pilot study comparing modified, in-home, individual CBT (n = 18) to usual care (n = 18) in pregnant women who screened positive for depression on a 3-item screener. Their CBT approached focused on recognition of the way in which maternal beliefs affected mood, obstacles to implementing behavioral activation, and enhancing communication and social support. Results indicated that, at 15 weeks following randomization, approximately 69% of clients who received CBT no longer met ICD-10 criteria for depression, relative to approximately 39% of clients who received usual care. At 33 weeks following randomization, approximately 81% of clients who received CBT no longer met criteria for depression, relative to approximately 36% of the clients who received usual care. Women who received CBT also scored lower on self-report inventories of depression and reported better mental health quality of life than women who received usual care at 33 weeks post-randomization.

What can be concluded from this literature? There is currently mixed evidence that supports the efficacy and effectiveness of CBT for perinatal depression or the prevention of perinatal depression, and the evidence is less conclusive than it is for the general adult population. This conclusion was confirmed in a meta-analysis by Cuijpers, Brännmark, and van Straten (2008), who determined that the ES capturing post-treatment differences between CBT and control conditions was 0.36, which is less than that found in the literature reviewed earlier in the treatment for depression for adults in general and less than the ES found for psychotherapy for postpartum depression (i.e., 0.51 after excluding one outlier). This ES indicates that there is a small effect in favor of CBT outperforming control conditions post-treatment, but that it is not as favorable as that obtained for other approaches to the treatment of perinatal distress (e.g., IPT).

A number of methodological caveats must be kept in mind when evaluating this literature. In many of the studies, only a subset of women who met study inclusion criteria agreed to participate (e.g., 38.9% in Austin et al., 2008). Thus, the samples of women who participated in these studies might not be representative of the population of perinatal women who would benefit from CBT. It could be, for example, that women with less severe clinical presentations were more likely to participate. It is conceivable that women with less severe clinical presentations would benefit even from minimal contact with a healthcare professional, such as that provided in usual care conditions, and do not require more sophisticated cognitive and behavioral interventions. Such a scenario would result in a paucity of significant differences in the performance of CBT relative to usual care. In addition, some studies found that attendance was problematic; for instance, Le et al. (2011) reported that 12% of women allocated to the Mothers and Babies course did not attend even one session, and Milgrom et al. (2005) found that 32.7% of the women randomized to their active treatments did not attend. Other methodological limitations include small sample sizes in some of the studies, making it difficult to achieve statistically significant differences between the CBT and control conditions; reliance on self-report inventories, rather than gold-standard structured clinical interviews, to diagnose depression; and lack of sufficient follow up, as the true effect of prevention programs can only be observed with a follow-up period that is long enough to capture new cases of depression (Nardi, Laurenzi, Di Nicoló, & Bellantuono, 2012).

From our reading of the literature, however, the most significant issue that bears on the interpretation of this pattern of results lies in the definition of CBT. Some of the practices reflected in the descriptions of CBT were inconsistent with the contemporary practice of CBT. For example, in their description of their cognitive behavioral counselling intervention, Applby et al. (1997, p. 933) stated, "Each session structured to offer reassurance and practical advice on four areas of concern." The offering of advice is inconsistent with the guided discovery environment that cognitive behavioral therapists strive to provide to their clients. Moreover, cognitive behavioral therapists typically offer reassurance judiciously in order not to reinforce unhelpful patterns of reassurance seeking. Charbol et al.'s (2002) study is one that is often cited as an example of CBT's efficacy. However, their intervention included many psychodynamic components, such that "the subject to acknowledge her ambivalence and link it with personal history, in particular Oedipal and separation-individuation conflicts" (p. 1041). These psychodynamic components, while embraced by many mental health professionals who specialize in perinatal psychology, are unequivocally inconsistent with the way in which cognitive behavioral therapists conceptualize their course of treatment and deliver therapy. Moreover, Jesse et al.'s (2010) CBT protocol included thought-stopping activities, which are clearly contraindicated by research by Daniel Wegner demonstrating that thought suppression is ineffective in reducing the frequency of intrusive thoughts (e.g., Wegner, Schneider, Carter, & White, 1987) and are considered to be out of favor in by expert cognitive behavioral therapists. We agree with the use of Milgrom et al.'s (2011) term, "counselling informed by CBT principles," and we suspect that this characterizes a number of the CBT packages for perinatal depression that have been evaluated in the literature. It is likely that there is a difference between CBT interventions that follow protocols that have been deemed empirically supposed (Chambless & Ollendick, 2011) and therapy "informed" by CBT principles, although this is an empirical question that should be tested in research.

Thus, it is unclear whether many of the perinatal women who participated in the clinical trials described in this section received CBT as developed by Aaron T. Beck (cf. O'Hara & McCabe, 2013), which is an approach characterized by a cognitive case conceptualization (see Chapter 2), guided discovery using Socratic questioning, and attention to the therapeutic relationship (see Chapter 4). We highlighted the A. Burns et al. (2013) study in this section; although it is a pilot study with small samples, it may be the closest to the Beckian approach described in this book, as it adapted CBT to address specific cognitions (e.g., maternal beliefs) and behaviors (e.g., balancing valued goals with time sensitive pressures) that are core issues with which perinatal women struggle. Results from this study indicated that CBT was highly effective in reducing depression relative to usual care, both post-treatment when the clients were still pregnant, and in the follow-up period when clients were postpartum. These results raise the possibility that Beckian, conceptualization-based CBT is an especially good match with perinatal women.

It was surprising that the majority of the studies examining group CBT approaches found that CBT did not outperform usual care, as many of the protocols were grounded in established theory and adapted established CBT strategies to the needs of perinatal women (e.g., Milgrom et al., 1999; Muñoz et al., 2001), and group treatments tend to be received well by perinatal women because they value the support and camaraderie of others with similar experiences (O'Mahen et al., 2012). Because many of these groups included a great deal of psychoeducation, it is possible that they did not allow sufficient time for the development of group cohesiveness or a strong therapeutic relationship with the facilitator. If this explanation is correct, it speaks to the power of relationships, either with the therapist or with other group members, in facilitating treatment success in perinatal women.

Perinatal Anxiety

The few cognitive behavioral interventions to address anxious clinical presentations closely approximate empirically supported treatment protocols for anxiety disorders for the general adult population. For example, Lilliecreutz, Josefsson, and Sydsjo (2010) conducted an open trial examining two sessions of a CBT group intervention for pregnant women with blood/injury phobia ($n = 30$). During the group sessions, clients engaged in prolonged exposure to different phobic stimuli, including lancets, syringes, injection needles, and intravenous catheters. In addition, a midwife performed procedures such as pricking clients' fingers, administering a vein puncture, and inserting an intravenous catheter. Clients took home the objects between the first and second group sessions, with the idea that they would continue exposure by looking at them and touching them. Results indicated that injection-related anxiety, general anxiety, and depression decreased following each of the two group sessions and that scores on inventories measuring these symptoms were significantly lower than scores reported by untreated women. This study provided important evidence that exposure is tolerated well by pregnant women and that it is efficacious in reducing anxiety and other symptoms associated with perinatal distress.

Timpano, Abramowitz, Mahaffey, Mitchell, and Schmidt (2011) developed a CBT program to prevent postpartum obsessive compulsive symptoms. They delivered their intervention in the context of regular childbirth education courses, such that an additional 30 minutes was added onto each of six sessions. Topics covered in the CBT component of the course included psychoeducation about obsessive compulsive symptoms and the cognitive model of intrusive thoughts, instruction in cognitive restructuring, instruction in the use of exposure as a behavioral experiment to test and modify unhelpful beliefs, and review and wrap-up. They compared childbirth education + CBT ($n = 38$) to childbirth education + control ($n = 33$), the latter of which included general education about anxiety disorders and videos that told the stories of several expecting couples. Results indicated that at 1, 3, and 6 months postpartum, mothers who received the CBT condition reported significantly lower levels of obsessions, compulsions, and cognitive distortions than women who received the control condition.

Finally, Shaw et al. (2013) described the development of a treatment protocol that adapted trauma-focused CBT (Resick & Schnicke, 1992) to prevent postpartum posttraumatic stress in mothers of infants born between 26 and 34 weeks' gestation and receiving treatment in the Neonatal Intensive Care Unit (NICU). The six-session treatment included the following components: (a) development of the therapeutic relationship and hearing of mothers' stories; (b) cognitive restructuring; (c) progressive muscle relaxation; (d) education about trauma-focused CBT and preparation for exposure by creating a trauma narrative; (e) exposure to thoughts and memories of childbirth by reading the trauma narrative, coupled with cognitive restructuring of self-blame and other unhelpful thoughts; and (f) redefining mothers' views of their infants and of parenting, as well as discussion of parenting and infant care. Twenty mothers who scored above a threshold on self-report inventories of anxiety, depression, and/or traumatic stress completed the treatment. Results indicated that mothers were highly satisfied with the treatment and that anxiety decreased from pre- to post-treatment in a subset of eight mothers who completed outcome measures. Although this treatment is in the early stage of development, it shows promise in being able to adapt an established cognitive behavioral intervention for PTSD for the unique concerns of distressed mothers of premature infants.

Conclusion

A vast literature has accumulated over the past forty years that demonstrates the efficacy of CBT for adults who struggle with depression, anxiety disorders, obsessive compulsive-related disorders, and trauma- and stressor-related disorders. Although there is no reason to believe that this evidence base would not apply to perinatal women, it is important to confirm that it is efficacious for perinatal distress because perinatal women are often excluded from large RCTs examining CBT in treatment-seeking adults. Surprisingly, research examining the efficacy of CBT for the treatment and prevention of perinatal depression is mixed, as some studies have found that it outperforms usual care, and other studies have found that it is equivalent to usual care. Although one can conclude from the extant research that CBT is a reasonable option to use with perinatal women, the magnitude of effects is not as impressive as it is in the general adult literature.

However, a close examination of the descriptions of the protocols used in these studies raises the possibility that not all of the cognitive behavioral interventions were fully consistent with cognitive and behavioral principles and strategy. Moreover, key features of the Beckian approach, such as the development and use of the cognitive case conceptualization to drive the selection of strategic interventions, appeared to be absent in many of the protocols. Instead, many of the protocols followed a session-by-session format, and some included strategies that expert cognitive behavioral therapists have cautioned against using.

We advocate for the delivery of the Beckian approach to perinatal women, such that treatment follows from an individualized cognitive case conceptualization in a collaborative manner that balances cognitive behavioral change with attention to the therapeutic relationship. A key feature of this approach is that it uses guided discovery to facilitate skill acquisition and solutions to life problems, rather than an exclusive reliance on didactics or the provision of advice. Chapters 5–11 of this book comprise the treatment manual that can guide therapists in delivering this treatment. It describes the flexible delivery of CBT, which is highly dependent on the cognitive case conceptualization, the preferences of the client, and the "data" obtained in treatment that speak of the degree to which the interventions are achieving their desired aims in the client's life. It does not require that any particular intervention must be delivered in a particular session. Instead, it requires that therapists be familiar with cognitive and behavioral principles of change and implement interventions to achieve those principles of change with integrity and by using careful observation. Moreover, it allows therapists to balance all three legs of the "three-legged stool" of evidence-based practice so that practice that is guided by the empirical literature is balanced with clinical expertise and client preferences.

4

THE THERAPEUTIC RELATIONSHIP

A commonly heard stereotype about CBT is that it is dry and rigid and discounts the importance of the therapeutic relationship. In reality, many classic writings on CBT emphasize that a strong therapeutic relationship must be in place in order for therapy to be successful, and they describe specific aspects of the therapeutic relationship to be cultivated throughout treatment (e.g., A. T. Beck et al., 1979). This chapter does the same, in light of discourse that emphasizes the centrality of the therapeutic relationship to perinatal women who seek treatment for emotional distress (e.g., Kleiman, 2009).

The therapeutic relationship is unique among the professional relationships that people have in their lives. The therapist is delivering an important service to the client, and the client agrees to logistical parameters such as the time and place to meet and the fee that will be paid. At the same time, there is a sense of caring, compassion, and intimacy that is felt by both parties. The therapist has the formidable task of cultivating and maintaining the therapeutic relationship while balancing the delivery of strategic interventions that are expected to bring relief to the emotional distress with which the client presents for treatment, all the while maintaining appropriate professional boundaries and bringing quality care to the client.

Perhaps the main component of the therapeutic relationship is the therapeutic or working alliance (Castonguay, Constantino, & Grosse Holtforth, 2006). Bordin (1979) described the *therapeutic alliance* as consisting of "three features: an agreement on *goals*, an assignment of *task* or series of tasks, and the development of *bonds*" (p. 253, italics added). In other words, there is a clear focus of the work that is done in therapy, strategic interventions are delivered in order to achieve goals, and there is an interpersonal connection between the client and the therapist. Meta-analyses have determined that the effect size for the relation between the therapeutic alliance and treatment outcome ranges from 0.22 to 0.26 (Horvath & Bedi, 2002; D. J. Martin, Garske, & Davis, 2000); in other words, there is a small but noticeable effect of the therapeutic alliance on the degree to which clients respond to treatment. Other key aspects of the therapeutic relationship include therapist empathy, positive regard, and congruence (Castonguay et al., 2006).

Developing a strong relationship early in the course of therapy is associated with better outcome and higher client retention (D. J. Martin et al., 2000), prompting expert psychotherapy researchers to recommend that therapists attend to the therapeutic relationship even in the first moments of interaction with their clients (e.g., Castonguay et al., 2006). Hardy, Cahill, and Barkham (2007) indicated that the main task early in therapy is engagement, which includes empathy, warmth, genuineness, negotiation of goals, collaboration, support, guidance, and affirmation. Empathy is particularly important; it alone accounts for 7–10% of variance in outcome and has been shown to be even more important in achieving positive outcomes in CBT than in other types of psychotherapy (Bohart, Elliott, Greenberg, & Watson, 2002). It is not difficult to imagine that therapist demonstration of empathy is critical with perinatal women, who often report excessive self-criticism, guilt, and a profound sense of failure. As therapy progresses, therapists continue to foster the therapeutic relationship by providing an environment that promotes openness to the process of therapy, commitment to the process of therapy, and trust in the therapeutic relationship (Hardy et al., 2007).

Over fifty years ago, Winnicott (1963) likened the therapeutic relationship to the mother-infant relationship, describing it as a "holding environment" characterized by unconditional acceptance, interest, and empathy. Although Winnicott practiced from a psychoanalytic orientation and approached therapy in a very different manner from cognitive behavioral therapists, the parallel is clear. When new mothers are called on to provide acceptance, care, and patience to their newborns, they may be in dire need of it themselves. Thus, it is of utmost importance for therapists to create a secure, welcoming environment characterized by mutual respect and unconditional acceptance. In many cases, perinatal women regard the therapeutic relationship as the most trusted relationship in their current lives, even as a sanctuary away from the demands of their lives (Kleiman, 2009).

The Therapeutic Relationship and CBT

Many core features of CBT also contribute to the development of a strong therapeutic relationship. *Collaboration* between the therapist and client gives the client the sense that her wishes and preferences are just as important as the tools that the therapist has to offer. Cognitive behavioral therapists have a great *respect for clients' individual differences*, as evidenced by the development of an individualized case conceptualization that drives treatment that is tailored to the needs of the unique clinical presentation.

In addition, cognitive behavioral therapists show an appreciation for clients' individual differences when they modify strategic interventions to fit the current demands in clients' lives, their strengths, and their challenges. Throughout treatment, cognitive behavioral therapists make *periodic summaries* to ensure that they have understood the essence of what their clients have communicated to them, which in turn gives clients the sense that their therapist cares and is listening carefully. Finally, cognitive behavioral therapists share the rationale for their strategic interventions and outline the precise manner in which they are expected to bring relief from emotional distress, which in turn *instills hope* in clients that something can be done with the problems that they would like to address in treatment.

This latter point is especially relevant with perinatal clients, who often state that their lives have changed forever and that they cannot imagine feeling "normal" again. The tools that are offered by the therapist may be perceived by the client in distress as a tangible way to manage the chaos by which she feels so overwhelmed. Most perinatal clients are relieved when the therapist can present and deliver expertise in treating this population, with supportive language as well as specific strategies of intervention. At a time when almost everything feels out of control, perinatal women coming to therapy seek immediate relief from their symptoms and control in their lives.

There is a small but impressive body of empirical research on the relation between the therapeutic alliance and outcome in CBT. Working alliance in these studies is typically measured by the self-report version or the observer version of the Working Alliance Inventory (WAI; Horvath & Greenberg, 1989; Tracey & Kokotovic, 1989; Tichenor & Hill, 1989), which measures the three components of the therapeutic relationship advanced by Bordin (1979; i.e., goals, tasks, and bonds). Interestingly, studies examining the association between the therapeutic relationship and symptom change in CBT find that symptom reduction precedes improvement in the therapeutic relationship, particularly the bond between the client and therapist, not vice versa (DeRubeis, Brotman, & Gibbons, 2005; DeRubeis & Feeley, 1990; Feeley, DeRubeis, & Gelfand, 1999; Webb et al., 2011). Moreover, clients who experience *sudden gains* in CBT, or abrupt and substantial reductions in their reports of depressive symptoms, subsequently endorse higher scores on measures of the working alliance (Tang, Beberman, DeRubeis, & Pham, 2005; Tang & DeRubeis, 1999). This pattern of results suggests that the benefit afforded by strategic interventions in CBT enhances clients' views of the therapeutic relationship. Furthermore, it raises the possibility that the implementation of strategic interventions early in the course of treatment, even when it seems that the therapeutic relationship is still being established, would be good practice. However, it should be noted that recent research has found that one aspect of the therapeutic alliance—the agreement between the therapist and client on the goals and tasks of therapy—predicted symptom change when it was measured early in the course of treatment (Webb et al., 2011), suggesting that this agreement is important to secure before strategic interventions commence.

Cultivating the Therapeutic Relationship

Figure 4.1 summarizes techniques that expert psychotherapists have described as cultivating a strong therapeutic relationship. Techniques that are important in achieving this aim include demonstrating attentiveness to verbal and nonverbal communication, making reflections, paraphrasing and summarizing what the client has stated, linking the client's

• Demonstrating attentiveness to verbal and nonverbal communication.
• Making reflections.
• Paraphrasing and summarizing what the client has stated.
• Linking the client's statements to statements that she has made previously.
• Validating the client's psychological experiences.
• Expressing an understanding of the client's unique needs.
• Educating the client about her symptoms.
• Refraining from being overly enthusiastic or optimistic.
• Modeling the same approach and behaviors that clients learn and acquire in CBT.
• Refraining from restructuring or correcting every negative thought or unhelpful behavior that the client describes in session.
• Demonstrating sensitivity to clients' reluctance to do homework, or more generally, to embrace cognitive and behavioral change strategies.
• Addressing ruptures in the therapeutic relationship in a manner that is sensitive and respectful, that models the core tenets of CBT, and that allows the client to have an important learning experience.

Figure 4.1 Techniques that Cultivate the Therapeutic Relationship.
Sources: Gilbert & Leahy (2007); C. F. Newman (2007).

statements to statements that she has made previously, and validating her psychological experiences (Gilbert & Leahy, 2007). These techniques are often regarded as nonspecific in nature because they are important to the outcome of any type of psychotherapy, not only CBT. Many perinatal women present for treatment stating that they feel alone and that others do not understand their subjective psychological experience during the transition to parenthood. This sense of isolation can actually reinforce their negative thoughts and further increase their distress. The therapist represents a model of unconditional acceptance as well as a safe place for a woman to disclose her most painful thoughts. It is crucial for therapists to express an understanding of her unique needs. It is also helpful for the therapist to provide some initial psychoeducation about perinatal depression and anxiety in order to connect with the client's current situation and establish a position of expertise in the treatment of perinatal distress. This will reassure the client that she is in the right place and enable her to experience the early stages of an alliance with the therapist, which is so crucial to the healing process.

Although the installation of hope is an important component of establishing the therapeutic relationship early in the course of therapy, it is important to refrain from being overly enthusiastic and optimistic. Most perinatal clients are tired and sleep-deprived, and excessive enthusiasm can feel like too much to them. In addition, some clients have adverse reactions to expressions of optimism, interpreting it as invalidation or as a sign that the therapist does not appreciate the difficulties that they are experiencing (Leahy, 2001). Thus, cognitive behavioral therapists balance the acknowledgement of clients' real problems while leaving room for intervention so that things can be different or better.

Cognitive behavioral therapists believe that it is important to demonstrate the same approach and behaviors that they hope their clients will learn and acquire in CBT. In this way, therapists are good role models for clients (C. F. Newman, 2007), serving as a resource for clients to consult as they are applying the tools in their own lives. In addition, it is important for cognitive behavioral therapists to have practiced the same homework that they encourage their clients to complete in between sessions and to actively use cognitive behavioral tools in their own lives. One of us (AW) tells her clients that she does not suggest that they practice anything that she, herself, has not practiced at some point in her life. Therapist modeling the CBT approach and CBT-consistent behaviors communicates to clients that they are universal phenomena that can benefit all people, regardless of whether they are a client in psychotherapy. It is also hoped that clients will view themselves as an equal member of a team if both the therapist and client are practicing the same behaviors.

Thus, cognitive behavioral therapists believe that the therapeutic relationship is enhanced when both the therapist and client actively apply cognitive and behavioral strategies in session. At the same time, however, it is important to balance change strategies with the nonspecific techniques described previously (cf. Wenzel et al., 2011). For example, perinatal clients often verbalize a large array of negative and unhelpful thoughts about themselves, their parenting, their spouse or partner, the grandparents, and so on. Attempting to restructure every thought might feel like micromanagement to the client, and it could interrupt the flow of the session and the connection with the therapist (cf. C. F. Newman, 2007). In addition, cognitive behavioral therapists should demonstrate sensitivity to clients' reluctance to complete homework in between sessions, or more generally, to embrace cognitive and behavioral change strategies. This can be done by acknowledging how overwhelming it must feel to have one more thing asked of them and how counterintuitive it might feel to them. Validating this with words and nonverbal reassurance can help engage a reluctant client. Because perinatal clients often present for therapy feeling quite overwhelmed, the prospect of having another obligation seems daunting for them. Cognitive and behavioral change strategies should never be forced on them. Perinatal clients are more likely to embrace change strategies when they feel ready to do so. Motivational interviewing techniques are often used in the early sessions of treatment with these clients in order to help them grapple with reasons for changing and to dig deep to find their motivation for change from within (see Chapter 5). In addition, throughout the rest of the book, we provide suggestions for how homework can be adapted for the demanding lives of perinatal women.

Despite therapists' best efforts, there might be ruptures in the therapeutic relationship, or they will find themselves in a situation in which there is a potential for a rupture. A rupture is "a tension or breakdown in the collaborative relationship between patient and therapist" (Safran, Muran, & Eubanks-Carter, 2011, p. 80). Cognitive behavioral therapists address ruptures in the therapeutic relationship in a manner that is sensitive and respectful, that models the core tenets of CBT, and that allows the client to have an important learning experience. For example, if the therapist senses that the client has had an adverse reaction to something that was said or done in session, the therapist gently brings this to the client's attention, offering it as a hypothesis and obtaining evidence to examine the accuracy of the hunch, which models an effective approach to handling interpersonal disputes in their own lives (C. F. Newman, 2007). Strauss et al. (2006) found that the successful repair of a rupture in the therapeutic relationship was associated with better outcome following treatment, suggesting that ruptures can actually enhance the therapy experience if they are handled well. However, doing so requires flexibility and interpersonal effectiveness, as qualitative data suggest that therapists' rigid adherence to technique when faced with a rupture in the therapeutic relationship may actually make the rupture worse (e.g., Castonguay, Goldfried, Wiser, Raue, & Hayes, 1996).

Techniques for maintaining and enhancing the therapeutic relationship occur in the following dialogue, in which Lyla's therapist sensed that Lyla was having an adverse reaction to her attempt at cognitive restructuring.

Therapist: So you saw your neighbor at the park, and she didn't wave to you. What was running through your mind when that happened?

Lyla: My mind? I don't know. Just another example of the crap that happens in my life. [looks bored]

Therapist: [using the skills described in Chapter 6 to help Lyla identify a relevant automatic thought associated with emotional distress] Well, might you have been thinking something benign, like "she didn't realize it was me," or might you have been thinking something that could bring you down, like "she's purposefully trying to ignore me"?

Lyla: [frowns a bit] What does it matter? [escalating] The end result is still the same! I have no friends! I've gotten feedback my entire life that people don't like me. No matter how much you want me to rationalize it, that's my reality!

Therapist: [backing down from cognitive restructuring and speaking gently and patiently] Lyla, I'm sensing that you're a bit frustrated with what we're doing in therapy right now. Am I accurate?

Lyla: Yes! I can't just think away my problems. It's like you expect me to just look at the positives, putting on rose-colored glasses. And that's just not the way my life works. [shakes head] Nobody gets me. Not even therapists, who I *pay* to get me.

Therapist: I appreciate that you told me this. I certainly apologize if I've given you the message that you can just think your problems away, or that you should put on rose-colored glasses. That's not what I meant to convey.

Lyla: [backing down] Well, I don't know if you actually conveyed it like that.

Therapist: Well, nevertheless, it's my job to check in with you to ensure that you and I have the same understanding of what we're doing together. I will be sure to do that more often. It's essential, in fact, that you feel "gotten" by me, and I will continue to do everything I can to appreciate what you are experiencing in your life.

Lyla: [looks stunned] You mean, you're not mad at me?

Therapist: Mad at you? Why would I be mad at you? This type of feedback is essential to our work together. You're allowed to be frustrated, and you're allowed to express that frustration in a safe environment.

Lyla: It's, it's just different than how it usually goes.

Therapist: How what usually goes?

Lyla: When I have a confrontation with people.

Therapist: Say more about that.

Lyla: Well, it's just that, my relationships, they all eventually go south. Something happens, and then, kaput, they're over.

Therapist: Do you think that's going to happen with us?

Lyla: As soon as I started unloading, I wondered.

Therapist: A minute ago, I told you that I appreciated your feedback and would use the feedback to check in with you more frequently in therapy to make sure that we're on the same page. How much do you buy that?

Lyla: [hesitates] I guess I do.

Therapist: I sense some hesitation in your voice. Speak from the place of that hesitation.

Lyla: I guess it's just that there have been a lot of other times that people have acted like we're all good after a confrontation, but in reality, we're not. It's really awkward the next time I see them.

Therapist: How much do you believe that's going to happen the next time we see each other?

Lyla: I guess not much. Maybe 10%.

Therapist: What do you think makes our situation different than the other instances in which you thought all was well in the relationship, but then the relationship went south?

Lyla: That's a good question. [thinking] Well, for one, you're a professional. [pauses] But I guess even that doesn't give me any guarantees. I've had some bad experiences in therapy before.

Therapist: [making a reflection] You've had some issues arise in therapy before that affected your relationship with the therapist.

Lyla: Yeah, exactly. But I think this is different. I mean, we're really talking it out right now. It doesn't seem like there will be any hard feelings either way.

Therapist: I can assure you, from my point of view, that there won't be any hard feelings. In fact, I'm viewing this as an important event in our relationship that we were able to work through.

Lyla: I don't have any hard feelings either. I was just venting, I guess. Things just feel so badly right now.

Therapist: So if we've been able to work through this together, what does this tell you about problems in other relationships, like when you have a difference of opinion with another person?

Lyla: It gives me hope that the relationship won't just end even if we have some sort of tiff. That if we just talk it out, things will be OK.

In this dialogue, the therapist quickly shifted gears when it was clear that Lyla was not responding to the therapeutic intervention. The therapist checked out two assumptions about possible ruptures in the therapeutic relationship: first, that Lyla was frustrated with the therapeutic intervention, and second, that Lyla did not truly believe that the therapist welcomed her feedback and would adjust her behavior. All the while, Lyla's therapist conducted herself with openmindedness, patience, and respect for Lyla's experience with their interaction. She allowed Lyla to talk about the possible rupture in the therapeutic relationship and be present with her experience of it. This sort of dialogue reflects *metacommunication skills,* or communication about what is happening in the therapeutic relationship (Safran, Crocker, McMain, & Murray, 1990), which have the potential to improve the quality of the bond between the client and therapist and refocus the pain on their collaborative work together (Castonguay et al., 2006). Toward the end of the dialogue, the therapist applied the learning that occurred to incidents that occur in other relationships in order to achieve generalization of the messages that Lyla was taking away, which allowed Lyla to take away an important message about viewing future interpersonal conflict.

Conclusion

This chapter clearly demonstrates the centrality of the therapeutic relationship in delivering CBT to perinatal women. On the one hand, the research described in this chapter has demonstrated that the early implementation of cognitive and behavioral strategic interventions is associated with a reduction in symptoms, which in turn enhances the client's view of the therapeutic relationship. On the other hand, perinatal experts have emphasized the importance of creating a sanctuary for perinatal women to experience support from their therapist, perhaps like no other person could give at this point in their lives.

The majority of perinatal women who present for treatment are more scared and unsure of themselves than they have ever been in their lives. For many, the thoughts and feelings they have that are expressed as symptoms, but experienced as self (Kleiman, 2009). That is, they have a strong belief that everything they are feeling and thinking now contributes to their distorted belief that they are bad mothers or weak in character. It is difficult for them to recognize that these are symptoms that will resolve with treatment rather than expressions of who they are. Therapists need to clarify this distinction and remind them that it is acceptable for them to approach therapy at their own pace and that they are in an environment in which they can expect support, empathy, and understanding. Cognitive behavioral therapists who work with perinatal women are sensitive to this balance and should strive to continually obtain feedback from perinatal clients in order to meet their clients' needs.

At times, clinicians who are training in CBT believe that further attention to the therapeutic relationship is somehow "off-limits" in CBT. As was demonstrated in dialogue between Lyla and her therapist, this is an incorrect assumption. Issues that arise in the therapeutic relationship, whether positive or challenging, serve as the optimal context to demonstrate respect, warmth, empathy, and patience, as well as to illustrate, model, and practice CBT principles and strategies. If a client is having a positive experience in therapy, she and her therapist can identify exactly what makes the experience positive, reflect on the emotional experience associated with these positive aspects, consider how her therapy experience is inconsistent with unhelpful beliefs that she has about the way relationships work, and discuss ways to replicate these positive aspects in her other relationships. If a client is having a negative experience in therapy, as Lyla did in the dialogue, she and her therapist can proactively address it, which provides further opportunity for the therapist to demonstrate empathy, patience, and respect, as well as for the client to have a corrective learning experience. That corrective learning experience may provide the realization that relationships do not have to end simply because there is a negative interaction or a conflict, it may help the client realize that people can still show care and affection even if they express discontent about the relationship, or it may be the opportunity to acquire communication skills that will help them to manage conflicts in relationships in the future. In fact, some of the best CBT work happens in the context of issues that arise in the therapeutic relationship, as it allows for the experiential learning of many cognitive and behavioral principles.

We encourage researchers to design future studies that will, empirically, identify the role of the therapeutic relationship in facilitating outcome in the treatment of perinatal distress. Because a strong therapeutic relationship is viewed as so central to perinatal experts, data that identify the amount of variance in outcome accounted for by the therapeutic relationship, the degree to which the therapeutic relationship serves as a mediator of change, and the specific components of the therapeutic relationship (e.g., empathy) that are particularly important to attend to with perinatal women. In addition, future research should identify characteristics of perinatal women for whom the therapeutic relationship is particularly associated with outcome, as recent research has demonstrated that a poorer therapeutic relationship predicts relapse in people who have chronic depression (i.e., five or more episodes; Weck et al., 2013).

Cognitive behavioral therapists believe that a strong therapeutic relationship is essential for a good outcome in therapy. At the same time, they believe that it is not sufficient and that cognitive and behavioral strategic interventions are necessary to modify unhelpful cognitive and behavioral patterns that maintain emotional distress. Fortunately, in most cases, it is possible to maintain a strong therapeutic relationship and deliver cognitive and behavioral strategic intervention; the therapist does not have to choose *either* to attend to the therapeutic relationship *or* to deliver a strategic intervention. The development of cognitive case conceptualizations and the delivery strategic interventions can be done in an authentic, genuine, and caring manner that enhances the therapeutic relationship, which can be a powerful combination in helping clients to obtain relief from perinatal distress.

5

COGNITIVE BEHAVIORAL THERAPY FOR PERINATAL DISTRESS

An Overview

As the reader has seen to this point in the book, CBT is a system of psychotherapy that has the potential to be a strong match for perinatal women. It is highly efficacious and effective for depression and anxiety, which are symptoms that are commonly reported by perinatal women seeking treatment. It offers tangible tools that women can adopt immediately in managing their emotional distress. It is also individualized in that the interventions follow from a cogent cognitive case conceptualization that accounts for the etiology and maintenance of women's clinical presentations and points to specific targets in treatment.

This chapter provides an overview of CBT for perinatal distress. First, an overview of the course of CBT is presented, with a special focus on how ambivalence about treatment affects clinical decisions and how psychotherapy proceeds. In addition, the structure of each CBT session is described, highlighting the fact that session structure need not be followed rigidly, but proceed according to the natural unfolding of the session and the client's needs. Finally, we discuss the way cognitive case conceptualization facilitates treatment planning, which provides a context for the subsequent chapters on the delivery of specific strategic therapeutic interventions.

Course of Treatment

Many CBT experts divide the course of treatment into three phases: an early phase, a middle phase, and a late phase (e.g., Wenzel et al., 2011). The *early phase* of treatment occurs at the beginning of treatment and can last one to three sessions (but can last longer if it is indicated by the client's clinical presentation). The aim of the early phase of treatment is to orient the client to treatment, ensuring that she understands what the treatment entails and is on board with the rationale. The early phase of treatment is also used for the therapist to gather information that is used in formulating the cognitive case conceptualization and in developing a treatment plan. Specific activities that may go on in the early phase of treatment are as follows:

- *Psychological assessment*: The therapist administers a diagnostic interview and/or self-report inventory in order to establish psychiatric diagnoses, which will be incorporated into the cognitive case conceptualization and used to focus the specific therapeutic interventions selected.
- *Psychoeducation about CBT*: The therapist describes the general features of CBT, including: (a) its active, problem-solving focus; (b) the types of things that the client can expect to do with the therapist in session; (c) change to the structure of sessions; (d) the importance of collaboration; and (e) reasons it is a good match for perinatal distress.
- *Psychoeducation about the CBT model*: The therapist describes the basic premises of the model, perhaps sharing a diagram such as the one in Figure 2.2, and works with the client to determine how it applies to her life.
- *Identification of obstacles to engagement in treatment*: The therapist works with the client to identify any obstacles that might prevent her from fully engaging in treatment, helps her to brainstorm ways to overcome those obstacles, and encourages her to commit to enacting one or more of the ways to overcome those obstacles.
- *Formulation of the cognitive case conceptualization*: The therapist takes the information from the client's history, the diagnostic interview, behavioral observation, and collateral reports and develops the beginning of a cognitive case conceptualization.
- *Development of a treatment plan*: The therapist works with the client to identify key targets for treatment, taking care to operationalize them in terms that are observable and measurable and identifying ways to measure progress toward these goals across the course of treatment.
- *Practice with one or more CBT tools*: The therapist responds to the client's current emotional state by sharing with her one or more tools that are expected to relieve distress and that will be practiced further in the next phase of treatment.

Although these are the "typical" activities that occur in the early phase of treatment, it is important not to follow them as one would a recipe in a cookbook without consideration of the client's needs and preferences. Indeed, all of the tools and strategies described in this book are meant to be delivered in a fluid manner that flows from the natural interaction between the client and therapist. As mentioned in Chapter 4, the therapist is continually mindful of the balance between the here-and-now interaction in the therapeutic relationship and the advancement of cognitive and behavioral change. When clients express a need to focus on something they view of utmost importance, in the early stage of treatment the therapist will comply in order to show respect for their wishes.

These features of CBT are especially important to remember when working with perinatal women. Many are scared to death, feeling less like themselves than they have ever felt before and petrified that they will cause harm to a helpless infant who is solely dependent on them. Most are so sleep-deprived that they say they are having trouble thinking straight. Many are desperate, believing that they are destined to live a life consumed by anxiety and a pervasive sense of inadequacy. As mentioned in Chapter 4, they are seeking support and nurturing just as much as they are seeking tools to manage their emotional distress.

Thus, the psychological assessment will probably not proceed as straightforwardly as it might with non-perinatal clients. These clients want help right away and often cannot wait to start treatment in order to complete an entire psychological assessment. Thus, therapists should have enough familiarity with the structure and process of CBT to accomplish many tasks at once—providing support, allowing the client to tell her "story," orienting her to treatment, advancing the cognitive case conceptualization, and setting the stage for an intervention that will begin to reduce her emotional distress. Although this might sound daunting to the novice clinician, therapists are encouraged to be mindful of the core principles of CBT to guide their clinical decisions in any one moment (Wenzel, 2013). This balance is illustrated in the following dialogue with Donna, who presented for her first session with grave fears that she had postpartum psychosis.

Donna: [with wide eyes, escalating as she is talking] I just know I'm psychotic. I feel like all of this isn't even real. Here I have this beautiful daughter, and I'm just numb. I don't deserve her. I think I made a big, big mistake. [pauses] What do you think? Am I going crazy? Am I going off the deep end?

Therapist: [leaning in and using a soft, soothing voice to provide supporting and nurturance] I don't think you're going crazy at all. You're going through what so many other women go through—an abrupt transition that isn't all it's cracked up to be.

Donna: [looks incredulous] Really? This is normal? Then how come I've never heard of anyone else going through this?

Therapist: [continuing to use a soft, even voice] There are lots of different versions of normal that characterize women after they've had a baby. You're right, some women don't go through this. But many, many women do [an example of psychoeducation, which the therapist viewed as a strategic intervention to normalize Donna's concerns]. In fact, over two-thirds of new mothers report having thoughts that they experience as quite scary. Would you say that your concern about being psychotic is a scary thought?

Donna: Yeah, definitely. It freaks me out. [pauses] But how do you know *for sure* that I'm not psychotic?

Therapist: Well, let me ask you some more questions about your thoughts and feelings.

[Therapist goes on to assess for the presence of psychotic symptoms, as well as the severity of obsessive compulsive symptoms, given Donna's psychiatric history. This accomplishes two aims. First, it allows the therapist to ask key questions for the purpose of psychological assessment, which allows her to clarify Donna's diagnosis and advance the cognitive case conceptualization. Second, it provides the therapist "data" to focus the type of psychoeducation that she communicates to Donna regarding Donna's clinical presentation.]

Therapist: On the basis of these questions I've asked you, what are you concluding about whether you are psychotic?

Donna: I guess . . . I mean, I don't have hallucinations. People are worried about me, yeah, but not worried that I will hurt Ellie. They just want me to relax and enjoy her a bit.

Therapist: I'm not worried that you're going to hurt Ellie, either. Your responses to my questions suggest that you are having persistent and intrusive thoughts about being psychotic, which are very inconsistent with how you view yourself. [pauses] Have there been other times in your life when you've fixated on concerns that, in reality, are very, very unlikely, or even non-existent?

Donna: Lots of times. A couple of years ago, I had this thing where I was convinced that I had run someone over when I was driving. It even got to the point where I would turn around and look all over the place to make sure there weren't any dead bodies. [thinking] And, when I was in my late teens, I was convinced that I was going to get AIDS. I got tested five times even though I was in a serious relationship with the same person.

Therapist: So what does all of this tell you about what's happening now?

Donna: [sighs] That this is my OCD kicking in.

Therapist: Tell me, how did you manage in the past when your OCD started to kick in?

[Here, the therapist is moving toward identifying a specific cognitive behavioral tool that Donna might be able to practice between sessions in order to attain some relief from her emotional distress.]

This dialogue illustrates how Donna's therapist wove together many aims of the early phase of CBT during their first appointment. In this excerpt, she provided support, which enhanced the therapeutic relationship; she conducted part of a psychological assessment, which advanced her conceptualization of Donna's clinical presentation; she provided psychoeducation, which gave Donna facts to normalize and make sense of her current emotional distress, and she worked toward identifying a cognitive behavioral tool that Donna could practice so that she could obtain immediate relief from her distress. In the remaining time in session, Donna's therapist: (a) conducted additional psychological assessment targeting other psychiatric diagnoses, such as depression; (b) educated Donna about the basic principles of CBT and how she expected that they would make a difference in Donna's life; (c) shared her conceptualization of Donna's intrusive thoughts in light of the cognitive behavioral model described in Chapter 2 (cf. Kuyken et al., 2009); and (d) obtained Donna's commitment to practice thought modification (see Chapter 6), which Donna has learned in a previous course of CBT for a different manifestation of OCD. At the time of the second session, Donna and her therapist solidified a treatment plan, and they moved into the next phase of treatment.

The early phase of treatment does not always run as smoothly with many clients. The classic stages of change model (e.g., Prochaska & DiClemente, 1982, 2005) indicates that clients present for treatment with a wide range of readiness for change. Only a small percentage of clients are in the *action* stage of change, meaning that they have made a firm commitment to make positive changes in their lives (Prochaska, DiClemente, & Norcross, 1992). Most clients who present for treatment are in one of three other stages of change. Those in the *precontemplation* stage of change do not see themselves as having any behaviors or issues that require change. Those in the *contemplation* stage of change admit that they have problems that need to be addressed, but they are ambivalent about moving forward, either because they see benefits from problematic behavior or because they believe it is too difficult to change. Those in the *preparation* stage of change admit that they have problems that need to be addressed and have taken small steps to put themselves in a position to make those changes, but they have not yet taken action. Psychotherapy researchers believe that it is crucial to identify the stage of change in which clients present, as the likelihood of dropout or treatment failure increases when there is a mismatch between the intervention that the therapist delivers and the client's readiness for change (Norcross, Krebs, & Prochaska, 2011).

The majority of perinatal women seen in outpatient treatment are beyond the precontemplation stage. They *know* there is a problem. They *know* that they are feeling worse than they have ever felt in their lives.

There can be a great deal of ambivalence about treatment. It is not that they necessarily see benefits to staying where they are. It is that the distress that they are feeling is so enormous that they do not know where to start, do not know when they can take the time to do therapeutic work, and do not believe they have the wherewithal to do it because they are so overwhelmed. In addition, another source of ambivalence that is unique to perinatal women is their fear that a mental health professional really will think she is crazy and take measures to take her child or children away. Because of this concern, many perinatal women approach treatment cautiously, refraining from disclosing the thoughts and emotional experiences that they consider to be most disturbing.

Thus, assessment and careful observation of ambivalence about treatment are key factors for therapists to consider in working with perinatal women. Fortunately, there is a well-established counseling approach for working with ambivalent clients. *Motivational interviewing* (Miller & Rollnick, 2013) is a style of counseling that was originally developed to give problem drinkers space to decide, on their own, that they were ready to reduce their drinking. It is a client-centered approach in which the therapist refrains from giving advice or telling the client what to do, and instead uses reflective listening and evocative questioning for clients to begin to see a discrepancy between the current manner in which they are living their lives and the way they want their lives to be. This approach has been honed over the past 25 years, and it is now used to address ambivalence in clients with a wide range of clinical presentations, not only problem drinking (cf. Westra, 2012).

Motivational interviewing has particular relevance to the successful delivery of CBT; they share many basic principles, including an emphasis on the therapeutic relationship, respect for individual differences, and a teamwork orientation between the therapist and client (Wenzel, 2013). Moreover, accumulating research has demonstrated that the delivery of motivational interviewing prior to a full course of CBT ultimately improves outcome (Westra, Arkowitz, & Dozois, 2009; Westra & Dozois, 2006). Other research has shown that motivational interviewing increases the likelihood that clients will follow through with treatment (Buckner & Schmidt, 2009). What this suggests is that motivational interviewing has the potential to be a key component of the early phase of treatment with perinatal women before a therapist launches into the next phase of treatment, in which cognitive and behavioral interventions are administered in their entirety.

Entire books that provide instruction in the delivery of motivational interviewing have been published (Miller & Rollnick, 2013; Westra, 2012), so we will not provide an elaborate description here. From a general standpoint, according to Miller and Rollnick (2013), four principles that underlie the "motivational interviewing spirit" include compassion, collaboration, acceptance, and evocation of the client's strengths that are present, rather than attempting to correct some sort of fault. Therapists who practice motivational interviewing with their clients engage their clients in order to form a connection, focus on the issues that the client hoped to address, evoke the client's own motivations for change, and plan to develop a commitment to change and put together a specific course of action. They use skills such as the asking of open-ended questions, affirmation, reflective listening, summarizing, informing, and advising with permission.

The following dialogue provides an illustration of how Lyla's therapist assessed for ambivalence and then used principles of motivational interviewing in order to help Lyla become more comfortable with the idea of therapy and make a decision to commit to treatment.

Lyla: [stroking her baby's hair as she speaks] I just don't have a lot of confidence that this will make a difference. I've been in therapy off and on ever since I was 16.

Therapist: You've been through a lot of therapy, and here you are again. You're not sure that this will be helpful.

Lyla: And now look at me. I'm 35. You're probably going to say that I shouldn't have had a baby in the first place if I'm this messed up.

Therapist: You're concerned that I will judge you.

Lyla: Why wouldn't you? I judge myself. I judge myself all the time. What kind of a life am I going to give my child if I am chronically depressed?

Therapist: [noting a hint of change talk] So you want your child to have a good life?

Lyla: Wouldn't any parent want that for their child? I just don't know where to start. [places head in hands] I'm so tired. All I want to do is sleep. Every day I need to call my mother and have her take care of Jack just so I can sleep the afternoon away.

Therapist: [first providing a statement of support, then making a statement that asks for elaboration of her change talk] I can tell how tired you are. It's so exhausting to have a little one. [pauses] You certainly want what's best for your son. What would that be?

Lyla: [tearful] I just want to be a normal person for once. I don't want to screw up my son.

Therapist: It sounds like you care so deeply for his well being.

Lyla: [nods] But where do I start?

Therapist: [asking permission] I believe I have something quite powerful to offer you. Would you like to hear more about my approach to treatment?

Lyla: [nods again]

65

[Therapist goes on to provide a small bit of psychoeducation about CBT to Lyla, taking care to refrain from providing too much detail so that Lyla does not become overwhelmed and back down, as well as to present the information in a manner that instills hope that things can be different.]

Lyla: I've never done anything like this before. I have always just gone into my appointment, gave an update on the week, talked about how I am feeling, and left, but things were still the same.

Therapist: [obtaining feedback] What do you think of this approach to therapy?

Lyla: It sounds like a lot of work.

Therapist: Right. And what new mother has the time to do a lot of work, on top of taking care of the baby?

Lyla: Don't get me wrong, I really think I need to figure out a way to make this work. If not for my own sake, then for Jack's sake.

Therapist: You'll do what it takes to do the best you can by your son.

Lyla: Yeah. Exactly. [pauses] This whole thing makes me nervous, though. In the past, when I commit to things, I usually don't follow through. And that makes me feel even worse about myself.

Therapist: I hear what you're saying. We certainly want to set you up for success rather than disappointment. I have an idea. What if you were to commit to just four additional sessions? I can share some of the tools I have to offer you, and you can try them out during that time. Then, at the end of four sessions, we can evaluate how it's going. We can see what's working and what's not working. If it's working, then that's great, you'll start to see some differences in your life. If it's not working, you can certainly decide to discontinue treatment. And, if some things are working and some things are not working, that will be important feedback so that we can put our heads together and make some adjustments so that we ensure that what we are doing is individualized for your needs?

Lyla: [brightens up slightly] This is a relief. Sometimes, with other therapists, I've felt trapped. Like I have to keep coming in, week after week, even though I don't want to.

Therapist: [taking the opportunity to reinforce another basic tenet of CBT] This is very important information. During every visit, I will get feedback from you. Feedback on what you are getting out of our work, feedback on whether I have gotten anything wrong, and so on. If you at all have the sense that you are trapped and just coming to therapy because you feel obligated, I invite you to share that with me. That will be a signal that we need to rethink what we're doing in here.

Several aspects of this dialogue deserve note. First, notice that early in the interaction, Lyla expressed concern that the therapist was judging that she should not have a baby. This is an example of an automatic thought (see Chapter 2), which has the potential to bring on negative emotions (e.g., resentment toward the therapist) and influence behavior in an unhelpful manner (e.g., no show at the next session). During the middle phase of CBT, a cognitive behavioral therapist might use the techniques described in Chapter 6 to help Lyla recognize that this is an automatic thought, rather than a fact, and examine the evidence that both supports and refutes the notion that the therapist is judging her. Here in the early phase of treatment, Lyla's therapist chose not to go this route, even though the automatic thought was clearly exaggerated, because she recognized that Lyla was in the contemplation stage of change and that the administration of a directive cognitive behavioral strategy might result in Lyla backing further away from therapy. In other words, Lyla's therapist was aware that the administration of a standard CBT strategy was probably a mismatch for Lyla's readiness for change, so she instead reflected Lyla's statement to communicate that she had heard Lyla's concern and was taking it seriously.

Toward the end of the dialogue, Lyla had expressed some change talk, while at the same time, maintaining some ambivalence about her commitment to treatment. Her therapist used a common strategy called a *behavioral experiment* in order to embrace Lyla's stance, moving treatment forward by asking her to commit to a handful of sessions while, at the same time, alleviating any pressure to commit to more than Lyla was ready for. Therapists who implement behavioral experiments have their clients enact a certain behavior without preconceived notions (e.g., attending four CBT sessions) and then evaluate how it went. Lyla's therapist anticipated that she would be able to model many of the central principles of CBT (e.g., collaboration, feedback, development of a targeted treatment plan) that would instill hope in Lyla that things could be different and that would show respect for her opinions and needs. Lyla's therapist was hopeful, then, that Lyla would have a "taste" of many aspects of CBT that many clients find attractive, which would help her to commit to additional sessions.

Although we emphasize the importance of motivational interviewing in this discussion of the early sessions of treatment, the principles of motivational interviewing are incorporated into effective CBT at any point in treatment when a client expresses or demonstrates ambivalence. Change is not linear; it is more of a process that waxes and wanes and is influenced by the course of the client's psychopathology, things that are going on in the client's life, and the client's response to the interventions applied in treatment. As a result, there is a continual dance between the therapist and client in which they circle back and forth between motivational interviewing and the delivery and practice of cognitive behavioral tools. In no circumstance is this more evident than with perinatal women, whose children are jetting through developmental stages at lightning speeds, requiring their psychological equilibrium to be continually re-balanced. Thus, therapists are encouraged to assess for the presence of ambivalence throughout the course of treatment, suspend any "agenda" they might have for cognitive behavioral change when they detect ambivalence, verify their perceptions with their clients, and use motivational interviewing to allow clients the space to decide if and when to recommit to treatment.

There is no question that a lot happens in the early phase of treatment, and what occurs in the early phase of treatment might set the stage for the flavor that the middle and late phases ultimately take. By the end of this phase of treatment, the client will have a solid understanding of what CBT entails. She may have gotten a glimpse of some of the tools and observed the manner in which they made a difference in her life. She and her therapist will have a clear, mutual understanding of the work that they expect to do in treatment. She will also know how to measure change so that she can determine whether therapy is helping her.

However, all of this is only achieved when the client has resolved her ambivalence and has committed to attend at least a subset of sessions. Although we initially indicated that the early phase of treatment usually occurs in between one and three sessions, in reality, there is no limit to the amount of time that a therapist might devote to the early phase depending on the client's readiness for change. Therapists are strongly encouraged to move at the client's own pace and only move to the middle phase of treatment when the client is ready to do so. From the therapist's standpoint, it might seem as if treatment is moving slowly, or that the client is not gaining maximal benefit from CBT. Do not underestimate the healing power of the therapeutic relationship itself and the space that is allowed for the perinatal woman to make decisions about her mental health. This could be the only time in the day that she has to herself, or the only time when someone is *not* telling her what to do, and she might hold this time sacred even if she is not diving into the cognitive and behavioral change tools that CBT has to offer.

The *middle phase* of treatment is where the "action" occurs. Clients move into the middle phase when they have made a commitment to treatment and express a willingness to try understanding their problems from a cognitive behavioral perspective and implementing the tools that are most appropriate for relieving the distress that they are experiencing. Although cognitive and behavioral change strategies are emphasized in this phase of treatment, cognitive behavioral therapists continue to be mindful of the balance between the implementation of these change strategies and nurturance of the therapeutic relationship.

No middle phase of treatment looks the same for any two clients. Remember that CBT is a flexible approach to treatment that relies on the underlying principles of cognitive behavioral theory to direct the therapist to select or develop a strategic intervention that matches their client's clinical presentation (i.e., cognitive case conceptualization). Chapters 6–10 of this book describe the application of standard CBT strategies to perinatal women. These standard strategies include cognitive restructuring, behavioral activation, affective coping skills, exposure, problem solving, and communication skills training. It is likely that therapists who deliver CBT to perinatal women will use some combination of many, but not all, of these strategies with their clients. However, cognitive behavioral therapists could implement other strategies, even those from other schools of psychotherapy, if they are called for by the cognitive case conceptualization. The key in the selection and the delivery of therapeutic interventions is that they are strategic, such that they: (a) logically follow from the case conceptualization; (b) are decided collaboratively by the therapist and client; (c) allow the client to leave the session with something more than she brought to the session; and (d) are seen through in their entirety before moving to another issue or concluding that they are ineffective (Wenzel, 2013). More about the strategic delivery of CBT interventions is discussed in Chapters 6–10.

Finally, clients enter into the *late phase* of treatment when they have made significant gains in the middle sessions and their emotional distress has decreased. From a stages of change perspective, they are moving from the action stages of change into the maintenance stage of change, meaning that they have demonstrate sustained success in making positive changes in their lives and are ready to make a lifelong commitment to making their new cognitive and behavioral set habitual. The aims of the late stage of treatment are to consolidate clients' learning, increase the likelihood that they will be able to generalize the cognitive and behavioral tools and principles to their lives after therapy has ended, and develop a relapse prevention plan. When clients enter into this stage, they develop a plan with their therapist to taper sessions and eventually end treatment. These and other activities that occur in the late stage of treatment are described in greater detail in Chapter 11.

Session Structure

In addition to the structure that characterizes the course of treatment, there is also a structure that shapes each individual session. The purpose of this structure is to ensure that everything considered to be important by both the therapist and client are covered in the session and that the time in session is used as effectively as possible. Figure 5.1 summarizes the CBT session structure components (cf. J. S. Beck, 2011).

BRIEF MOOD CHECK: The therapist obtains a quantitative estimate of the client's mood state, which will allow the therapist and client to monitor the client's progress in treatment.

BRIDGE FROM THE PREVIOUS SESSION: The therapist asks the client what she took away from the previous session in order to orient her to the current session and ensure that a thread runs across sessions.

AGENDA: The therapist and client collaboratively agree on the issues to address during the current session.

DISCUSSION OF AGENDA ITEMS: The therapist and client address the items on the agenda, taking care to balance attention to the therapeutic relationship with cognitive and behavioral change strategies. During this discussion, the therapist makes *periodic summaries* to ensure that she understands what the client is communicating and that they are in agreement with the direction that the session is taking.

HOMEWORK: The therapist and client review the homework that the client completed in the time since the previous session, and they collaboratively develop new homework to be completed before the next session.

FINAL SUMMARY AND FEEDBACK: The therapist invites the client to summarize what she is taking away from the current session and provide other feedback.

Figure 5.1 CBT Session Structure Components.

Many therapists who are learning about CBT balk at the notion of session structure. Reactions range from concern that the structure is too rigid, to concerns that the structure will somehow be off-putting to clients or stifle spontaneous expression, to concerns that it is inauthentic and will damage the therapeutic relationship. However, session structure has many benefits. First, many clients seek treatment because they are overwhelmed by their life problems. They have not been able to make sense of them and seem to be "spinning their wheels." CBT session structure models an organized approach to dealing with life's problems, demonstrating to clients a new way of approaching their problems and instilling hope that their problems can be addressed. Second, it ensures that a strategic intervention is delivered in a way that advances treatment, such that the client learns something tangible that she did not know when the session started and has a plan for implementing it in her life outside of session. Without session structure, sessions can take one of three forms: (a) clients spend the majority of the session "venting" about the details of their problems without working with their therapist to develop a plan for addressing them; (b) clients jump from topic to topic, falling into the same pattern as they do outside of session when they think about their problems and leaving them just as confused and overwhelmed as they were at the beginning of the session; or (c) the client and therapist engage in unstructured exploration of the past in a manner that neither advances the cognitive case conceptualization nor gives the client any direction on how to manage her emotional distress that she is experiencing in the here and now.

Session structure has the potential to be *particularly* important to implement with perinatal women. It is natural that many perinatal women are *more* overwhelmed than the average client due to the new demands of parenthood, abrupt mood shifts, and sleep deprivation. They might be craving structure to make sense of their experience. When therapists work collaboratively with perinatal clients to implement session structure, they are giving them the message that there is something they can do *right now* to address their emotional distress. They are giving clients the message that their experiences are not alarming and can be addressed effectively with the tools they have to offer. They are giving clients some relief from their confusion and hopelessness.

It is equally as important for sessions to run in a smooth, fluid manner, as opposed to a rigid manner in which the therapist seems to be checking off the session structure components using a checklist. Although we discuss the session structure components in a particular order in the remainder of this section, this does not mean that these components *must* be implemented in this particular order. Above all, cognitive behavioral therapists are mindful of their clients' needs and preferences in any one moment, being 100% present and in tune with their clients. Will there be times when the best-intentioned cognitive behavioral therapist does not cover all of these components in their session? Of course. Will there be certain clients for whom this session structure approach is not a good match? Of course. Instead, this heuristic for session structure can be regarded as a guiding principle of which therapists remain mindful as the session unfolds. With time, these session structure components become the natural manner in which cognitive behavioral therapists conduct business.

The *brief mood check* typically occurs at the beginning of the session after the therapist has greeted the client. It is a check in to monitor the client's mood in the time between sessions, and its purpose is to provide objective "data" that will allow the therapist and client to monitor the client's progress. Although it is tempting to ask a general question, such as "How are you feeling?" or "How is your mood?", therapists are strongly encouraged to use a quantitative scale, such as a 0–10 likert-type scale (0 = absence of depression, 10 = most depression that the client has ever experienced). The goal is to obtain precise information that is as straightforward as possible for the therapist to interpret. If the therapist asks, "How is your mood?", and in one session the client responds with "down," and in the next session the client responds with "not good," it is unclear whether the two mood states are different from one another and which one is more severe than the other. With quantitative data, the therapist can more readily make a determination of whether the strategies that are being implemented in session are making a difference in the client's level of emotional distress. If the mood ratings gradually decrease, then the therapist can conclude that the interventions are appropriate; if the mood ratings remain the same or increase, then the therapist considers the hypothesis that a different intervention might be a more effective strategy for the client.

Any symptoms can be monitored during the brief mood check; the symptoms that are monitored with any client depend on the symptoms that are most distressing to the client. With many clients, cognitive behavioral therapists obtain ratings of depression and anxiety. If a client has a unique symptom that is also being targeted in treatment (e.g., sleep disturbance, reassurance seeking), then the therapist might also obtain a quantitative estimate of its severity. Risky and/or potentially life-threatening symptoms (e.g., alcohol or drug use, suicidal ideation) are also monitored during the brief mood check.

In addition to the brief mood check, cognitive behavioral therapists typically encourage their clients to make a *bridge from the previous session* before jumping into the contents of the current session. The purposes of the bridge are to orient the client to the current session and ensure that a thread runs across sessions so that the client can build on her learning and practice. It is best to ask the client an open-ended question, rather than a close-ended question, to initiate the bridge so that the client can actively put words to the learning that occurred. Asking the client whether the previous session was helpful will almost undoubtedly yield a short response such as "yes." Although it is gratifying to know that our clients find sessions helpful, the goal of treatment is for clients to become their own cognitive behavioral therapists, and one way to achieve this goal is to ask questions that allow them to put words to the principles that they are learning. Helpful bridging questions include "What did you take away from our previous session?", "What nugget from our previous session ended up sticking with you, or making a difference in your life?", or "What take-home message did you take away from our previous session?"

The implementation of the bridge from the previous session should be balanced with the realization that many perinatal women will be so overwhelmed and sleep-deprived that they will not remember the previous session. On the one hand, this is perfectly understandable, given their current life circumstances. On the other hand, CBT will only be as effective as the degree to which clients are able to remember the principles and tools learned and practiced in sessions and apply them to their own lives. If any client, perinatal or otherwise, repeatedly has difficulty remembering the previous session, it is important to address that systematically in session in order to devise creative ways for the take-home messages to remain with her in between sessions (e.g., reminder notes).

The *agenda* is the plan for how the time in session will be spent. The therapist and client, in collaboration, decide in advance what they want to cover in the session. Setting an agenda helps to ensure that discussion is targeted and focused; that there is time for issues that both the client and therapist believe are important to be covered, and that the session does not end, only for the therapist and/or the client to realize that other topics needed to be covered. Some expert cognitive behavioral therapists recommend writing the agenda on a piece of paper or a white board to help both the therapist and client stay focused. This practice is especially helpful for clients who repeatedly tend to veer off on unhelpful tangents, or clients who provide so much description that they get lost in the detail and have difficulty clarifying the fundamental issue that needs to be addressed with CBT strategy. Questions that therapists can ask in formulating the agenda include "What would you like to put on the game plan for today?", and "What would you like to be sure to address today?" If clinicians find that clients put tangential issues on the agenda and hypothesize that they are avoiding addressing the core issues in their cognitive case conceptualization, they can ask a question such as, "What should we focus on today in the service of meeting the goals that we set at the beginning of treatment?"

Cognitive behavioral therapists are mindful of CBT's collaborative nature. Applied to agenda setting, this means that both parties equally contribute to the agenda. Clients will usually want to discuss stressors, challenges, or conflicts that arose in the time between sessions. Cognitive behavioral therapists will want to check in about the client's between-session work (i.e., homework) and continue to educate about or practice a particular cognitive or behavioral tool. A typical agenda for a perinatal client might be a review of her homework, discussion of discord with her mother-in-law, addressing of continued mood disturbance, and advancement and practice of a cognitive or behavioral tool. Thus, some of the agenda items are content-based (i.e., discord with mother-in-law, continued mood disturbance), and some of the agenda items are strategy-based. However, even when the focus of discussion is on the content area that the perinatal client hopes to address, the therapist will bring a strategic mindset, understanding the issue in light of the cognitive case conceptualization, encouraging the client to apply the tools she has already learned to manage her emotional distress or solve the problem, and creating a context for the implementation of a new strategic intervention to address the issue.

Attention to the agenda does not end after the agenda is developed. Indeed, good cognitive behavioral therapists are mindful of the agenda throughout the session and periodically revisit it when necessary. In almost every session, discussion goes in a direction that was not anticipated when the agenda was initially developed. Rather than being swept off course by this new direction, and rather than insisting that clients remain on the topic that was identified for the agenda, cognitive behavioral therapists assume a "middle ground" stance and work collaboratively with their client to reassess the agenda. The therapist might make an observation like, "This seems like an important issue that is different from what we had hoped to cover. We have about 20 minutes remaining in the session. How do you think we should best use our remaining time?" In this way, the therapist and client thoughtfully decide the direction of the session, in light of the new topic that was introduced. Regardless of whether they agree to stick with the original topic or shift to the new topic, a systematic approach to dealing with problems and challenges has been modeled.

Thus, the brief mood check, and bridge from the previous session, and the setting of the agenda typically occur in the first five minutes or so of the session. This does not have to happen sequentially; more often there is an interplay among these three session structure components. This interplay is illustrated in the following dialogue between Tara and her therapist.

Therapist: Come on in, Tara. It's good to see you today.
Tara: [a bit shaky] Thanks. I'm glad you could squeeze in the appointment.
Therapist: You seem a bit tired today. [Tara nods her head] Tell me, on our 0 to 10 scale, with 10 being the most depression you've ever experienced, where have you been in the time since our previous session?
Tara: [tears rolling down her cheeks and shaking her head] It hasn't been good. It hasn't been good at all.
Therapist: [gently] I'm so sorry to hear that. I know how tough things have been for you lately, and you could really use a break. [Tara nods and smiles weakly] Last week, you told me that you were an 8 out of 10 on our depression scale. Is it safe to say that you are even higher this week?
Tara: [looks down at her hands in her lap] Yeah. I think it's gotten to a 10 out of 10 now. [pauses, and then begins to escalate]

It's just that everyone expects so much of me, you know? I *should* be breastfeeding exclusively. I *should* be doing more tummy time. Should this, should that. I'm so sick of it!

Therapist: It sounds like there is a real mismatch between what you perceive others' expectations to be and what you feel you can do at the moment.

Tara: There sure is.

Therapist: I wonder if this is something for us to focus on in our session today? So that we can see if we can figure out a way for you to get some relief from these unrelenting expectations?

Tara: Yeah, definitely. I can't take this anymore.

Therapist: So your depression has worsened in the past week. What about your anxiety on our same 0 to 10 scale?

Tara: That's off the charts, too.

Therapist: A 10?

Tara: Yeah, a 10.

Therapist: Is the increase in the anxiety related to the expectations of others, or is there another source of it?

Tara: Well, I'm still waking up panicking. Even if I'm not really thinking of anything. So I don't know. Is it all of those expectations? Is it lack of sleep? Is it just life? Who knows?

Therapist: So, what you view as others' expectations probably also contribute to the anxiety, but they don't account for all of it. We've been working on tools to manage your panic. Should we also put that on our game plan for today so that we can evaluate what's working and what's not working?

Tara: Yes, we better. Because *nothing* is working.

Therapist: Tell me what you learned from our previous session that might have some relevance to making sense of how you're feeling today?

Tara: Honestly, I don't even remember what we talked about. I'm so sleep deprived.

Therapist: Would you like a reminder?

Tara: Please.

Therapist: A big part of the session was spent practicing controlled breathing so that you can learn to manage the physiological aspects of your nighttime panics. Does that ring a bell?

Tara: Oh, well yeah, I tried it a little. I'm not sure if it did anything, though.

Therapist: Tell you what, why don't we revisit that when we evaluate the degree to which the tools we've practiced so far are working.

Tara: Yeah, OK, that sounds good.

Therapist: So, it looks like our focus of today will be on managing what you view as other's expectations during these early

75

	postpartum months and evaluating the degree to which your CBT tools are working in managing your nighttime panic. Is there anything else that you had hoped to cover today?
Tara:	Well, I've just had this overwhelming sense of dread, like I shouldn't have had a child. Like I was selfish for having a baby if I can't even take care of him.
Therapist:	What a painful idea that is.
Tara:	[tears welling up] It is. I hate it.
Therapist:	So we have three very important issues to cover today—your view of others' expectations for you, the coping tools, and the dread. Which is the most important one for us to cover?
Tara:	[pauses, thinking] The dread, I think. I think it underlies everything.
Therapist:	OK, let's focus on that. And how is this for a plan, I'll keep track of time. And if I notice that there are only 20 minutes or so left in the session and we're still talking about the dread, is it OK if I bring that to your attention so that we can decide together whether to table the other two items that we had hoped to cover, or whether to shift gears?
Tara:	Yes, thanks, I'd be grateful for that. Time seems to get away from me these days.

Several aspects of this dialogue deserve note. First, notice the therapist's response when Tara indicated that "things were not good." It would have been tempting for the therapist to run with that statement and say "tell me about that." Although this response is not unreasonable, it likely would have led to unstructured discussion about a number of things that Tara was experiencing. The therapist would not have finished the quantitative mood check, might not have learned that Tara had difficulty remembering the previous session and that her panic coping tools seemed ineffective to her, and might not have gotten to the heart of the issue—Tara's dread associated with her perception that her family would be better off without her—that ultimately served as the focus of much of the session. Also note that the therapist did not rigidly insist that Tara supply a quantitative estimate of her depression. Rather, the therapist first responded with an empathic statement and then gently asked about her level relative to the level that she had reported at the time of the previous session.

A second point of this dialogue to notice is the process by which Tara and her therapist set the agenda. It did not occur in one single instance, such that the therapist asked Tara what she wanted to cover, and Tara responded with an organized list of topics. Rather, the therapist caught on to important information that Tara communicated during the mood check and the bridge and asked, curiously, if those issues should be added to the agenda. Then, following the bridge, she asked if Tara had anything else to add to the agenda, at which time Tara identified an important issue that had not been touched on at that point. This example illustrates the fact that agenda setting often occurs simultaneously as other structure components are implemented at the beginning of a session.

A final point of this dialogue to notice is how Tara's therapist prioritized the three agenda items and firmed up the use of their time. Because the three issues all seemed important to address, Tara's therapist relied on Tara's preferences to determine which item to cover first. Sensing that the issues surrounding her dread could use the entire time of the session, the therapist proposed that she would watch the time and let Tara know when a substantial amount of time had passed so that they could make a collaborative and informed decision about whether or not to table the remaining items. This example illustrates that therapists are mindful of the agenda throughout the session and apply it in a systematic but flexible manner.

When the agenda has been set, and the therapist and client have agreed on the item to address first, *discussion of agenda items* ensures. As stated previously, when discussing content areas that the client expressed a desire to cover, the therapist does not listen passively, but makes an attempt to assimilate the client's content into the cognitive case conceptualization, understand the implications of the content in light of the cognitive case conceptualization, and create a context for an intervention to emerge. For instance, Tara's therapist allowed her to provide some examples of the thoughts she had that were related to the dread. Rather than responding with general reactions such as "uh-huh," "tell me more," or "that must be hard," Tara's therapist responded with statements and questions that set her up to implement a strategic intervention designed to soften unhelpful thoughts such as the ones that Tara was reporting (i.e., cognitive restructuring; see Chapter 6). Examples of these statements and questions include, "What was running through your mind when you experienced the dread?" and "Is there anything that you are not acknowledging that might suggest the opposite—that would suggest that you are a good wife and mother?" By the end of the discussion, Tara's therapist had taught her how to recognize thinking that might be overly negative and exacerbating her dread, which was a tangible tool that she could take away from the session and practice in between sessions.

During the discussion of agenda items, cognitive behavioral therapists take care to make *periodic summaries* to confirm that they understand the main points of what their client is communicating. When there is more than one agenda item, it is often helpful for therapists to encourage clients to make a periodic summary, in which they articulate what they are taking away from the discussion before they move on to another topic. Periodic summaries done in this manner provide yet another opportunity for clients' consolidation of learning, such that they summarize their cognitive behavioral understanding of the issue and how a specific tool or strategy can help to remedy it.

Throughout this chapter, we have alluded to between-session work that allows clients to implement the tools and principles that they learn in session to problems that arise in their daily lives. *Homework* is the term that we use for this between-session work, although it is perfectly acceptable to use a different label if the word "homework" is off-putting to the client. Research shows that homework is a vital component of CBT—the more the therapist emphasizes homework, and the more the client commits to homework, the better is the outcome by the end of treatment (e.g., Kazantzis, Whittington, & Dattilio, 2010). Therein lies the issue—when does a new mother have time to fit in homework? In many instances, it is too much for a perinatal woman to complete elaborate tracking forms or exercises at preplanned times. Cognitive behavioral therapists who work with perinatal women, then, must be creative in devising ways to generalize the work done in session to the lives of new mothers. Throughout the remainder of the book, we describe standard CBT homework exercises and ways to adapt them to the demands of new motherhood.

Homework is given attention in each session in two ways. First, the homework that had been developed in the previous session is reviewed systematically. The idea behind homework review is that it is much more than a simple check-in to determine whether the client completed the homework. Instead, time should be taken in session for the client to articulate what she learned from doing the homework, and if she found it helpful, ways to continue operating according to the principles of the homework to continue to manage her mood disturbance. If the client ran into obstacles in implementing the homework or found it to be unhelpful, then discussion ensues about what went wrong and ways to modify the homework to be more helpful. Even if the client made no attempt at all to do the homework, it is important to address it to ensure that the client understands the rationale for homework in general, as well as the rationale for the particular exercise she agreed to do. Failure to spend time discussing homework in session inadvertently gives the message that homework is not important, when we know from the research cited previously that it is actually very important. When clients know that homework will be discussed in session without fail, the likelihood increases that they will attend to it between sessions. In this way, therapist behavior shapes client behavior.

There is no prescribed time in session that homework must be reviewed. Some cognitive behavioral therapists review homework before they set the agenda, although my (AW) preference is to add homework review to the agenda in order to allow ample time for discussion. This is especially the case when the therapist is in the process of helping the client to acquire a specific skill set across sessions, such that discussion of the homework would lead logically into the presentation and practice of the "next step" in the skill set. At times, the client's homework involves the tracking of symptoms or problems in the time between sessions. In these cases, the notes that the client records logically form the agenda of items to be discussed. In still other instances, the client presents with a pressing issue, and she decides that she would like to address that issue first before reviewing the homework. Finally, the dialogue between Tara and her therapist illustrates another way in which previous homework is incorporated into the session, when her therapist suggested that they regroup and discuss what was working and what was not working from the tools that Tara had been learning thus far. Tara's therapist reasoned that, during that discussion, she would check in regarding the previous homework as well as the degree to which Tara was continuing to use the skills she had learned in previous sessions in her daily life.

In addition to reviewing the previous homework, cognitive behavioral therapists work with their clients to develop new homework that will be practiced in the time before the next session. Figure 5.2 presents tips for maximizing the likelihood that homework is successful. Although many therapists believe that homework is developed at the end of the session, in reality, homework is developed whenever it is logical on the basis of the agenda items that are discussed. It is preferable for homework to be developed before the last few minutes of the session so that there is ample time to: (a) tailor the homework to meet the client's strengths and preferences; (b) practice it in session; and (c) identify obstacles that could interfere with homework completion and ways to overcome those obstacles. Remember that homework is not something that is developed so that the therapist adheres to a CBT protocol—it is developed because the intervention follows from the cognitive case conceptualization, and the therapist anticipates that it will make a difference in the client's life.

At the close of the session, cognitive behavioral therapists ask their clients to provide a *final summary and feedback*. The final summary allows clients to review the topics that were covered in session, and more importantly, articulate what they are taking away from the discussion of each agenda item. By putting words to the strategies implemented and their rationale, clients begin to consolidate their learning and increase the likelihood that they will remember the cognitive and behavioral principles in their own lives. This is especially important for perinatal women, who are overwhelmed and sleep deprived. Actively describing what they are learning in the session encodes the principles and tools in memory to a much greater degree than by listening passively to the therapist. In addition,

- Develop homework that logically follows discussion of one or more agenda items.

- Ensure that the homework exercise matches the strategy that was implemented and the skill that was practiced in session.

- Develop homework collaboratively with the client, identifying ways that the homework might be adapted to account for the client's strengths and preferences.

- If possible, begin the homework in session.

- Ask the client to identify days and times when she can commit to doing the homework.

- Ask the client to identify a "back-up plan" if she is unable to complete the homework at the designated times.

- Identify obstacles to completing the homework and ways to overcome those obstacles.

- Ask the client to explain in her own words the expected benefit of doing the homework.

- Ask the client to rate the likelihood of completing the homework. If the likelihood rating is less than 90%, modify the homework so that it is more achievable.

- If homework was developed earlier in the session, remind the client of the homework before she leaves the session.

Figure 5.2 Tips for Successful Homework.

the therapist asks for feedback on the session, such as whether the client believes the strategies implemented were a sound match for her needs and whether anything occurred in the session that was bothersome. Soliciting this kind of feedback reinforces the collaborative nature of CBT, giving clients the message that their feedback is important and will be incorporated into their therapeutic work as it proceeds.

From Cognitive Case Conceptualization to Treatment Planning

The remaining chapters of this book describe specific cognitive and behavioral strategies that therapists may implement during one or more sessions. Although the treatment and session structures described to this point in the chapter help therapists to organize the session, as well as to organize their thinking about the course of treatment with any client, little has been said as of yet about strategy. Strategy lies at the heart of CBT (cf. Wenzel, 2013). It encompasses the specific way in which therapists bring their professional expertise about theory and empirical research regarding treatment outcome and mechanisms of change to address any client's clinical presentation.

How does a therapist know which strategy to select? Chapter 2 described the application of cognitive behavioral theory to the development of a cognitive case conceptualization that captures the unique clinical presentation of each client. Therapists use that conceptualization to identify specific targets for treatment. Each of those targets can be incorporated into a treatment plan, prioritized, and linked to one or more interventions. The conceptualization guides the course of treatment, and the treatment plan guides the work that is done in any session. In the remainder of this section, we describe the treatment planning process, which in turn serves as the blueprint to implement the strategies described in the subsequent chapters of this book.

Figure 5.3 summarizes Wendy's treatment plan. Recall that Wendy's therapist hypothesized that the core belief, "I'm in danger," was associated with overestimations of the probability that harm would befall her children and her husband. As a result, she engaged in safety behaviors such as not allowing her oldest child to attend pre-school and excessive checking to ensure that her children were not hurt. She avoided turning on the news when it was covering a tragedy involving the death of children. Her anxiety was also directed at her husband's health, as she worried that his poor diet and exercise habits pointed to an early death, and she often scoured the internet to rule out various medical conditions and to identify symptoms that she could catch early before they progressed.

When Wendy presented for treatment, she identified the goal of reducing her anxiety. It is common for most new clients to identify vague, abstract goals, such as "reduce anxiety," "reduce depression," "feel better," and "feel normal." Although, of course, therapists want their clients to feel better, it is important to construct an operational definition of what that means so that progress toward goals can be monitored in treatment. In other words, it is important for goals to be as specific and measurable as possible. Thus, notice in Figure 5.3 that Wendy's goal to reduce anxiety was broken down into four components: (a) decrease in catastrophic thinking; (b) increase in the number of activities in which she allows her children to engage; (c) decrease in checking and reassurance seeking behaviors; and (d) decrease in excessive anxiety reactions when the news covers tragedies involving children. For each of these targets, Wendy and her therapist further identified specific indicators that she

Treatment Target	Treatment Strategy
PRIMARY GOAL: REDUCE ANXIETY	
Decrease in catastrophic thinking, as evidenced by client self-report and consistent use of therapeutic tools	Cognitive restructuring
Increase in the number of activities in which client allows her children to engage, as evidenced by allowing her oldest child to go to pre-school and her children to ride on previously forbidden amusement rides, play on previously forbidden playground equipment, and play while supervised in an unfenced yard	Cognitive restructuring, exposure with response prevention
Decrease in checking and reassurance seeking behaviors, as evidenced by refraining from hovering next to children while playing, fully engaging in conversation with other mothers at the playground, and refraining from searching the internet regarding her husband's health	Cognitive restructuring, exposure with response prevention
Decrease in excessive anxiety reaction when news covers tragedies involving children, as evidenced by client self-report and appropriate reading/watching of news stories	Cognitive restructuring, exposure with response prevention, controlled breathing
SECONDARY GOAL: IMPROVED SELF CARE	
Balance of needs of children with own needs, as evidenced by getting a sitter and reserving one morning a week for pleasurable activities of client's choice	Cognitive restructuring, behavioral activation, problem solving
Improved sleep, as evidenced by going to bed by 10pm each night and refraining from engaging in activating activities after 8pm	Sleep hygiene, problem solving

Figure 5.3 Wendy's Treatment Plan.

was making progress toward these goals, and Wendy's therapist aligned one or more cognitive and behavioral treatment strategies with each of the targets so that there was a clear sense of exactly how Wendy would achieve these goals.

Although, in many instances, clients come to treatment requesting to work on a specific goal, therapists should be vigilant for other, related goals that would be reasonable aims of treatment to enhance clients' functioning and quality of life. When Wendy's therapist conducted the psychological assessment, she learned that Wendy took almost no time for herself, which wore her down and likely depleted her psychological resources, making it likely that she would respond with an anxiety reaction when she was triggered. She also noticed that Wendy stayed up many nights until midnight or 1am using the internet, which only allowed 5–6 hours of sleep before her children woke up for the day. During treatment planning, Wendy's therapist communicated these observations and asked Wendy whether these were additional targets to address in treatment. Wendy readily agreed, although she wanted to focus first on reducing her anxiety as a primary goal and work toward improved self-care as a secondary goal.

Treatment plans focus the work done in each session. They give perinatal women hope that something can be done to address their emotional distress. They provide a glimpse of how things can be different. Moreover, they serve as an anchor for the therapist when clients present in crisis or with high affect. Although throughout this book we tout CBT as a collaborative approach to treatment wherein the therapist and client are equal members of a team, in our experience, many perinatal women rely on their therapist to take the lead in developing the treatment plan in the early phase of treatment. They are lost and do not know the pathway to recovery. They are tired and want to be taken care of. As they begin to get relief from emotional distress, they will be able to assume a greater role in the direction that treatment takes.

It is not uncommon for therapists to develop an intricate treatment plan, only to let it sit in the back of the client's chart. Thus, therapists should be sure to review the treatment plan periodically across the course of treatment. For example, after four or six sessions, therapists can ask the client's permission to add review of treatment goals to the agenda. During those reviews, they can assess the degree to which the client has met the specific targets, decide whether to shift the goals that deserve priority, and add any new goals to the plan that might not have been anticipated in the early phase of treatment.

Conclusion

A structure is evident in how the course of CBT unfolds over time, as well as how each session is directed. This structure is in place to organize the many issues and problems that are associated with emotional distress and to ensure that clients get maximal benefit from each session. It is implemented flexibly, rather than in a manner that seems rigid or as if items are being crossed out on a checklist.

It is tempting to abandon CBT structure when clients are in acute distress, and many perinatal women indeed present in acute emotional distress. Many therapists report that they worry that the implementation of structure will send the message to the client that they are uncaring, or that it will somehow be off-putting to the client. Remember that such concerns are, themselves, automatic thoughts, and should be evaluated carefully before they are taken as fact and dictate a clinical decision. Therapists who sense that their clients are not responding favorably to structure check out these assumptions with their clients and then modify the structure only when their clients state explicitly that they would like to approach the session in a different manner. In many cases, therapists who do this usually find that their clients are not having a negative reaction and even appreciate the structure because they want to make sure that they are working actively toward their treatment goals. Not only does this yield important information when the therapist makes a clinical decision about the implementation of structure, it models an important CBT strategy of checking out assumptions before taking them as fact and using the information that is gathered in order to make a decision.

The treatment plan arguably represents the intersection between structure and strategy. It is an organized list of problem areas to be addressed in treatment. However, it goes beyond a mere listing of treatment targets and provides direction about the specific strategic interventions that have the potential to help the client achieve her goals. When clients and therapists alike are overwhelmed by crises, an abundance of life problems, or high levels of affect, the treatment plan is the foundation from which the therapist can begin to intervene.

6

EVALUATING UNHELPFUL
COGNITIONS

According to the cognitive behavioral model described in Chapter 2, how people make meaning of their life experiences plays a large role in determining their emotional experiences and behavioral choices. It follows, then, that a central activity in CBT is helping clients to ensure that they are thinking in the most balanced, accurate, and helpful manner as is possible. The strategy that cognitive behavioral therapists use to achieve this aim is called *cognitive restructuring*, which is defined as the process by which clients learn to identify, evaluate, and if necessary, modify unhelpful cognition that is exacerbating their emotional distress and driving behavioral responses that might make their situations worse. Using guided discovery, cognitive behavioral therapists ask their clients questions to stimulate critical evaluation and alternative viewpoints to cognitions that might be keeping them entrenched in their emotional distress. Cognitive behavioral therapists might help clients to recognize their automatic thoughts during the early phase of treatment in order to give clients a glimpse of the types of activities in which they might engage during the course of treatment. However, cognitive restructuring in its entirety, as is described in this chapter, is typically executed in the middle phase of treatment, after treatment goals have been clearly been established.

Cognitive restructuring can be implemented at two levels. At the most basic level, cognitive restructuring is aimed at modifying situational automatic thoughts that exacerbate emotional distress in any specific instance. At a more sophisticated level, cognitive restructuring is aimed at modifying unhelpful underlying beliefs that can explain, in part, the types of automatic thoughts that are triggered in any situation. Cognitive behavioral therapists typically help their clients acquire skill in cognitive restructuring at the automatic thought level before addressing underlying beliefs. This is so because: (a) clients usually want to see some effect of treatment in a timely manner, and modifying unhelpful automatic thoughts is a straightforward way to get some relief; and (b) it takes some time to identify the precise nature of underlying beliefs and to modify them once they are identified, as they are often painful, difficult to articulate, and entrenched. Many cognitive behavioral therapists find that after clients have acquired skill in working with their automatic thoughts, they are better equipped to handle their underlying beliefs.

This model works well for perinatal women. As has been stated frequently throughout this book, most perinatal women are in acute distress when they present for treatment, and they want to feel better immediately. Cognitive restructuring of their unhelpful automatic thoughts is one way to achieve this aim. In addition, the concerns with which perinatal women initially present are usually focused on the here and now, stemming from the transition to parenthood. Examples of these concerns include worries that something is wrong with the baby, worries that they are not good enough mothers, and worries about finances and going back to work. All of these worries can be considered situational automatic thoughts that have been prompted by the change of environment post-childbirth.

This being said, many perinatal women realize that their difficulties during the transition to parenthood can be traced back to unhelpful beliefs about themselves, others, the world, and the future. These women often opt to remain in therapy after their acute distress has subsided in order to work on belief modification. The idea behind belief modification for perinatal women with depression and anxiety is that it will allow them to develop a healthier view of themselves and the world, thereby putting them in a better position to cope with the stressors of parenthood as their child grows up and handle any additional pregnancies. Thus, this chapter is divided into two main sections: cognitive restructuring of situational automatic thoughts and cognitive restructuring of underlying beliefs. It should be noted that the techniques described in this section are not unique to this book; they have been described and illustrated at length in many important CBT texts, such as those written by J. S. Beck (2011), Dobson and Dobson (2009), and Wright, Basco, and Thase (2006). However, they are applied here to concerns that are typically expressed by perinatal women.

Cognitive Restructuring of Automatic Thoughts

Cognitive restructuring of situational automatic thoughts typically progresses in three stages: (a) the identification of automatic thoughts; (b) the evaluation of automatic thoughts; and (c) the modification of automatic thoughts. These are not skills that are typically acquired in one session. Clients usually practice the identification of their thoughts, and as they gain skill in identifying the thoughts that are the most directly associated with emotional distress, their therapist then provides them tools to evaluate and modify these thoughts. Each of these activities is discussed in this section.

Identification of Automatic Thoughts

As clients share their stories, describe their frustrations, and express their fears, cognitive behavioral therapists help them to identify the automatic thoughts that are associated with emotional distress. Figure 6.1 lists some common questions that cognitive behavioral therapists ask to help clients identify their automatic thoughts. Although the most common question is, "What was running through your mind in that situation?", it is important for therapists to have an array of prompts at their disposal, as, at first, many clients have difficulty identifying what they were thinking. When this occurs, it can be helpful to let clients know that this is to be expected; after all, automatic thoughts are named as such for a reason, as they often arise so quickly that we often just know that we feel upset in a situation, and we are not necessarily aware that we are thinking about the situation in a certain way. Thus, this first step in the cognitive restructuring process—identification of automatic thoughts—is crucial to help clients slow down, interrupt the barrage of catastrophic thoughts that might be plaguing them, and recognize the key thoughts that are fueling their emotional distress. Over time, clients will learn to ask themselves the questions to identify their automatic thoughts, rather than rely on their therapists to do so. Consider the following dialogue with Lyla, who had

•   What was running through your mind in that situation?
•   What do you guess might have been running through your mind in that situation?
•   Did you have a picture in your mind of something awful that might happen?
•   Did you have a memory of something awful that happened in the past?
•   Might you have been thinking _____ (something opposite to what would be expected) or _____ (something similar to what would be expected)?
•   What did that situation mean to you?
•   What did that situation mean about you?
•   What is the fundamental issue that is so upsetting to you?

Figure 6.1 Questions to Elicit Automatic Thoughts.

Note: Some of these questions can be found in J. S. Beck (2011).

agreed to continue with CBT after four sessions with her therapist and made a commitment to focus on cognitive restructuring.

Lyla: But I don't *know* what I'm thinking. I just feel down all the time. There are no thoughts.

Therapist: I can see how it feels that way. But let's do a little more investigating. Can you think of a specific instance that happened during the past couple days when you noticed that you were even more upset and depressed than usual?

Lyla: I guess so. This morning, for example, my husband left without saying goodbye. I couldn't believe he'd just leave like that.

Therapist: When you realized that he had left the house without saying goodbye, what ran through your mind?

Lyla: That he didn't even make the effort to say goodbye to me.

Therapist: It sounds like this was quite upsetting for you.

Lyla: [nods, becoming tearful]

Therapist: Tell me, what did it mean to you that he left without saying goodbye?

Lyla: [crying] It means that he's fed up. Done. He's sick and tired of me being depressed.

Therapist: [gently] What do you mean by fed up and done?

Lyla: [shaking] He's gonna leave. I just know it. I've put him through so much.

Therapist: And this idea is associated with an increase in depression?

Lyla: [nods]

Therapist: What a powerful idea that is. That he's going to leave you. It makes a lot of sense that your depression would increase when this is in your mind.

Lyla: Yeah, I'm just waiting for the shoe to drop.

Therapist: So is it safe to say that this idea, that he's going to leave you, is most associated with your depression? Rather than the fact that he left without saying goodbye?

Lyla: Well, it's both I guess.

Therapist: Fair enough. On our 0–10 scale, with 0 being no depression, and 10 being the most depression you've ever experienced, how much depression is associated with the idea that your husband left without saying goodbye?

Lyla: It's high. Like a 7.

Therapist: And how much depression is associated with the idea that your husband is going to leave you?

Lyla: [looks down at her hands] That's the worst. A 10 out of 10.

Therapist: I wonder if we should start to really take a look at this prediction you're making, that your husband will leave you?

Lyla: OK, I think we should.

Several points about this dialogue deserve note. At first, Lyla was speaking in generalities, stating that she was always depressed and that she could not think of specific thoughts associated her depression. This sentiment is not uncommon. Although it is important not to directly challenge clients and try to convince them that they are indeed thinking negative automatic thoughts, it is equally important not to take that report at face value and simply abandon cognitive restructuring. It is likely that they are having difficulty identifying automatic thoughts because they are not focused on a specific instance or situation. Thus, Lyla's therapist adopted an inquisitive stance (i.e., "Let's do a little more investigating") and helped her to focus on a specific situation that occurred in the past couple of days, with the reasoning that the more recently a situation occurred, the more likely it is that Lyla would be able to identify automatic thoughts.

In addition, notice what happened after Lyla was prompted to indicate what ran through her mind when she noticed that her husband had left without saying goodbye. Her initial automatic thought was, "He didn't even make the effort to say goodbye." Although there is some judgment associated with this automatic thought (i.e., saying he "didn't even make the effort" communicated a negative connotation), the bulk of it was largely factual, as he did not say goodbye to her before he left. After providing some empathy, Lyla's therapist asked what it meant to her that he left without saying goodbye. It was at this point that Lyla expressed a number of automatic thoughts (e.g., that her husband is fed up, that he is going to leave her) that evoked even more emotional distress than the fact that he left without saying goodbye. These thoughts are called "hot thoughts" (Greenberger & Padesky, 1995; Padesky & Greenberger, 1995) and are the most fruitful thoughts to subject to cognitive restructuring because they are predictions and assumptions, rather than factual. Although it is understandable that Lyla would be upset about her husband leaving the house without saying goodbye, subjecting it to cognitive restructuring likely would not led to as much relief from her emotional distress because it is indisputable that this occurred. Thus, when cognitive behavioral therapists notice that clients are reporting facts as automatic thoughts, they ask additional questions to get to the *meaning* of those facts to their clients.

Finally, notice that Lyla's therapist asked Lyla to rate the emotional intensity of two of her automatic thoughts—the fact that her husband left without saying goodbye, and the idea that her husband was going to leave her. Obtaining these ratings of emotional intensity is one way to focus on the "hot thought," with the idea that the automatic thought associated with the highest rating of emotional intensity would be the "hot thought." However, ratings of emotional intensity also serve another purpose. Later, when therapists help their clients to modify inaccurate and unhelpful automatic thoughts, they ask their clients to rerate the level of emotional intensity associated with the modified thought. This allows clients to compare and contrast their ratings of emotional intensity, giving them tangible evidence that cognitive restructuring is useful in reducing their emotional distress in the moment.

There are times when clients have great difficulty identifying automatic thoughts even when the therapist has asked a number of the questions listed in Figure 6.1. In these cases, it can be helpful to engage clients in an experiential exercise, such that they evoke the same intensity of emotional distress that they experienced during the situation in question and report their thoughts in "real time." This can be achieved by asking clients to close their eyes and use mental imagery to bring themselves back to the problematic situation or by using role play in order to recreate the situation.

Evaluation of Automatic Thoughts

Typically, cognitive behavioral therapists devote a session to helping their clients acquire skill in identifying their automatic thoughts, and for homework, clients track their automatic thoughts and bring in examples of their automatic thoughts at the time of the next session. If clients were unable to complete their homework or if they had difficulty with the exercise, then it is sensible to devote the subsequent session to continued practice in identifying automatic thoughts. However, if clients completed their homework, and it is clear that clients have the capacity to identify automatic thoughts that are reasonably related to their emotional distress (i.e., the thoughts are reasonably "hot"), then therapists can begin work with their clients to develop skill in evaluating their automatic thoughts.

One word of caution deserves note here. Many authors of CBT texts describe this process as "challenging" automatic thoughts. A more neutral way of view this process is one of "evaluation." Cognitive restructuring was meant to be a process in which the therapist and client work collaboratively and curiously, without preconceived notions, to examine all of the pieces of information that go into making meaning of a particular situation. It is only after that critical examination that the therapist and client then make a determination as to whether the thought is inaccurate, unbalanced, or otherwise unhelpful. Adopting a "challenging" stance presupposes that there is something wrong with the client's thinking. Unless a therapist has a client with postpartum psychosis, it is likely that there might be a grain of truth in her thinking. A full-on "challenge" might invalidate her emotional distress. Moreover, the

EVALUATING UNHELPFUL COGNITIONS

"challenging" stance subtly communicates that the therapist is the sole expert in the room, which is contrary to the fundamental tenet of collaboration. One way to view the "evaluating" stance is that the therapist and client are co-detectives, gathering all of the evidence, then drawing a conclusion, or co-scientists, collecting the "data" and drawing a conclusion after data analysis. Thus, evaluating automatic thoughts is done in the spirit of *collaborative empiricism*, such that the therapist and client work together as a team (i.e., collaboration), and they based the conclusions that they draw on the evidence or data that are collected (i.e., empiricism).

In our experience, the "evaluating" stance is the ideal match for perinatal women. It is true that some perinatal women are experiencing such acute emotional distress that they just want to be told what to do in order to feel better, and "challenging" would indeed fit this bill. However, in this case, there is a danger that the client becomes reliant on the therapist to solve her problems for her. When the client learns to question her automatic thoughts on her own, she gains valuable practice that will allow her to more easily rely on these skills the next time she is faced with a stressor or challenge. The idea is for clients to examine their own thinking and draw their own conclusions, rather than be told what and how to think.

Figure 6.2 displays some common questions that cognitive behavioral therapists ask to facilitate the evaluation process. These questions are not asked in isolation, but in combination. No one evaluation question is optimal for every automatic thought; the evaluation questions that are posed must be a logical match for the content of the automatic thought. For example, if a pregnant woman seeks therapy after learning that her unborn child has a rare genetic disorder, asking "What's the likelihood of the worst-case scenario occurring?" would be inappropriate. Moreover, cognitive behavioral therapists need not be limited to the evaluation questions listed in Figure 6.2. *Any* question can be posted as long as it facilitates critical evaluation. Some of the best cognitive restructuring occurs when the therapist poses unique and creative questions that speak eloquently to the individualized situations and thoughts reported by the client. I (AW) once worked with a postpartum client who struggled with the automatic thought, "I'm the worst mother in the world." We attempted to examine the evidence that both supported and did not support that statement. Despite a thorough evaluation, she continued to report a high level of depression, as well as a high level in the idea that she is a bad mother. It was only after I asked specific questions such as, "How often do you hug your children?", "How often do you tell your children you love them?", "How often do you prepare meals for your children?" that she began to conclude that she was dismissing some important parenting activities in which she was engaging.

• What evidence do I have that supports this thought? Is that evidence truly factual? What evidence do I have that does not support this thought? Which evidence is more significant—the evidence that supports this thought, or the evidence that does not support this thought?
• What other explanations might be at work in this situation?
• Does _____ have to lead to or be equal to _____?
• What is the worst that can happen? What is the best that can happen? What is the most realistic thing that will happen? Is the most realistic thing that can happen closer to the best-case scenario or the worst-case scenario?
• If the worst were to happen, how, specifically, would I cope? How bad would it really be? Is there a chance that things would ultimately work out?
• What is the likelihood of the worst-case scenario occurring?
• Is this situation really so important or consequential?
• Does _____'s opinion really reflect everyone else's? Might there be another explanation for _____'s opinion?
• What is the effect of focusing on my automatic thought? What is the effect of changing my automatic thought?
• How useful is it to be focusing on this automatic thought? What kinds of things might it be interfering with?
• What would I tell a friend in this situation?
• What would my spouse/partner/parent/close friend think about my automatic thought?
• How can I model healthy thinking from my child/children? How would I want my child/children to view this situation?
• If this automatic thought is largely factual, what should I do about the situation?
• If this automatic thought is largely factual, how can I arrive at a place of peace or acceptance?
• If this automatic thought is largely factual, and I must be in this awful situation, what wisdom can I gain? How can I achieve personal growth?

Figure 6.2 Evaluation Questions.

Note: Some of these questions can be found in J. S. Beck (2011).

The following dialogue illustrates the back-and-forth flow between the therapist and client during the evaluation of automatic thoughts. This dialogue occurred when Wendy expressed fear that her son would be killed in a school shooting.

Wendy: I know it's irrational, but I just can't let him go to pre-school. Every time I go, I look around at the doors, the way the school is set up, and I see a million ways a shooter could get in and wreak havoc.

Therapist: So the fundamental automatic thought is what?

Wendy: It's that . . . it's so hard to say, I know it sound stupid . . . but that my son will be the victim of a school shooting.

Therapist: I don't think you sound stupid. You sound like a mother who very much loves her son and who has been affected by all of the recent news. Nevertheless, it sounds like such thoughts are affecting your life.

Wendy: They sure are. I can't keep making my son stay home. I know he needs to go to school. He asks about it all the time.

Therapist: What do you think the likelihood is that he would be the victim of a school shooting?

Wendy: These days? A lot. Well, [rethinking], maybe only like 1%. But still, I can't even bear that chance.

Therapist: I wonder if 1% is really accurate?

Wendy: Yeah, I don't know, it might not be.

Therapist: How might you go about finding the most accurate information?

Wendy: Hmmm, I never thought about that. That's a good idea. I guess I should figure out how many kids, in total, go to school in this state, and how many have actually died from a school shooting.

Therapist: I think that's a terrific idea. Might that be something you do for homework?

Wendy: [brightens up] Yeah, I really like that idea.

Notice in this dialogue that Wendy's therapist started with a standard evaluation question (i.e., "What's the likelihood that your son would be a victim in a school shooting?") then asked other questions, such as the degree to which Wendy's estimate was accurate and how she might go about finding more information. In the subsequent section, we will see how Wendy used the information she gathered in order to modify her initial automatic thought that her son would be the victim of a school shooting.

This dialogue with Wendy represents an instance in which the client is open to the questioning of her thoughts. Other clients are so entrenched in their negative thinking that they make sweeping, generalized, and judgmental automatic thoughts that are more difficult to test and for which evidence to the contrary is easily dismissed. Lyla, for example, often expressed automatic thoughts, such as "I'm the lowest of the low. I'm like a grub. I'm a failure. I don't deserve happiness." These are inherently subjective impressions that are difficult to measure against a standard metric, as there is no universally accepted measurement that determines success versus failure and deserving versus undeserving. Her therapist took a much different approach than Wendy's therapist did in helping her to evaluate and get distance from and perspective on her automatic thoughts.

Lyla: I'm the lowest of the low. I'm like a grub. I'm a failure. I don't deserve happiness.

Therapist: What makes you judge yourself so harshly?

Lyla: I just stay in bed all day. Jack doesn't even keep normal baby hours. He's up at 6 for a feeding, and then we go right back down to bed until 10, 11, maybe longer. I'm not giving him what he needs.

Therapist: Might you be forgetting to acknowledge some of the things about you, some of the things that you've accomplished that go against that idea that you're a failure?

Lyla: What, you mean like the fact that I graduated from college?

Therapist: What do *you* think? Do *you* think that people who have graduated from college are failures?

Lyla: [disqualifying the positive] That's irrelevant here. That has nothing to do with my worth now.

Therapist: What *does* have to do with your worth now?

Lyla: Taking care of Jack. Being a good wife. Keeping up the house. *None* of which I'm doing right now.

Therapist: I wonder if we can examine this more closely. [goes on to work with Lyla to identify the precise behaviors that she would be doing to take care of her son, be a good wife, and keep up the house]

Therapist: Summarize for me what you are and are not doing to take care of Jack.

Lyla: Lots that I'm not doing. Not keeping him on a healthy sleep schedule. I skip baths sometimes. I don't take him out for walks as much as I should. I haven't even looked at his baby book.

Therapist: And . . .?

Lyla: Yes, OK, there are a few things that I *am* doing. I have to nurse him when he's hungry. He won't let me sleep if I don't. And I guess I'm better with him than my husband is. He screams whenever my husband picks him up.

Therapist:	So which wins out—the things that suggest that you're doing OK, or the things that, in your mind, make you a failure?
Lyla:	It's hard to see anything but failure when you sleep as much as I do.
Therapist:	What if you were to present these things to your husband? What do you think his view would be?
Lyla:	He says that I'm great with Jack. [pauses] But what does he know?
Therapist:	Yes, what *does* he know?
Lyla:	Well, he isn't even around during the day, so he really doesn't know.
Therapist:	Is anyone with you more than he is?
Lyla:	Well, no.
Therapist:	And is he around during non-work hours, such as evenings, weekends, and holidays?
Lyla:	Well, yes.
Therapist:	So might he know at least a little bit?
Lyla:	[softly] I guess he does, at least a little bit.

In this dialogue, Lyla's therapist demonstrated an important tactic when clients make sweeping, judgmental generalizations, such as "I'm a failure"—she worked with Lyla to identify more specific components in observable and behavioral terms and asked Lyla to consider where she stood on those components. When clients do this, they usually realize that they fall short in some of the behavioral components and that they are doing adequately on other components. This more detailed consideration, then, helps them to reevaluate their all-or-nothing automatic thoughts and realize that there are many shades of gray in between, allowing them to be easier on themselves. Lyla only partially responded to this intervention—although she was able to acknowledge some of her positive parenting behaviors, she simultaneously dismissed them because she perceived that she slept all the time. Thus, her therapist added another evaluation question, asking what her husband would think of her automatic thoughts. Lyla tried to dismiss the fact that he would view her parenting in a favorable light by pointing out that he does not know anything. Her therapist followed with some targeted questions to help Lyla soften her perspective that he does not know anything.

Modification of Automatic Thoughts

Cognitive behavioral therapists work with their clients to modify their automatic thoughts when they conclude, as a result of the evaluation process, that their automatic thoughts are inaccurate, unbalanced, or otherwise unhelpful. Using the fruits of the critical analysis, therapists will work with clients to develop *balanced responses*. A balanced response is a new thought that is more accurate, nuanced, and helpful than the original automatic thought. We say "nuanced" because balanced responses are often lengthier and account for more information than the original automatic thought. The following dialogue illustrates how Wendy constructed a balanced response after she completed her homework exercise of researching the precise numbers that would form an accurate estimate of the likelihood that her son would die from a school shooting.

Therapist: Well, what's the verdict?

Wendy: It was *so* interesting. When I looked at how many kids are in school in the entire state, and then how many have been in a school shooting, I realized that the chance was 1 in 250,000,000 that something like that would happen.

Therapist: Terrific, you really did your research.

Wendy: And my brother-in-law, who was helping me, pointed out something else that was interesting. My son only goes to school three days a week, and not even for a full day. So it you take that into consideration, the chances are 1 in 850,000,000.

Therapist: What an astute observation. What do you conclude from this? [attempting to elicit a balanced response]

Wendy: That the chances are so minuscule that this would ever happen.

Therapist: Before, when you had the idea that your son would die in a school shooting, you rated your fear as a 10 on our 10-point scale. When you acknowledge the fact that the chances are 1 in 850,000,000, where is your level of anxiety now?

Wendy: Down, oh way down.

Therapist: Let me play devil's advocate for a moment. Let's say it is a Monday morning, getting your son ready to go to school, and you start to worry about a shooting at his school. You remember that the chances are only 1 in 850,000,000 of that happening, but you can't shake your anxiety. What would you tell yourself?

Wendy: I'm glad we're talking about this because I can totally see this happening to me. Um . . . Well, one thing I know in my heart is that it's important for him to go to school. When I keep him home, he asks about the other kids. He misses it. He gets socialization there that I can't give him at home.

Therapist: Ah, so you focus on the advantages that school offers him?

Wendy: Yeah, exactly.

Therapist: Are there any additional advantages?

Wendy: There are lots of them. He's learning new things, even read-
               ing a little bit. And this is great practice so that he adjusts
               well when he goes to kindergarten.
Therapist: In your mind, do the advantages of sending him to school
               outweigh the 1 in 850,000,000 chance of a school shooting?
Wendy: Definitely.
Therapist: Let's put all of this together into a balanced response that
               you can remember every time you have anxiety about this
               issue. So, next time you are anxious about a school shooting,
               how will you respond to that?
Wendy: [looking thoughtful] I'd say that the chances of my son being
               involved in a school shooting are 1 in 850,000,000. By
               keeping him home from school for such an unlikely event, I
               will be depriving him of valuable learning and socialization
               opportunities. Plus, I will be modeling an anxious way of liv-
               ing your life, rather than a balanced way, and I don't want to
               pass this on to my children.
Therapist: I wonder if you should write this down so that you have it as
               a reminder?
Wendy: Yes, I think I should.

Wendy's balanced response contained the fruits of her careful consideration of the true likelihood that her son would be involved in a school
shooting and the advantages of sending her child to school in spite of the
small likelihood of a school shooting. The consideration of the advantages of sending her son to school arose only after the therapist played
devil's advocate and asked her what she would do if acknowledging the
low likelihood of a school shooting did not decrease her anxiety. Her
therapist's rationale for this intervention is that many anxious clients can
objectively acknowledge a low likelihood of catastrophic events, but they
continue to have difficulty tolerating the uncertainty of whether or not
the event will occur. Thus, continued questioning allowed Wendy to identify other important points to consider—the advantages of sending her
son to school despite the low risk—that could be incorporated into the
balanced response.

The key point about balanced responses is that they must be compelling and believable, even in the midst of acute emotional distress. Simplistic responses to automatic thoughts, such as "Everything will be OK" or
"Just get over it," tend not to be helpful or believable during emotional
upset. Compelling balanced responses must account for all of the ways
in which a client might dismiss it by saying "yeah but" in the moment
in which it is needed. For this reason, balanced responses tend to include
several statements that can counteract these "yeah buts."

Tools for Cognitive Restructuring

Some of cognitive restructuring occurs through dialogue between the therapist and client in session, as illustrated in the examples above. However, some of cognitive restructuring also takes place in the client's own environment. When clients are first acquiring skill in cognitive restructuring, it is often helpful for them to have some sort of structure or template to guide them through the process. After all, cognitive restructuring is a very different approach to dealing with upsetting thoughts than many clients are accustomed to, and even if the process is clear in the therapist's office, it is easy to forget how to apply it when faced with everyday stressors and challenges. This section describes some specific tools that can help clients to implement cognitive restructuring in the lives between sessions.

Thought Record

A *thought record* is a sheet of paper in which clients can record the automatic thoughts that they experience between sessions and their associated emotional responses (cf. A. T. Beck et al., 1979; J. S. Beck, 2011). The most typical thought records are displayed in Figures 6.3 and 6.4. The three-column thought record allows clients to hone their skill in identifying "hot" thoughts when they are first introduced to cognitive

Situation What happened?	Automatic Thought What ran through your mind? What did that situation mean to you?	Emotion Rate on 0 (low)–10 (high) scale.

Figure 6.3 Three-Column Thought Record.

Situation What happened?	Automatic Thought What ran through your mind? What did that situa- tion mean to you?	Emotion Rate on 0 (low)–10 (high) scale associated with the automatic thought.	Balanced Response Evaluate all aspects of the automatic thought and compose a more balanced appraisal of the situation.	Emotion Rate on 0 (low)–10 (high) scale associated with the balanced response.

Figure 6.4 Five-Column Thought Record.

restructuring. Once clients have mastered the ability to identify auto-matic thoughts associated with emotional distress, then they can begin to use the five-column thought record, where they also record the balanced response and the degree to which their emotional distress has decreased as a result of developing the balanced response.

On the one hand, many clients find that thought records are convenient ways to organize their cognitive restructuring work. Therapists who choose to make use of thought records typically will introduce them early in ses-sion, such that clients can record their automatic thoughts associated with the various items they have included on the agenda as they arise. In this way, clients gain practice in completing thought records in "real time" and have a template that they can follow in their own lives between sessions.

On the other hand, many perinatal women have indicated that they find it too difficult to maintain a running thought record between ses-sions. They have trouble remembering where they put the sheet. The baby spits up on the sheet. They can't complete the sheet in the dark when they are nursing their babies. These are legitimate obstacles and, rather than meaning that cognitive restructuring cannot be implemented with perinatal women, they mean that cognitive behavioral therapists who work with perinatal women must be creative in developing convenient ways for perinatal women to generalize the skills that they are gaining in therapy to their everyday lives. The remainder of tools described in this section have the potential to be a better match for perinatal women than the thought records.

Coping Card

A *coping card* is a brief reminder of the fruits of therapeutic work that can be consulted quickly when needed (J. S. Beck, 2011). They are particularly useful when they contain compelling balanced responses to automatic thoughts that clients experience over and over. On a 3 x 5 index card, a business card, or simply a sheet of paper, clients can write their original automatic thought as well as the balanced response. They are then encouraged to keep the coping card in an easy-access location (e.g., diaper bag) and consult it whenever they detect their original automatic thought and associated emotional distress. One of us (AW) had a postpartum client who purchased a spiral bound package of index cards, which allowed her to record many balanced responses that addressed various aspects of her life stress. Figure 6.5 is an example of a coping card that Wendy developed in session with her therapist.

Behavioral Experiments

Behavioral experiments allow clients to test negative predictions in their own environment, gathering evidence in their own lives that speak to the validity of their automatic thoughts (J. S. Beck, 2011). Behavioral experiments are especially useful for cases in which clients believe their balanced

---

AUTOMATIC THOUGHT: My son will be the victim of a school shooting.

BALANCED RESPONSE: The chances of my son being involved in a school shooting are 1 in 850,000,000. By keeping him home from school for such an unlikely event, I will be depriving him of valuable learning and socialization opportunities. He likes being at school and asks about his friends when I do not let him go. If I don't let him go, I will be modeling an anxious way of living life, and I don't want to pass this onto my children.

Figure 6.5 Sample Coping Card.

responses intellectually, but not emotionally. They often need to see the "proof" with their own eyes to truly invest in the balanced response.

The behavioral experiment was particularly powerful for Tara, who was beginning to avoid going out in public places for fear that she would have a panic attack or begin crying hysterically. She also predicted that if this happened, others would judge her as being crazy and think she was an unfit mother. Although she was able to acknowledge that this had never happened to her before, she was convinced that this was going to occur. The following is dialogue between Tara and her therapist as they set up a behavioral experiment to test her predictions.

Tara: I know, I know. It seems like I've been able to keep it together in the past. But, I don't know, it just *feels* like the next time we go out, I'm going to lose it.

Therapist: Well, perhaps we can test this out.

Tara: You mean by going somewhere and seeing if it actually happens?

Therapist: Yes, that's exactly what I mean.

Tara: Oh boy. [pauses] But I guess that would be the best way to find out, wouldn't it?

Therapist: It's certainly a powerful way to find out. Tell me, where might you go to test out this prediction?

Tara: I guess the grocery store. That's the place I've been avoiding the most for some reason.

Therapist: OK, the grocery store. When will you go?

Tara: I could go tomorrow morning after Thomas wakes up from his morning nap.

Therapist: And what groceries do you need to get?

Tara: Milk, eggs, yogurt, produce, stuff to make stir fry tomorrow night.

Therapist: OK, so tomorrow you'll go to the grocery store after Thomas wakes up from his nap and get the groceries you mentioned. Let's prepare for the worst-case scenario. Suppose you start to panic. How will you cope with that?

Tara: I could use some of the breathing exercises we've been working on. And I could go to the frozen aisles. For some reason, the cool air in the frozen aisles soothes me.

Therapist: That sounds like a terrific plan. Anything else for a back-up, in case breathing and going to the frozen aisle don't work?

Tara: I'll have my phone with me, and I can call my mom. Sometimes I do this when I am panicking at home, and it usually helps.

Therapist: So *either* you're going to show yourself that your prediction that you will "lose it" is overstated, *or* you're going to show yourself that even if you panic, you'll be able to cope and get through it?

Tara: [brightens up] Yeah, I guess I am. [pauses] But if I do panic, what will the other people think? They'll think there's a raging lunatic loose in the store.

Therapist: Let me ask you this. Have you ever been in a public place and noticed someone in acute distress?

Tara: Yes, a couple of times. Once in the mall. And another time at the park.

Therapist: Did you think those people were raging lunatics?

Tara: [laughs] No. No, I didn't. I just thought something was really wrong. I would have even tried to help, but in both cases, other people were already helping.

Therapist: What does that tell you?

Tara: I get it. That most people would probably be more concerned than judgmental.

Therapist: How much do you believe that?

Tara: I do. I believe it a lot, like 90%.

Therapist: OK. We've addressed when you'll go to the grocery store, what you will buy, how to cope if you start to panic, and how to handle concerns that others will judge you negatively if you have an emotional reaction. Is there anything else that we need to prepare in advance for? Any obstacles that might interfere with executing this experiment?

Tara: If I wake up tomorrow morning, and I'm feeling really off. [pauses] I've been off a lot lately. Then I just feel like holing up in the house, not going anywhere.

[Tara and her therapist go on to discuss how to center herself when she wakes up and feels off, how to commit to executing the experiment in spite of how she feels, and when to schedule a back-up visit to the grocery store in the event that she does not follow through the next morning.]

Notice, in this dialogue, that the behavioral experiment took some time to unfold. First, Tara's therapist helped her to identify the specifics of the experiment, including the particular public place to which she was going to visit, the time of day she would go, and the products she would buy when she arrived. It is important to plan the experiment as specifically as is possible so that clients know exactly what to do. When behavioral experiments are vague and general, when it comes to execute them in their own lives, clients often do not know where to start. In addition, notice that Tara's therapist encouraged her to develop a specific plan for coping with the worst-case scenario. This is called a *decatastrophizing plan* (J. S. Beck, 2011), and it helps to demystify the worst-case scenario and instill confidence in clients that they would be able to survive it. Then, Tara's therapist identified the fact that Tara would really be testing two competing predictions—either that her worst fear would not be realized, or that she would be able to cope effectively with her worst fear. Thus, this behavioral experiment was regarded as a "win-win" scenario, as regardless of what happened, she would be able to test a prediction that was maintaining her emotional distress. Finally, at the end of the dialogue, Tara's therapist helped her to identify other obstacles that might interfere with the execution of the behavioral experiment, and they brainstormed ways to overcome those obstacles and even developed a back-up plan so that Tara would have another opportunity to execute the experiment if she did not do so at the scheduled time.

The implementation of the behavioral experiment is the typical homework exercise that the client completes between sessions. At the time of the subsequent session, it is important to place the results of the behavioral experiment on the agenda so that some time is devoted to debriefing and careful evaluation of the client's original automatic thoughts in light of the results of the behavioral experiment. The client can then develop a balanced response to which she can refer in subsequent instances in which she makes similar predictions of bad things happening.

Applications

The age of technology has made the practice of CBT more convenient than ever. As of the writing of this book, there are consistently new applications (i.e., apps) being created and marketed that help clients implement their CBT homework between sessions. Typing in "CBT" in the app store will bring users to an array of CBT apps, many of which were developed in collaboration with expert cognitive behavioral therapists. Because cognitive restructuring is a central strategy in CBT, most of these apps allow users to record and modify their automatic thoughts. If an app is not appealing to a particular client, she can consider simply recording automatic thoughts and balanced responses in the notes function of her telephone, or even record her automatic thoughts and balanced responses using a voice recording function. Many perinatal clients have reported that recording their cognitive restructuring work on their phones, whether it be through an app, the notes function, or voice recording, significantly increases the likelihood that they complete their homework between sessions.

Cognitive Restructuring of Beliefs

As stated previously, many perinatal women obtain a great deal of relief from the restructuring of situational automatic thoughts, and this meets their treatment goals. Other women, however, recognize that their thinking during the transition to parenthood reflects more pervasive themes of self-deprecation, mistrust, or hopelessness, some of which might stem from unresolved pains from childhood. In these latter cases, it is possible that these clients are characterized by unhelpful underlying beliefs that rear their heads in times of life stress, such as during the childbirth, and that these clients could benefit from belief modification techniques after they have demonstrated skill in modifying unhelpful situational automatic thoughts.

Identification of Beliefs

The first step in belief modification is to put words to the belief. At the beginning of treatment, most clients find that their underlying beliefs are difficult to articulate. It is almost as if they have a filter by which they view the world and thus interpret events that happen, but that they are not entirely cognizant that such a filter is activated. Over time, as they work with their situational automatic thoughts, clients develop increasing awareness as to the presence and contents of underlying beliefs.

Many strategies exist for identifying underlying beliefs. Certainly, a therapist could ask about them directly, although many clients are unable to spontaneously indicate a precise belief that has plagued them for so long. Another way to identifying underlying beliefs is to be alert for themes that characterize the situational automatic thoughts identified as clients acquire skill in cognitive restructuring. Influenced by the pioneering work of J. S. Beck (2011), I (AW) view four general themes that characterize underlying beliefs. *Unlovable beliefs* are beliefs that reflect a sense of undesirability, such as "I'll be rejected" and "People don't like me." *Failure beliefs* are beliefs that reflect a lack of accomplishment, such as "I'm incompetent" and "I'm stupid." *Helpless beliefs* are beliefs that reflect a lack of controllability, including "I'm trapped" and "I'm powerless." Finally, *worthless beliefs* are those that often cut across two or three of these other dimensions, being particularly pervasive and associated with particularly high levels of negative affect. Examples of worthless beliefs include "I'm a waste" and "I don't deserve to be alive" (Wenzel, 2013).

Underlying beliefs can also be determined using a technique called the *Downward Arrow Technique* (D. D. Burns, 1980). Cognitive behavioral therapists who use this strategy continually drill down to the meaning underlying reported automatic thoughts until there is no greater meaning that can be uncovered. Consider this dialogue with Tara, which her therapist could have initiated instead of the behavioral experiment.

Tara:　　　I know, I know. It seems like I've been able to keep it together in the past. But, I don't know, it just *feels* like the next time we go out, I'm going to lose it.

Therapist:　If you were to lose it, as you say, what would that mean?

Tara:　　　[crying] It would mean that something is wrong with me.

Therapist:	And if something is wrong with you, what does that mean about you?
Tara:	That I'm never going to get out of this. That I will always be different.
Therapist:	And say that something has changed, that you are different. What does that mean?
Tara:	[crying even harder] I'm an unfit mother! Thomas deserves a better mother. He should be with someone else.
Therapist:	Is that what you truly believe? That you're an unfit mother and that he deserves someone else?
Tara:	[nods head] When I'm feeling like this, yes.

Finally, as the above dialogue also demonstrates, when a client demonstrates high affect, it is likely that she has hit upon a belief of some significance. Signs for which the therapist can be alert include tears, avoidance of eye contact, fidgeting, defensiveness, blushing and blotchiness, and a change in speech volume.

Modification of Beliefs

Our goal is for clients to shift from beliefs that are excessively negative or unhelpful to more helpful and healthier beliefs. Thus, it is important to define the new belief to which the client is shifting. As with the balanced responses, it is important that the new beliefs be as believable and as compelling as is possible. Consider a person who carries the belief, "I am a failure." If she has a history of adversity of difficulties attaining goals, it might not be realistic to shift to a belief such as "I am successful." However, most clients can embrace belief such as "I'm just as good as the next person," and "I'm a good person, warts and all." In this section, we present some strategies for achieving a shift from an old, unhelpful belief to a new, more helpful belief.

Pie Chart

Often, when clients make sweeping all-or-nothing statements about being a failure, being worthless, and so on, they are focusing in on one aspect of their lives that they perceive is not going well, ignoring the other aspects of their lives that are going just fine. Nowhere is this more true than with perinatal women. Understandably, they are focused in on parenting and caring for their child during this time. However, their perceived failures in these domains often bleed into a general sense that they have failed in life.

The pie chart is a technique that allows clients to clarify the characteristics or roles that they view as contributing to their positive belief. Like Tara, Donna had the belief that she was a bad mother because she was convinced that she had postpartum psychosis. When she presented for treatment, this had generalized into, "I'm a bad person." However, when she laid out all of her most valued roles in a pie chart, she began to revise her view that she was a bad person, as there were several domains in which she perceived that she was "measuring up."

Figure 6.6 is an example of Donna's pie chart. The five domains that she identified as having importance in her life were being a parent, being a wife, being a daughter and sister to the members of her family of origin, being a friend to her close friends, and her spirituality. When she first viewed the pie chart in its totality, Donna remained convinced that she was falling short in the domain of being a parent. Although she was critical of herself in the domains of being a wife, daughter, sister, and friend, she was able to see that she was not falling short 100% in these domains. Moreover, she indicated that throughout her perinatal distress, she remained close to her God and believed that she was engaging in faithful spiritual practice. After completing her pie chart, her therapist asked her, on the basis of these data, if she now viewed herself as being a bad person. Donna responded that she believed she had a long way to go to be a good mother, but she also acknowledged the areas of her life in which she was fulfilling her valued roles. Thus, she could no longer make the blanket statement that she was a "bad person." On the basis of the "evidence" she constructed the more balanced belief, "I'm a work in progress."

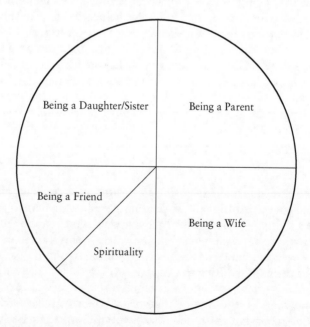

Figure 6.6 Sample Pie Chart.

Next, Donna and her therapist developed a list of specific behaviors in which she could engage to be more consistent with her values of being a good mother, wife, daughter, sister, and friend, and her therapist encouraged her to enact one of these behaviors between sessions. The goal of this intervention was for Donna to begin to behave in a manner that was consistent with her most cherished values and roles (i.e., those that contributed to being a good person), with the idea that the more she engaged in these behaviors, the more she would shift her underlying belief from "I'm a bad person" to "I'm a decent person."

Evidence Log

Evidence logs allow clients to track the evidence that supports their new, more helpful underlying belief. Clients can simply take a sheet of paper (or start a new note in the notes function of their smartphone) and begin a list of bullet pointed evidence that supports their new belief. However, this exercise is not as straightforward as it might seem. Most clients tend to dismiss most evidence that supports the new belief. Thus, therapists who work with clients who agree to keep an evidence log must thoroughly review the events of the previous week between sessions, keeping keenly aware of evidence that supports the new belief but that the client is dismissing. In addition, the therapist must probe for historical evidence that supports the new belief but that the client is dismissing because she believes it is not relevant to the present. For example, Donna helped her mother to raise her two younger sisters after her father passed away when she was a young age, which usually contributed to the notion that she is a good daughter and a sister. However, when she first presented for treatment, she believed that evidence did not "count" because it happened so long ago.

When clients keep evidence logs prospectively across the course of several weeks, they usually find, with their therapist's help, that there is a preponderance of evidence that supports their new belief. When the evidence accumulates, and they see it in their visual field in a list of bullet points, then they have a harder and harder time of refuting it. One consideration with the evidence log, as we mentioned previously with cognitive restructuring of situational automatic thoughts, is that it must be located in a convenient place. If clients are tech-savvy, we highly recommend that they keep their evidence log in their smartphone or in another easily accessible electronic file so that they can easily add to it when they encounter additional evidence.

When Donna kept her evidence log across four weeks of therapy, she was shocked by the amount of evidence that supported the notion that she was a decent person. She logged down everything she did to care for her daughter, and she realized that it was much more than that for which she was giving herself credit. Similarly, she logged down the positive comments that her husband expressed to her, and again, she realized that she was not failing as a wife. Her more balanced view was that they were both struggling, but that they were in the transition to parenthood as a unified team. In addition, she realized that she neglected to acknowledge the fact that she spent nearly an hour a day on the phone with one of her sisters, who was going through a difficult breakup with a boyfriend. Although Donna continued to wonder whether she was taking more from her mother than giving her, she realized that her mother had been longing to be a grandmother and that she was relishing the role. She also began to recognize that she was contributing to her family of origin in ways that she did not even define as important when she first created her pie chart, as she brought her daughter to visit her elderly grandmother once a week, and she served as an Alcoholics Anonymous (AA) sponsor for her cousin's wife who had recently had a number of struggles. Moreover, she logged down all of her activity with her church, which she had always viewed as a strong and positive part of her identity, and she realized that she was a more important part of the spiritual community there than she had once thought.

On the basis of four weeks of tracking, Donna realized how hard she was being on herself. In addition to refuting the belief that she was a bad person, she also realized that the fear that brought her into treatment—that she was having a postpartum psychotic episode—was no longer founded because she was functioning at a high level. After four weeks, she discontinued the active tracking of evidence because she had readily adopted the new, healthier belief. However, she occasionally reviewed her list for months thereafter whenever she recognized that the old belief was becoming activated.

Cognitive Continuum

The *cognitive continuum* is a belief modification strategy that targets all-or-nothing beliefs, such as "I am a failure" or "I am worthless" (J. S. Beck, 2011). Cognitive behavioral therapists who use this strategy draw a continuum of polar opposites and ask their clients to rate where they fall on the continuum. As we have seen, many postpartum clients believe that they are bad mothers, so therapists applying the cognitive continuum strategy would have them draw a horizontal line and write "0%—Bad Mother" at one end and "100%—Good Mother" at another end. When clients are in the throes of emotional despair, most rank themselves very poorly on the continuum, such as 0% or 10%. However, the therapist then uses guided discovery questioning to encourage the client to think critically about where she falls on the continuum in light of the full population. Consider this dialogue with Lyla, who was struggling with the belief that she was a bad mother.

Therapist: Let's consider mothering as being on a continuum, with 100% representing the best mother that one could imagine, and 0% representing the worst mother that one could imagine. [draws out continuum and gives Lyla a pencil] Indicate the place on the continuum where you fall.

Lyla: Do you want me to rate myself? I'd put myself at a 0%. No question. I'm the worst.

Therapist: [writing Lyla's name under 0%] OK, we'll start here. But before you take 0% as fact, I'd like you to think about the full pool of people who are mothers, just to make sure that you're not being overly hard on yourself.

Lyla: Seriously. Everyone I know is a better mother than I am.

Therapist: Who's the best mother you know?

Lyla: My sister-in-law, Dawn.

Therapist: [writing Dawn under "100%"] And what makes Dawn the best mother you know?

Lyla: She does everything for those four kids. And all with a smile on her face. Everyone says she's a saint, especially because she's married to my brother who works all the time and who is never around.

Therapist: Can you think of anyone, besides yourself, who you would not view as a good mother?

Lyla: Um . . . [thinking] um, maybe this girl I know from high school, Maureen.

Therapist: And what makes you view her as someone who is not a good mother.

Lyla: She's really gotten herself in a lot of trouble. She has three kids, all with different guys, and her boyfriend beats her. They both drink. A lot. My mother told me that she had child protective services called on her.

Therapist: Hmmm, have you ever had child protective services called on you?

Lyla: [hesitating] Well . . . no.

Therapist: Do you drink a lot, especially when you are taking care of Jack?

Lyla: No, I haven't had anything to drink since before I was pregnant.

Therapist: So what do you make of all of this?

Lyla: Well . . . I guess I have to be above Maureen. Like maybe she can be written at 0%, and I can be written at 1%?

Therapist: OK, we can change that. But before we do, I wonder if there are any other people who might have even more problems with parenting or with their kids than Maureen. In other words, does Maureen really represent a 0%?

Lyla:	I guess not. I mean, there are women who give birth and leave their babies in trash cans, right? And mothers who get their kids taken away permanently. [pauses] I just read an article about a woman who died, and her children wrote an obituary describing all of her abuse.
Therapist:	Should we revisit our ratings?
Lyla:	Yeah, I guess we should.

[Lyla and her therapist made ratings for all of the people who she had mentioned whom she viewed as bad mothers. She then moved Maureen up to 10%, and she moved herself up to 20%.]

Therapist:	On the basis of these ratings, can you still continue to conclude that you are the worst mother?
Lyla:	No, I guess not, not if you include all of the people who abuse their children and who leave their children out for dead.
Therapist:	Can you still conclude that you are a bad mother?
Lyla:	Yes, I think that's still valid. Being at 20% is not great at all.
Therapist:	[wondering if she could continue to help Lyla evaluate the accuracy of her rating of 20%] Just out of curiosity, who would be right in the middle of the scale? A 50%.
Lyla:	[thinking] I guess that would be my cousin Luanne.
Therapist:	[writing "Luanne" under 50%] And what makes her right in the middle?
Lyla:	Her daughter just turned 1. She had postpartum depression, like me. So it was a real struggle for her. But I know she really loves her daughter. And her daughter seems to be doing just fine.
Therapist:	Take a moment to reflect on what you just said. [pauses] What makes Luanne any different than you? What makes her a 50% and you a 20%?
Lyla:	Well, she eventually went back to work. I don't even have a job to go back to.
Therapist:	Is there anything that you have working in your favor that she doesn't?
Lyla:	No, there's nothing. [pauses] Oh, maybe here's something. When she was at her worst, someone else had to take care of the baby full-time. She was that bad. She really didn't even start bonding with her daughter until she was like 4 months old.
Therapist:	Has anyone else had to take care of Jack for you?
Lyla:	No, I've done it all myself. Believe me, I wouldn't want to have any of my family members step in and take care of him.

Therapist: And when did you start bonding with him?
Lyla: Oh, right when he was born. Before he was born, actually. He's the one thing that keeps me going.
Therapist: [sits back] Should we revise the rating of 20% in light of what you've just said?
Lyla: [sighs] OK. I can see how I'd be at 50%.
Therapist: The next time you start to go down the road of viewing yourself as a bad mother, maybe even the worst mother in the world, what will you say to yourself?
Lyla: I have to remember all of the people who don't care for their children at all, who maybe even abuse their children, and know that I'm not perfect, but that I'm actually giving him everything I can.
Therapist: When you acknowledge that, what happens to your depression?
Lyla: I feel a lot better.

Notice that the cognitive continuum strategy takes some time to unfold. Clients do not usually alter their ratings easily; it is only after careful consideration of the full universe of people that they realize that they are judging themselves harshly and not giving themselves credit. When therapists implement the cognitive continuum, they take care to define specific behaviors that underlie the ratings to ensure that ratings are made on the basis of specific facts, rather than generalizations, stereotypes, or partial truths.

Acting as If

Acting as if is a belief modification strategy that rests on the assumption that adaptive behavior can facilitate important cognitive change (J. S. Beck, 2011). It is as if the client leads with her behavior, then her mind follows. Many clients report that they cannot engage in adaptive behaviors until they start to feel better emotionally and think differently about themselves; acting as if shows clients that their behavior is not mood dependent, and that behaving in a more adaptive, effective manner provides important evidence that they *can* make good choices, have success, and act according to a more helpful belief system.

Tara, for example, found that when she focused on her belief that she was a bad mother, she lost confidence in her parenting skills and became hesitant, tentative, and reassurance seeking. These behavioral responses simply reinforced her belief that she was a bad mother. Her therapist suggested that she act "as if" she was a confident, effective mother. Tara and her therapist spent time in session outlining what she would do if she were a confident, effective mother, including taking her baby out every day, chatting in a friendly manner with new mothers at stores or at her yoga class (rather than avoiding them), refraining from asking other parents for advice in handling challenges, and refraining from being overly apologetic when her baby was fussy in the presence of others. Tara agreed to experiment with these behaviors for homework (in the same spirit as a behavioral experiment). When she returned for her next session, she reported that her depression and anxiety levels had dropped to their lowest levels since she had given birth. When her therapist asked her to what she attributed these low ratings, Tara replied that she had surprised herself with just how competent she was with her baby. Another new mother approached her to ask how she managed to care for her baby with such ease, as this other new mother was struggling, herself, and perceived that Tara "had it all together." On the basis of this exercise, Tara drew two conclusions: (a) that she was at least an adequate mother; and (b) that behaving in a manner consistent with a healthy belief, even if she did not always feel like it or believe the healthy belief applied to her, was associated with an improvement in self-esteem and a decrease in anxiety and depression.

Conclusion

Cognitive restructuring is a powerful took that can help clients to get some relief from their emotional distress by viewing their life circumstances as accurately and as helpfully as is possible, focusing on the "big picture" while not getting bogged down with details of how bad aspects of their lives are going at any moment. However, cognitive restructuring is anything but simple positive thinking. Therapists who implement cognitive restructuring help their clients to acquire tools to be accurate and balanced in their thinking, acknowledging what is not going right in their lives but recognizing their strengths, resources, and past successes.

In this chapter, we identified one obstacle that perinatal women often experience when they attempt to try cognitive restructuring for homework between sessions—that they simply do not have the time and energy to track their thoughts and balanced responses in a systematic manner. In our experience, there are two other obstacles that perinatal women commonly report when they attempt to use cognitive restructuring. One is that they are so overwhelmed and sleep-deprived that they report having trouble "thinking straight." Here, we encourage the combined use of affective coping skills described in Chapter 8 with straightforward cognitive restructuring tools that minimize sustained attention, such as the coping card. As is described in greater detail in Chapter 8, affective coping skills can help to center perinatal clients, quieting their minds and reducing agitation, so that they are able to make use of other CBT tools. One of us (AW) calls this the "one-two punch"—"one" being the affective coping skill, and "two" being the subsequent application of a CBT tool, such as the coping card.

A second obstacle that has been reported by perinatal women is that their concerns are too great to be subjected to cognitive restructuring, reasoning that childbearing is perhaps the most meaningful and important thing that they will ever do in their lives, and having something go wrong would be the most devastating life event they could ever experience. Thus, they remain entrenched in a pattern of worry that can only be allayed after they give birth to a healthy child. For example, one woman going through her first pregnancy acknowledged that the odds of having a child with a developmental disability were almost nothing, given the negative sequential screening results she had achieved earlier in her pregnancy, but she was consumed by the "what ifs" when she presented for therapy. When her therapist implemented appropriate cognitive interventions, such as developing a decatastrophizing plan if such an event were to occur (e.g., focusing on the positive and enriching lives that people with disabilities can have) and considering the benefits of tolerating the uncertainty, the woman put her hand up and shook her head, stating that the possibility of a disability was so threatening to her that she simply could not allow herself to "let her guard down," despite the fact that she was in her third trimester and could do nothing about it. For these women, the provision of support and affective coping skills may be all that they can tolerate, with the idea that a strong therapeutic relationship will increase the likelihood that they resume CBT following childbirth so that they can begin working on this intolerance of uncertainty with less threatening situations.

Regardless of the specific techniques that a cognitive behavioral therapist uses to achieve cognitive restructuring, the overall aim is for these healthy cognitive habits to last a lifetime. They will bring relief from emotional distress in the short-term. However, to prevent relapse, it is important that clients develop ways to continually approach stressors, challenges, and disappointments with accuracy and balance. Thus, therapists who use cognitive restructuring ensure that their clients can articulate the way skills generalize to other situations that are not discussed in therapy sessions, as well as other situations that might occur after therapy has ended.

7

BEHAVIORAL INTERVENTIONS
FOR PERINATAL DEPRESSION

As any clinician knows, clients who suffer from depression find it excruciating. They lack energy. They lack motivation. When they do engage in their usual activities, they find that they are dragging and uninterested and that they have difficulty obtaining pleasure from things they used to enjoy. As a result, they isolate. They procrastinate. The more unfinished tasks pile up, the more overwhelmed, dejected, and hopeless depressed clients become.

These behavioral sequelae of depression are especially pronounced in perinatal women. Pregnant women in their first trimester often report fatigue as their body adjusts to the hormonal increases that typically occur following conception. Pregnant women in their third trimester often report fatigue as they carry around much more mass than they are used to carrying, and they have trouble getting around. Postpartum women are often up multiple times a night tending to their infants, disrupting their sleep. In other words, pregnancy and the postpartum period are times in which it is logical that women would lack energy and have difficulty completing their usual activities simply because of the demands on their bodies. When these demands are coupled with depression, the fallout can be enormous. Depressed clients are in great need of a strategic approach that will help enable them to become more engaged in their lives.

Behavioral activation refers to a set of techniques that helps depressed clients actively engage in their lives and overcome patterns of avoidance and procrastination. It was developed as a stand-alone behavioral treatment for depression (Addis & Martell, 2004; Martell, Addis, & Jacobson, 2001), consistent with research showing that it is just as efficacious as a full package of CBT (which includes the cognitive restructuring techniques described in the previous chapter; Dimidjian et al., 2006; Jacobson et al., 1996). However, many fundamental techniques of behavioral activation were included in early versions of CBT for depression (e.g., A. T. Beck et al., 1979), and contemporary approaches to CBT place great emphasis on the techniques and underlying strategic principles of the work of Jacobson, Addis, and Martell (e.g., J. S. Beck, 2011; Wenzel, 2013; Wenzel et al., 2011). Thus, behavioral activation can be delivered to

114

depressed clients on its own, or it can be delivered to clients as part of a larger cognitive behavioral treatment package. In the latter case, therapists select behavioral activation when their clients' individualized case conceptualization suggests that lack of positive reinforcement from their client's life due to inactivity seems to be maintaining and exacerbating her depression. It is this approach that we describe in this chapter.

Techniques of Behavioral Activation

Increasing Engagement

With moderately to severely depressed clients, a first step that cognitive behavioral therapists often take is to help them engage positively with their environments. In order to achieve this, however, cognitive behavioral therapists need to know how their depressed clients are spending their time. In a typical course of CBT, the therapist ask their client to commit to *activity monitoring*, which is the tracking of how clients are spending each hour of the day in the days between sessions (J. S. Beck, 2011). Clients typically record these activities on a grid called an *activity log* and give two ratings: (a) a rating of the degree to which they got a sense of accomplishment from the activity (i.e., 0 = no sense of accomplishment; 10 = the highest sense of accomplishment that they could imagine); and (b) a rating of the degree to which they found the activity pleasurable (i.e., 0 = no pleasure; 10 = the most pleasure that they could imagine). At the end of the day, they rate their overall level of depression (i.e., 0 = no depression; 10 = the highest level of depression that they could imagine). Most clients observe an inverse correlation between their ratings of accomplishment and pleasure and their depression ratings. In other words, they usually see that the more they are engaging in activities that give them a sense of accomplishment and pleasure, the less depressed they feel.

It is not difficult to see that this activity would be challenging for women with young children, particularly postpartum women who are caring for an infant and quite possibly one or more other young children. Although activity monitoring yields important data that can be used to tailor additional interventions to promote engagement, it is onerous to record what one is doing every hour of the day. Some women have difficulty remembering to record their activities. Other women are just too consumed with the basics of child care to add another task to their "to do" list. Still other women have good intentions, but when they are faced with the decision of whether to record activities and associated ratings or nap when their baby is napping, they understandably do the latter.

On the one hand, it is important not to simply rely on your client's memory of how she spent her time. Memory is malleable, and retrospective accounts of how time was spent in the previous days and the associated sense of accomplishment and pleasure one attained from them would be difficult for anyone to report accurately, and particularly so for a sleep-deprived postpartum women. On the other hand, therapists who work with perinatal women will need to be creative in devising a manner in which prospective data can be gathered in a manner that is not overwhelming for their clients.

There are many ways to be creative. Tara's therapist reasoned that behavioral activation would be useful on the basis of Tara's report that she spent hours ruminating about whether she was a good mother and whether her husband and son would be better off without her, which in turn increased her depression and anxiety. Her therapist anticipated that as Tara began to engage in more activities that gave her a sense of accomplishment, she would begin to give herself credit for the many things she did in her roles as a wife and mother. Although Tara was game for recording her activities, she did not think it would work to record them on a piece of paper, as her son was colicky, and she reported that he was almost always in her arms. As an alternative, she used the voice recording function on her smartphone, indicating how she was spending her time at eight pre-designated times during the day (prompted by her smartphone's alarm). She voiced what she was doing at the moment, her accomplishment rating, and her pleasure rating. At the end of the day, she voice recorded her overall depression level. During her subsequent session, she played the voice recordings for her therapist, her therapist recorded them in her chart, and they examined the patterns in her ratings. Figure 7.1 is an example of the information that Tara's therapist helped her to compile.

Lyla simply found the idea of making so many ratings to be overwhelming. In the spirit of collaboration, Lyla and her therapist made the thoughtful decision to forego the ratings of accomplishment and pleasure. Because she slept so much during the day, her therapist hypothesized that demonstrating the simple association between the number of activities in which she engaged during the day and her overall mood would provide a context for subsequent behavioral activation interventions. Lyla's

	Thurs	Fri	Sat	Sun	Mon	Tues	Wed
T1	Feeding Thomas A = 3 P = 4	Sitting and thinking A = 0 P = 0	Cleaning up after breakfast A = 4 P = 0	Feeding Thomas A = 2 P = 4	Doing laundry A = 5 P = 1	Feeding Thomas A = 5 P = 6	Sitting and thinking A = 0 P = 0
T2	Yoga A = 2 P = 4	Going for a walk A = 1 P = 7	Running errand A = 4 P = 1	Church A = 1 P = 3	Going for a walk A = 3 P = 8	Yoga A = 3 P = 6	Sitting and thinking A = 0 P = 0

Figure 7.1 Tara's Activity Log.

T3	Talking to mom on phone A = 0 P = 3	Feeding Thomas A = 4 P = 5	Watching TV A = 0 P = 4	Coming home from church A = 0 P = 0	Talking to neighbors A = 1 P = 8	Watching TV A = 0 P = 4	Feeding Thomas A = 1 P = 2
T4	Eating lunch A = 0 P = 2	Dusting A = 5 P = 2	Ordering baby supplies online A = 2 P = 2	Sitting and thinking A = 0 P = 0	Eating lunch A = 2 P = 6	Eating lunch A = 2 P = 5	Talking to mom on phone A = 0 P = 2
T5	Sitting and thinking A = 0 P = 0	Going for another walk A = 2 P = 6	Feeding Thomas A = 3 P = 5	Sitting and thinking A = 0 P = 0	Swimming with Thomas A = 6 P = 9	Going for a walk A = 4 P = 7	Sitting and thinking A = 0 P = 0
T6	Making dinner A = 5 P = 1	Eating take-out A = 0 P = 6	Making dinner A = 5 P = 4	Sitting with husband while he makes dinner A = 0 P = 0	Making dinner A = 7 P = 7	Making dinner A = 6 P = 5	Sitting and thinking A = 0 P = 0
T7	Talking to husband A = 1 P = 3	Tummy time with Thomas A = 7 P = 5	Visiting with sister A = 1 P = 4	Tidying Thomas' room A = 2 P = 0	Cuddling with husband and Thomas A = 1 P = 10	Playing with Thomas and his baby gym A = 3 P = 7	Arguing with husband A = 0 P = 0
T8	Giving Thomas bath A = 3 P = 3	Singing to Thomas A = 2 P = 7	Feeding Thomas A = 3 P = 5	Giving Thomas a bath A = 2 P = 2	Paying bills A = 5 P = 1	Watching TV A = 0 P = 5	Feeding Thomas A = 1 P = 1
DEP	7	4	5	8	3	4	8

Figure 7.1 Continued.

therapist also suspected that making the recording form as straightforward as possible would maximize the likelihood that Lyla would comply with recording in between sessions. Thus, together in session, Lyla and her therapist developed a pool of possible activities in which she might engage in the time in between sessions. Her therapist developed a format for her to simply check off whenever she engaged in the activity on a particular day and then make one mood rating at the end of the day. Figure 7.2 is an

Activity	Wed	Thurs	Fri	Sat	Sun	Mon	Tues
Feed Jack.	X	X	X	X	X	X	X
Take a shower.	X			X	X		
Take Jack on a walk through the neighborhood.				X		X	
Empty the dishwasher.		X		X		X	
Tidy up the living room.							
Call a family member or friend.	X	X		X		X	X
Go on a play date.		X					
Attend Mommy and Me story time at the library.				X			
Prepare a meal.	X				X		X
Practice tummy time with Jack.	X						X
Read a chapter in a novel.		X			X		
Give Jack a bath.	X	X	X	X	X	X	X
OVERALL DEPRESSION LEVEL (0 = no depression; 10 = the most depression I have ever experienced)	5	7	9	4	6	8	7

Figure 7.2 Lyla's Modified Activity Log.

example of this modified activity log. Using this format, she indeed completed the activity monitoring in the time between sessions.

Other suggestions for simplifying the process of activity monitoring are as follows:

- Rather than having the client record activities and their associated ratings for all days during the session, the client can choose three representative days. Clients who choose this option should be sure to record activities for two weekdays and one weekend day.
- Enlist the client's spouse or partner to assist with the exercise. For example, the spouse or partner could help the client to fill in her activities at a set time during the day. Or at minimum, the spouse or partner could attend a session to provide another viewpoint of how the client is spending her time.
- Use a smartphone or tablet device application (app). As stated in Chapter 6, there is a plethora of CBT apps that are being introduced to the market at the time of the writing of this book (e.g., MoodKit for iphone). Many of them contain functions to track activities in addition to other cognitive and behavioral strategies.

As stated previously, the purpose of activity monitoring is to identify the specific targets for behavioral activation interventions. Thus, when clients complete activity monitoring, it is important to spend time in the subsequent session discussing the conclusions that they are drawing from the exercise. It is best to give the client space to draw and articulate her own conclusions first before the therapist does so, in order for her to truly internalize the behavioral principle that underlies the association between her mood and activity level. One way to clearly organize the data obtained from activity monitoring is to translate the data into a graphical representation. Figure 7.3 displays the results from Lyla's efforts at activity monitoring. This graph provided a vivid illustration of the notion that her depression was generally worse when she was engaging in fewer activities. When clients make more elaborate ratings, such as the accomplishment and pleasure ratings that Tara recorded into her smartphone, therapists can simply take the average accomplishment and pleasure ratings for each day and plot three lines on a graph: one for the average accomplishment rating, one for the average pleasure rating, and one for the average depression rating. The expected pattern is an inverse association between the average ratings and accomplishment and pleasure and the daily depression rating.

On the basis of this information, cognitive behavioral therapists then work with their clients on *activity scheduling*, which, as it sounds, is the scheduling of activities that are expected to have a mood-enhancing effect. The therapist works with the client to identify activities that have the potential to produce a sense of accomplishment or pleasure and to figure out when she might pursue these activities. In traditional CBT,

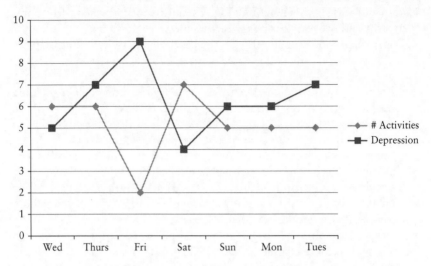

Figure 7.3 Graphical Representation of Lyla's Behavioral Activation Data.

therapist have their clients write in the accomplishment and pleasurable activities that they hope to engage in particular time slots on their activity log. During the week, they then indicate whether or not they engaged in the activity while they continue to log down the other activities in which they engage, the associated accomplishment and pleasure ratings, and the overall depression rating at the end of the day.

With perinatal clients, we recommend modifications to this procedure. As we saw in our discussion of activity monitoring, it is challenging for perinatal women to record every activity in which they engage and make associated accomplishment and pleasure ratings. Moreover, women with infants and young children face the additional reality that it is nearly impossible to schedule activities at specific times, given the unpredictability of small children and their needs, as well as the unpredictability of their energy level and need for sleep. Thus, what can be helpful with perinatal clients is to choose two or three activities that the client anticipates would be especially pleasurable or especially associated with a sense of accomplishment. Then, therapists can implement "flexible scheduling," such that clients identify a general time frame in which they engage in the activity (e.g., "Tuesday morning" or "Saturday afternoon"), as well as "back-up plans" if they are unable to enact the activity in the broad time frame that they had originally identified. Another way to use the "back-up plan" is to have a small pool of activities from which to choose during the scheduled time, so that the implementation of the activity can be achieved even when certain factors might interfere. Tara, for example, wanted to schedule runs using her new jogging stroller. However, running outdoors is dependent on good weather. Thus, she identified three activities all with the same level of expected accomplishment and pleasure that she could choose during the scheduled time of her activity, and she made her choices on the basis of the weather and the amount of sleep she got the previous night.

When clients schedule activities, cognitive behavioral therapists ask them to rate the actual degree of accomplishment and pleasure associated with them, as well as to provide an overall depression rating at the end of the day. It is hoped that clients will observe that their average depression rating improves in between sessions as a function of the degree to which they engage in activities that they associate with a sense of accomplishment and pleasure. Across the course of several weeks, clients can schedule more and more activities into their weeks. It is important to be reasonable and balanced in scheduling these activities, as it is overwhelming for most clients, and perinatal clients in particular, to be overscheduled. Over time, the activities that have the greatest mood enhancing effects are integrated into one's daily routine so that they become a natural part of the manner in which clients live their lives.

Although activity scheduling is a powerful technique in achieving behavioral activation, the course of activity monitoring and scheduling described to this point is more the exception than the rule. Many clients find activity monitoring and scheduling to be quite difficult, as it requires them to proactively break free of behavioral patterns that are deeply entrenched. Next, we describe some of the obstacles that therapists and clients experience in activity monitoring and scheduling, as well as ways to overcome those obstacles.

The Client Does Not Complete the Homework

All cognitive behavioral therapists will encounter instances in which their clients do not complete their activity monitoring or do not implement the activities that had been planned. In these instances, the therapist must undergo a thorough consideration of the factors underlying homework noncompliance. Many perinatal clients, for example, report that they are too depressed or overwhelmed to complete the activity log. If homework noncompliance persists even after creatively modifying the exercise to meet the client's needs, then additional interventions should be considered in order to alleviate the severity of the client's symptoms. Might it be helpful for the client to have a medication consult with a prescribing healthcare provider to determine whether psychotropic medications would be warranted? Is the client so agitated that she needs to learn self-soothing techniques (see Chapter 8) before attempting her homework? Might the client benefit from implementing one and only one activity into her life without the accompanying tracking in order to out the smallest dent in her mood disturbance before tackling a more complex exercise like activity monitoring and scheduling?

Other clients do not complete their homework because they are ambivalent about the exercise. They might be so hopeless that it is difficult for them to believe that anything will make a difference. Or they might not yet be in the action stage of change, such that they are ready, willing, and feel able to put in the effort required to maximize activity monitoring and scheduling's benefits. Therapists who encounter these obstacles can consider using the principles of motivational interviewing (Miller & Rollnick, 2013; Westra, 2012) to gain a better sense of the client's internal experience and ambivalence, foster the therapeutic relationship, and strategically ask reflective questions to help these clients embrace change. It is also important to be sure that the client understands the association between inactivity and low mood so that she has a clear understanding of this strategy's mechanism of action.

However, it just might be the case that the client is simply not ready to take on an exercise as systematic as activity monitoring and scheduling. She might need nurturing. She might need to take care of herself in her own way, which we elaborate on more in the next section of this chapter. She might want something other than a solution to her problems, when it seems like that is all others in her social support network are giving her. As was stated in Chapter 4, the therapeutic relationship is essential in healing from perinatal distress, and it is the springboard from which clients embrace cognitive and behavioral strategies when they are ready to do so.

The Client Cannot Identify Activities to be Scheduled

Depression often puts blinders on people, such that they can see straight ahead to the tasks that require immediate attention, but they have trouble using their peripheral vision to "dream" about other activities that would give them a sense of accomplishment, pleasure, and meaning. The perinatal client might be so overwhelmed that she cannot think of doing anything other than caring for the baby. Or she might have been depressed so long that she has forgotten what used to give her pleasure.

Fortunately, there are ready-made lists of pleasurable activities that therapists and their clients can consult. The original list, called the Pleasant Events Schedule, featured more than 300 items (MacPhillamy & Lewinsohn, 1976). An internet search for "Pleasant Events Schedule" will yield many links to web sites and PDF documents that contain various versions. Therapists can print out a Pleasant Events Schedule (sometimes called a Pleasant Activities List) and help their client to select potentially pleasurable activities that she otherwise would not have considered.

There is no Time in the Client's Schedule for New Activities

This obstacle is one that is frequently encountered by cognitive behavioral therapists who work with perinatal women. Parenting young children is a job that requires attention 24 hours, 7 days a week. If clients have identified activities that do not involve their child or children, then it is possible that they will need to use the problem solving skills described in Chapter 9 to obtain child care. In addition, clients should be encouraged to use creativity and flexibility in the activities that they choose in order to account for the reality of their life circumstances. For example, perhaps a client would like to get some exercise by going for a hike, but the hike is sufficiently rough that she could not take her baby with her. Instead, she might obtain similar benefit (i.e., exercise) by taking a class at a local gym that provides childcare.

The Client Becomes Discouraged When She Does Not Immediately Feel Better

It is important for clients to have accurate and realistic expectations regarding the benefits that they will obtain from activity monitoring and scheduling. Although on average, clients experience a reduction in depression when they engage in activities associated with a sense of accomplishment and pleasure, there is variability. A single attempt to engage in one of these new activities may or may not be associated with a noticeable change in mood. These effects are cumulative over time. Thus, it is important to help clients to identify any negative automatic thoughts about themselves or the potential for this exercise to be helpful and to use the cognitive restructuring techniques described in Chapter 6 to evaluate their accuracy and helpfulness.

Graded Task Assignment

Perinatal women are often so depleted that even the most straightforward of tasks seems daunting to them. Tasks that are particularly complex just seem out of the question. *Graded task assignment* is a behavioral activation strategy in which clients gain skill in breaking tasks into smaller pieces. When clients do this, they can then incorporate the smaller pieces into activity scheduling. Problem solving tools (see Chapter 9) are often used in conjunction with graded task assignment to help clients identify and prioritize the specific components of tasks with which they are faced.

Self-Care

Many perinatal women are so overwhelmed that they are engaging in minimal self-care, which has the potential to further sap the psychological resources that are crucial to handling the increased stress associated with parenthood. They may only be getting a few hours of sleep per day; they may be showering only sporadically; they may be eating poorly. Feeling badly physically increases the likelihood that people, especially those who are already struggling with depression, feel badly emotionally.

Cognitive behavioral therapists are encouraged to ask the following questions to assess for the degree to which their perinatal clients are adhering to basic aspects of self-care:

- How many hours of sleep are you getting, in total, in a 24-hour period?
- After you feed the baby, are you able to go right back to sleep, or do you lie awake?
- What (other than feeding a baby) is keeping you up from sleeping at night?
- How many meals are you eating each day?
- What are you eating during your meals? During your snacks?
- How many days a week have you been showering?
- Have you been drinking alcohol or using drugs? How much and how often?

By asking these and any other questions about self-care, cognitive behavioral therapists begin to identify unhealthy habits that might be exacerbating their client's clinical presentation. When therapists identify one or more areas of suboptimal self-care, they can then target those areas using behavior modification techniques.

Modifying unhelpful self-care behavior does not happen overnight, especially for a new mother who is already overwhelmed and sleep-deprived. Moreover, it is important to have realistic expectations, as it is almost certain that a breastfeeding mother of a newborn will have her sleep interrupted when she gets up in the middle of the night to nurse. Part of activity scheduling might involve a "do one and only one thing each day" rule, and the one thing that a new mother might choose to do is something basic like taking a shower.

Some cognitive behavioral therapists find that the best approach with a new mother is to instill healthy self-care behaviors before using activity scheduling to increase the degree to which she experiences a sense of accomplishment and pleasure in her life. Other cognitive behavioral therapists incorporate self-care behaviors into activity scheduling and use the activity schedule as a way to work on healthy self-care habits. Regardless of the specific way in which self-care is incorporated into CBT for perinatal distress, it is imperative to address if the client is not taking care of herself, as she will not be in a good position to embrace the other strategies described in this volume. In the next sections, we give some specific suggestions to help perinatal women enhance their self-care in a number of domains.

Healthy Sleep

Figure 7.4 displays principles of healthy sleep. It contains principles of *sleep hygiene*, which is a set of behaviors that can be enacted to maximize

• Set a regular sleep schedule (i.e., regular time to bed, regular time to wake) and stick with it seven days a week.
• Avoid naps.
• Use the bed only for sleep, sex, and nursing. Do not read, watch television, talk on the phone, or eat in bed.
• Go to bed only when sleepy.
• Engage in a relaxing activity an hour before bedtime. No working, doing chores, or answering emails.
• Develop a predictable bedtime routine (e.g., washing face, brushing teeth) to serve as a cue that it is bedtime.
• If awake for longer than a half hour, get out of bed and engage in a quiet, non-arousing activity (no computer, phone, or tablet device) until sleepy enough to go back to bed.
• Turn the clock so that it cannot be seen.
• Do not turn on smartphones or tablet devices in the middle of the night. Consider storing smartphones or tablet devices outside of the bedroom if their flickering lights are activating.
• Refrain from drinking caffeinated beverages after noon.
• Refrain from using alcohol as a sleep aid.
• Refrain from smoking cigarettes in the evening.
• Exercise regularly but do not do so within four hours of bedtime.
• Do not fixate on sleeping a certain number of hours.
• Make sure the bedroom is dark, quiet, and at a comfortable temperature. Use a white noise machine to minimize noise if needed.
• Make sure the bed is comfortable.
• Do not go to bed hungry, but do not eat a heavy meal before bed. A light snack before bed is fine.
• Avoid excessive intake of all liquids in the evening to avoid multiple bathroom trips in the middle of the night.
• Use cognitive behavioral strategies to minimize the degree to which problems, sadness, or anxiety are taken to bed.

Figure 7.4 Healthy Sleep Habits.

Note: Many of these tips for healthy sleep habits can be found in Hauri & Linde (1996), Perlis, Jungquist, Smith, & Posner, (2005), and Silberman (2008). Adapted with permission from Wenzel (2014b).

the likelihood that a person gets quality sleep at night and is alert the next day, and *stimulus control*, which is a set of behaviors that can be enacted to ensure that being in bed is associated with sleep, rather than arousal. Many cognitive behavioral therapists share these principles with their clients whose sleep is disrupted and work with them to systematically implement healthy sleep behaviors into their routines.

With perinatal women, it is important to be mindful that these are aspirational goals. Pregnant women usually have difficulty finding a comfortable position in which to sleep, and even if they refrain from drinking liquids before bed, they will wake up multiple times of night to use the bathroom. Most postpartum women will be getting up one or more times a night to care for their newborn. Some postpartum women co-sleep with their babies and will nurse in bed.

Thus, cognitive behavioral therapists who work with perinatal women review the principles of healthy sleep with them and collaboratively decide the most effective manner to implement as many of the principles as possible, with the reasoning that the more of these principles that perinatal women follow, the greater the likelihood that they will get a good night's sleep. For example, although perinatal women might balk of the idea of having a regular bedtime and wake time, striving to establish some semblance of a regular schedule will create healthy habits for their baby, as well as for themselves. The long-term payoff could have important implications for the prevention of emotional distress.

With most adults, cognitive behavioral therapists hold a strict "no napping rule." The reasoning behind this rule is that the pressure to sleep builds throughout the day, and when the time comes to fall asleep at night, enough "debt" has accumulated that the person is able to fall asleep (Perlis, Jungquist, Smith, & Posner, 2005). When a person naps, she has broken that cycle and increases the likelihood that there will not be enough pressure for sleep to facilitate sleepiness when it is time to go to bed. Typically, even when a person has had a poor night's sleep, she is instructed not to nap so that the sleep pressure is high enough that she will have a sound night's sleep the next night.

We are not as strict about the "no napping" rule with new mothers as we are with non-perinatal clients. Some perinatal women report that their newborns sleep only a couple of hours at a time, such that they are up and down through the night with broken sleep. On occasion, perinatal women describe even more challenging sleep patterns—one perinatal woman reported that her newborn was up every 20 minutes! When a client is still adjusting to the postpartum period and broken sleep patterns, she might need to nap until her infant is a little older. When cognitive behavioral therapists make this choice in collaboration with their clients, they carefully monitor their client's sleeping pattern. If she continues to report a great deal of difficulty sleeping at night when the baby is sleeping, then it is likely that she is, indeed, not building up enough pressure for sleep to fall asleep at night. Even if it does not sound attractive to the client, it may be in her best interest to experiment with the "no napping" rule and observe whether it affects her ability to fall asleep at night.

Many of the rules of sleep hygiene maximize the likelihood that people will encounter cues that signal to them that it is time to go to bed. Postpartum women and infants, alike, can benefit from these cues. For example, we advise perinatal clients to use their beds only for sleep, sex, and nursing. Doing so will pair the act of sleeping with being in bed; if clients are using their beds for other purposes, such as watching television or talking on the phone, then they are pairing the acts of being awake and active with being in bed. We also encourage perinatal clients to engage in a relaxing activity before bed, as well as to implement a predictable bedtime routine. Not only are these routines non-activating, they also provide additional cues to the body that it is time for sleep. From a practical standpoint, many new mothers will need to implement a bedtime routine that involves their newborn. An example might be a warm bath for the baby, then nursing, then rocking in a rocking chair and singing quiet lullabies.

Healthy Diet and Nutritional Habits

At the outset, we should say that we are mental health professionals, not dieticians or nutritionists, and a full set of scientifically-based recommendations for perinatal nutrition is beyond the scope of this book. If a client is in need of comprehensive diet and nutritional services, then cognitive behavioral therapists make appropriate referrals.

That being said, we take a similar approach as Marsha Linehan, the developer of Dialectical Behavioral Therapy (DBT; Linehan, 1993a, 1993b), who regards eating three meals a day (along with regular sleep and exercise) as the building blocks of emotion regulation. Without taking in the "fuel" to help themselves face the challenges of the day, perinatal women will be at increased likelihood of feeling lethargic, overwhelmed, and unable to cope with the demands of a newborn. Clients might need to work breakfast, lunch, and dinner into their activity schedules in order to ensure that they get the nourishment that they need. They might need to use problem solving skills (see Chapter 9) in order to figure out ways to prepare meals for themselves if they are the sole care provider for their newborn for much of the day. At minimum, clients can make efforts to have healthy choices in the house that they can grab quickly if they are unable to find enough time to prepare a meal, such as nuts, yogurt, fruits, vegetables, and whole grain bread.

Alcohol and Drug Use

The American Congress of Obstetrics and Gynecology warns that alcohol should not be used during pregnancy. Some prescription drugs may be used under the close supervision of a prescribing provider. Although guidelines for alcohol use while breastfeeding are less clear, the La Leche League International recommends that women plan ahead if they expect to have an alcoholic drink, such that they feed their infant stored breast milk or wait for the alcohol to clear one's system before nursing. Again, prescription drugs may be used under the close supervision of a prescribing provider. Use of illegal drugs is never recommended regardless of one's perinatal status.

Cognitive behavioral therapists treating perinatal clients who use alcohol or illegal drugs during pregnancy and/or the postpartum period should address this situation directly, making it a high priority target for treatment. Perinatal clients who use alcohol or illegal drugs to reduce emotional distress can be taught the other cognitive behavioral strategies described in this volume, such as cognitive restructuring (see Chapter 6) and self-soothing (see Chapter 8). Because these skills take some time to acquire and practice, therapists should closely monitor their clients' use of alcohol and illegal drugs. If their clinical judgment is that the client's use of alcohol or illegal drugs is putting herself or her infant at risk, then she should be referred immediately to a higher level of care.

Interplay Between Cognition and Behavior

The techniques described in this chapter represent those that involve enacting behavioral changes. However, it is important to recognize that behavior cannot be totally divorced from cognition, and that cognition plays an important role as clients practice these behavioral techniques. Thus, many cognitive behavioral therapists find themselves simultaneously delivering cognitive interventions with behavioral interventions.

For example, consider Lyla, who was severely depressed and often skeptical that the therapeutic interventions would make a difference in her life. When her therapist first proposed behavioral activation, she only made a halfway commitment to following through, remarking that the technique seemed too simple to be useful to her. That, in and of itself, was an automatic thought that was associated with pessimism and a lack of motivation that interfered with fully enacting the activities to which she committed for homework. Another way of viewing Lyla's cognitive orientation is that she was creating a self-fulfilling prophesy, such that she was skeptical that behavioral activation would work, and she was increasing the likelihood that it, indeed, would not be helpful because this attitude prevented her from fully embracing it. Thus, it was important that Lyla's therapist work with her to reshape this attitude in order to maximize the likelihood that behavioral activation would make a noticeable difference in her depression.

Conversely, much cognitive change can occur after enacting a behavioral activation technique. Success with behavioral activation provides evidence to clients that their lives *can* be different, instilling a sense of self-efficacy and motivating them to continue living by the same principles in order to manage their mood. That is, success with behavioral activation has the potential to alter clients' views of themselves, their world, and their future.

Perhaps the most interesting example of the interplay between cognition and behavior occurs in instances in which clients report the idea that they would engage more in activities associated with a sense of accomplishment or pleasure *if only they felt better*. In other words, they have the idea that they need to be less depressed before they can fully engage in their lives, which can prevent them from taking action in the here and now in order to get behavioral activation's antidepressant benefits. *Countering mood dependent behaviors* is a technique that helps clients to see that they can feel depressed and, *at the same time*, engage in valued activities that give them a sense of accomplishment and pleasure (Farmer & Chapman, 2008). The rationale behind this technique is that clients experiment with engaging in activities associated with a sense of accomplishment or pleasure even when they do not feel up to it due to their depression, and they reserve judgment about the degree to which it was helpful until after they have completed the activity. Clients who use this technique begin to learn that their behavior is not dependent on their mood.

Conclusion

Behavioral activation is a strategy that incorporates concrete behavioral techniques to provide fairly immediate antidepressant effects. It helps clients to become more actively engaged in valued activities associated with a sense of pleasure and accomplishment. Its targets range from basic self-care to breaking complex tasks, such as a finding a child care center, into smaller pieces. Although behavioral activation requires that clients enact different, and more adaptive, behaviors in their lives, its cognitive effects are just as powerful as its behavioral effects because it provides positive evidence to shape a healthy sense of self and optimism for the future.

As has been stated already in this chapter, at times this is "easier said than done" with depressed clients, and this is particularly so with perinatal women. Between adjusting to new and rigorous demands on their time and feeling physically suboptimal, it is difficult for them to think about scheduling activities associated with a sense of accomplishment and pleasure into their days. It is likely that, with many perinatal clients, activity scheduling will start with basic self-care and child care. Cognitive work may need to be incorporated to help perinatal women refine what it means to have a sense of accomplishment and pleasure, given the radical manner in which their life has changed.

That being said, perinatal women can also be given hope that the demands on their time will not stay this way forever. Many women with perinatal distress believe that their lives have been changed forever and that they will never reclaim parts of themselves that they valued and that enhanced their self-esteem. It can help to remind them that babies are the most dependent during their first year of life, and with each year, they become increasingly independent (so to speak), allowing them more time to engage in the activities that they once found to give them a sense of accomplishment and pleasure. Until that time, therapists can work with perinatal women to have reasonable expectations for the types of activities in which they engage, but also to be creative in finding new activities that reflect their core values and preferences in a new way.

8

BEHAVIORAL INTERVENTIONS FOR PERINATAL ANXIETY

The behavioral activation interventions described in the previous chapter represent just one set of behavioral strategies from which cognitive behavioral therapists draw. In this chapter, we describe behavioral strategies that are primarily targeted toward anxiety. We begin with a description of relatively straightforward behavioral exercises that can help perinatal women manage anxiety in any one moment. We then turn our attention to a discussion of how avoidance of intrusive thoughts, triggers for intrusive thoughts, and reminders of childbirth or other trauma perpetuate anxiety, as well as strategies for overcoming this pattern of avoidance.

Affective Coping Skills

Affective coping skills are tools that perinatal clients can apply to reduce high levels of anxiety and agitation to reasonable levels in order to become more centered, grounded, and able to address whatever challenges they are facing (Wenzel, 2013). Not only can affective coping skills help people survive moments of severe emotional distress, they also promote cognitive change when their successful application provides evidence that clients *can* manage their anxiety. Thus, when perinatal women experience a reduction in emotional distress, they begin to put a dent in the pervasive sense of helplessness that they often report when they first begin treatment.

Affective coping skills, when practiced consistently, can be powerful tools for managing emotional distress, but it is important to recognize that they are usually viewed as a short-term strategy to survive difficult moments, rather than long-term solutions to clients' problems and unhelpful patterns of behavior (cf. Linehan, 1993a, 1993b). Even in instances in which clients successfully reduce their anxiety using an affective coping skill, the problem or issue that triggered the anxiety still needs to be addressed. Moreover, if clients rely on these skills in order to reduce experiencing anxiety associated with triggers that they are avoiding, then their use might entrench anxiety further in the long run. Thus, cognitive behavioral therapists who use affective coping skills with their clients think critically about the function that these tools serve and ensure that they are moving treatment forward, rather than inadvertently making avoidance patterns more difficult to overcome in the future. Our rule of thumb is that if clients are so anxious or agitated that they have difficulty concentrating or focusing, interfering with their ability to embrace the cognitive and behavioral work being done in session (or applied outside of session), then affective coping skills are helpful to reduce their anxiety enough to be centered so that they can then take skillful action to address whatever is triggering them.

In the following sections, we describe the two most standard affective coping strategies used by cognitive behavioral therapists—controlled breathing and muscle relaxation. We view these strategies as tools that can be placed into perinatal clients' tool belts, similar to what a carpenter does with his hammers and wrenches. As much as perinatal clients want relief from their emotional distress right away, it is important that they have accurate expectations for the use of these tools. With time, they are expected to reduce emotional distress when they are practiced. However, sometimes this does not happen right away, as clients need to acquire skill in using these tools, much like what happens when we learn how to ride a bicycle. Thus, we encourage clients to practice in times of (relative) calm in order to strengthen their skills so that they are able to call upon them in times of emotional distress.

Controlled Breathing

Controlled breathing is a strategy in which clients learn to breathe at an even rate and depth. This strategy is especially useful for clients who report that overbreathing is a part of the way in which their anxiety manifests. It helps to regulate the amount of oxygen that clients take into their bodies, which in turn regulates their breathing physiology and instills a sense of controllability and predictability.

Many clinicians who use breathing techniques with their clients use the term "deep breathing." This is because they are encouraging their clients to breathe with their diaphragms, rather than with their chests. Diaphragmatic breathing is an important component of controlled breathing. It allows clients to fill their lungs fully with air. In contrast, when clients breathe from their chests, it is called "shallow breathing" because they are not fully filling their lungs with air. Clients will know when they are using their diaphragms to breathe because they will see their bellies expanding and contracting, almost as if they are filling and then deflating a balloon. Clients who have difficulty understanding this concept can lean back on a reclining chair or even lay on a flat surface so that they can better see their bellies moving up and down.

The danger, however, of referring to breathing tools as "deep breathing" is that clients mistakenly get the impression that they are supposed to take in as much air as they can. These clients, then, breathe more deeply than they would otherwise. In order to understand why this is problematic, it is important to have a working knowledge of the physiology of breathing. When oxygen is taken into the body, it is converted to carbon dioxide. The body is much more sensitive to levels of carbon dioxide in the body than it is to levels of oxygen. Thus, when the body detects that there is an overabundance of carbon dioxide, an array of physiological processes are initiated: (a) the acid content in the blood decreases (i.e., alkaline blood); (b) blood vessels constrict; and (c) hemoglobin, or the chemical in the blood that carries oxygen to various parts of the body, increases its "stickiness," meaning that less oxygen is released. The culmination of these physiological processes is that various parts of the body are receiving *less* oxygen than they would otherwise, rather than more oxygen. When this happens, paradoxically, the person experiences many of the same physiological symptoms of anxiety that she was trying to control. For example, when the brain does not get enough oxygen, people experience sensations of unreality, dizziness, and lightheadedness. When the extremities do not get enough oxygen, people experience coldness, clamminess, tingling, and numbing.

Thus, when clients are taught controlled breathing, rather than deep breathing, they are learning to take in normal amounts of air at a steady pace in order to regulate the oxygen-carbon dioxide balance in their bodies. The following is a simple protocol that clinicians and clients can follow (Wenzel, 2014b):

- Find a quiet, relaxing location, and dim the lights if possible.
- Sit in a reclined position or lay down on your back.
- Close your eyes if you are comfortable in doing so; otherwise, fix your gaze on one spot in the room.
- Breathe through your mouth or nose in to a count of 3 (1, 2, 3). Take a brief pause, and exhale through your mouth or nose to a count of 5 (1, 2, 3, 4, 5).
- Continue this practice for 10 breaths.
- Be sure to take in a normal amount of air in each breath.
- If you are lying down, check to make sure that your belly is moving up and down, as if a balloon is inflating and deflating. Your belly expanding and contracting in this manner is indicative of diaphragmatic breathing.
- Remain with your eyes closed until you are ready to open them.
- Assess what is different after going through this exercise. Taking the time to note the benefits of controlled breathing will increase the likelihood that you will use it in the future.

It is important to practice this in session, rather than simply talk about how to do controlled breathing without the experiential component. If the client presents in a state of distress or agitation, then in-session practice of controlled breathing can an effective tool for grounding her so that she is able to make use of the session in a way that will be helpful for her. In-session practice also allows the therapist to determine whether the client truly understands how to engage in diaphragmatic breathing. In addition, in-session practice allows the client to leave the session with increased confidence that she will be able to use it in her life outside of session.

Even when perinatal women successfully practice controlled breathing in session, they may have difficulty translating their success to their own home environments. They may forget the specific steps of the procedure. They might have trouble slowing down and finding the time to work it into their routines. For these and other reasons, therapists should take the time to maximize the likelihood that controlled breathing will be helpful to perinatal women outside of session. They can use problem solving strategies with their clients (see also Chapter 9) to determine when they might practice controlled breathing and who might be able to watch over the child or children while they take the time to practice. If perinatal clients are simply unable to sequester time or find someone to watch over their child or children, they can nevertheless find creative ways to integrate controlled breathing into their routines. Perhaps they practice breathing while the baby is nursing, when they are lying down with their toddlers for bed, or to the rhythmic steps of a walk with the stroller around the neighborhood. The beauty of the breath is that it is always present so that clients can mobilize it in any one moment.

The advent of modern technology has also been an asset to the practice of controlled breathing. At the time of the writing of this book, there are many breathing applications (apps) available for smartphones and tablet devices that are free or for a nominal cost. There are also audio tracks that are available from sources such as iTunes and amazon.com. The advantage of the apps and audio tracks is that the client can simply listen and follow the directions, rather than having to remember the steps to controlled breathing on her own. Many clients find that the voices on the recordings are soothing and enhance the experience.

Muscle Relaxation

Muscle relaxation refers to a family of relaxation tools aimed at achieving a state of relaxation, both physiologically in the muscles as well as emotionally. Perhaps the most commonly used type of muscle relaxation is *progressive muscle relaxation* (Bernstein, Borkovec, & Hazlett-Stevens, 2000), which is the systematic tensing and relaxing of sixteen different muscle groups in order to achieve a state of relaxation. Over time, clients learn to pair muscle groups and condense the procedure, such that they move toward tensing and relaxing right muscle groups, then four, and then two. With practice, they can cue the relaxation of all of their muscle groups at once.

Whereas controlled breathing is a staple in the cognitive behavioral treatment of many anxiety disorders, especially panic disorder (Barlow & Craske, 2007) and posttraumatic stress disorder (PTSD; Rothbaum, Foa, & Hembree, 2007), there is more controversy about the inclusion of muscle relaxation in the cognitive behavioral treatment of anxiety. Hofmann (2012) indicated that controlled breathing, rather than muscle relaxation, is a more central mechanism of change in the cognitive behavioral treatment of panic disorder. Moreover, he observed that panic is exasperated in some clients with panic disorder because they become more anxious, rather than less anxious, in a state of relaxation. In contrast, muscle relaxation has been demonstrated as an empirically supported treatment for generalized anxiety disorder (GAD) on its own (Siev & Chambless, 2007), although research has shown that full packages of CBT are more efficacious than muscle relaxation on its own in the treatment of GAD (Dugas et al., 2010). Thus, muscle relaxation has long been incorporated into CBT treatment packages for GAD (M. G. Newman & Borkovec, 1995). It also has been incorporated into CBT treatment packages for insomnia (Perlis et al., 2005).

How does the therapist know whether muscle relaxation is indicated for any one client? If the client's primary clinical presentation is one of panic attacks, then muscle relaxation is not indicated. If the client's primary clinical presentation is one of generalized anxiety or insomnia, then muscle relaxation is indeed indicated. If the client's primary clinical presentation is mixed or unspecified, therapists can rely on the collaborative therapeutic relationship and seek feedback from their clients about their clients' preferences.

If therapists choose to teach their clients muscle relaxation, the following is a simple progressive muscle relaxation protocol that they can use (Wenzel, 2014b):

- Find a quiet, relaxing location, and dim the lights if possible.
- Sit in a reclined position or lay down on your back.
- Close your eyes if you are comfortable in doing so; otherwise, fix your gaze on one spot in the room.
- Consider beginning the exercise with controlled breathing protocol such as the procedure that was described previously.
- Tense each major muscle group for 5–10 seconds and release the tension for 30–45 seconds. Major muscle groups include the feet, calves, thighs, abdominal region, hands and forearms, biceps, chest/

shoulders/upper back area, neck and throat, lower cheeks and jaw, and upper cheeks and forehead.

- When you release the tension with each muscle group, exhale through your mouth or nose so that you can infused your breath into the relaxation that you are experiencing.
- Remain with your eyes closed until you are ready to open them.
- Assess what is different after going through this exercise. Taking the time to note the benefits of muscle relaxation will increase the likelihood that you will use it in the future.

Like controlled breathing, we recommend that clients download an app or an audio-file to follow when they are doing muscle relaxation. Clients who follow written protocols report that the relaxation experience is interrupted when they must pause repeatedly to identify the next muscle group to be tensed and relaxed. Regardless of the specific modality used for learning and practicing relaxation, with time, the idea is that clients will achieve some muscle memory, and that they will be able to cue their bodies to relax when needed.

Exposure

Although most clients find affective coping skills to be helpful in managing distress, CBT experts regard exposure as the most powerful strategy for treating anxiety (Longmore & Worrell, 2007). *Exposure* is defined as prolonged and systematic contact with a feared stimulus or situation (Abramowitz, Deacon, & Whiteside, 2011). According to Abramowitz and Arch (2014, p. 2), exposure "promotes the cognitive goal of providing data to challenge mistaken beliefs and appraisals. It also promotes the behavioral goal of extinguishing conditioned fear responses to obsessional thoughts, doubts, and images and to external situations and stimuli that trigger obsessions." Figure 8.1 lists common types of exposures that are conducted with various anxiety, traumatic stress, and obsessive compulsive disorders. With perinatal women, the exposure targets manifest in many ways.

In vivo exposure is exposure to "real life" situations and stimuli that are feared and avoided. Clients with obsessive compulsive disorder (OCD), for example, often avoid situations that are the targets of their intrusive thoughts (e.g., contamination, harm coming to others). Clients with panic disorder often avoid situations in which they believe they will have trouble escaping if they were to have a panic attack (e.g., highways, elevators). Clients with posttraumatic stress disorder (PTSD) avoid situations that remind them of a previous trauma (e.g., hospitals). Clients with social anxiety disorder avoid situations in which they expect to be judged or evaluated negatively by others (e.g., mothers' groups).

In vivo exposure for GAD runs a bit differently. These clients do not typically report a feared situation or stimulus that is able to be

Disorder	Exposure Type	Target of Exposure
Generalized Anxiety Disorder (GAD)	In vivo exposure	Uncertainty-inducting situations
	Imaginal exposure	Narratives of worst-case fears with uncertain endings
	Interoceptive exposure	Bodily sensations associated with significant health anxiety
Panic Disorder	In vivo exposure	Feared and avoided situations and stimuli
	Interoceptive exposure	Feared bodily sensations
Social Anxiety Disorder	In vivo exposure	Feared and avoided situations and stimuli
Obsessive Compulsive Disorder (OCD)	In vivo exposure	Feared and avoided situations and stimuli
	Imaginal exposure	Intrusive obsessional thoughts; feared outcomes that cannot be simulated though in vivo exposure
Posttraumatic Stress Disorder (PTSD)	In vivo exposure	Feared and avoided situations and stimuli
	Imaginal exposure	Narrative of the traumatic event

Figure 8.1 Common Types of Exposure.

replicated in an in vivo exposure; instead, they have vague, diffuse anxious apprehension about hypothetical scenarios in the future. However, a key feature in the clinical presentation of GAD is the intolerance of uncertainty. It follows, then, that uncertainty would be targeted during exposure therapy. In vivo exposures can be devised that set up perinatal clients to intentionally place themselves in uncertain situations. According to Dugas and Robichaud (2007), common uncertainty-inducing situations including sending an email of low to moderate importance without spell checking and eating at a restaurant for which one has not read reviews. Although these uncertainty-inducing situations might seem like a far cry from the uncertainty that torments new mothers, engaging in these exposures can build up one's tolerance for uncertainty. This can be presented to clients as developing the "uncertainty tolerance muscle."

Imaginal exposure involves exposure to thoughts and memories using vivid imagery. Although in vivo exposure is typically the most powerful form of exposure, in some cases it is impossible (or inappropriate) to replicate a "real life" exposure to a feared situation or stimulus (e.g., childbirth, sexual assault, worry that a family member will be seriously harmed). Imaginal exposure is not typically used with clients with panic disorder and social anxiety disorder, unless their anxiety is so great that they must use imaginal exposure as a preliminary step before engaging in in vivo exposure (Abramowitz et al., 2011). However, imaginal exposure is pivotal in the treatment of GAD, PTSD, and OCD. Clients with GAD develop detailed, vivid narratives of their hypothetical fears, ensuring to incorporate many uncertainty-inducing elements (Dugas & Robichaud, 2007); clients with PTSD also develop vivid, detailed narratives, but instead target the traumatic experience that is the source of their PTSD (Rothbaum et al., 2007). In both cases, clients read the narrative aloud in session and continue to do so for homework in order to overcome avoidance of hypothetical fears and traumatic memories. Clients with OCD who experience intrusive thoughts intentionally verbalize the thought over and over; clients with OCD who have to do things in a certain way intentionally do things differently (or "wrongly") in order to tolerate the distress of disrupting their ritual (Abramowitz et al., 2011).

Finally, *interoceptive exposure* is the intentional provocation of feared bodily sensations. Many clients with anxiety disorders begin to fear the symptoms of anxiety themselves, which we term "fear of fear" (Chambless & Gracely, 1989). In other words, they find the symptoms of anxiety, especially those that are physiological in nature, so aversive that they go to great lengths to avoid them. Sensations such as racing heart, hyperventilation, restricted airway, and dizziness are targeted in interoceptive exposure using procedures such as running up and down stairs, overbreathing, breathing through a straw while plugging one's nose, and spinning in a chair (Barlow & Craske, 2007). Interoceptive exposure is the cornerstone in the cognitive behavioral treatment of panic disorder, as most panic clients have an aversion to physiological sensations that they experience during a panic attack. However, interoceptive exposure is also useful for generally anxious clients who report significant health anxiety, as well as for socially anxious clients who fear exhibiting noticeable physiological sensations in front of other people.

The most fundamental reason why exposure works is because it helps clients to overcome avoidance. Avoidance serves to maintain anxiety through negative reinforcement, or the removal of an aversive state. Most people experience anxiety as aversive. When they avoid, they experience relief from anxiety, which is reinforcing. When this cycle goes unchecked, it facilitates a habitual behavioral pattern of avoidance that further entrenches a person's anxiety. Although cognitive restructuring and affective coping skills are helpful in managing anxiety, if clients continue to avoid feared stimuli and situations despite the fact that they can reason through them and reduce emotional distress, then additional intervention is indicated.

Historically, exposure was theorized to work through the mechanism of *habituation* (Foa & Kozak, 1986; Foa & McNally, 1996). Habituation refers to the fact that people do not stay in a state of heightened alertness indefinitely; eventually, the body adapts and returns to a resting state. Exposure expert Jonathan Abramowitz and his colleagues have likened the process of habituation to getting used to the cold water in a swimming pool (Abramowitz et al., 2011). When a person first enters the swimming pool, the water feels cold to her. If she stays in the pool long enough, she will no longer feel cold. It is not that the temperature of the water has changed, but rather that the person's body has adapted to the temperature of the water. The same process of adaption happens with exposure. Given time, the level of arousal will decrease as the person has adapted to being in contact with a feared stimulus or situation. On the basis of this model, cognitive behavioral therapists who conduct exposure typically aim for anxious clients' anxiety to decrease across the course of a single exposure trial (called *within-session habituation*), as well as for clients' anxiety to be lowered in subsequent attempts to complete an exposure (called *between-session habituation*).

Recently, Michelle Craske and her colleagues reviewed the state of the literature on the mechanisms of change associated with exposure, evaluated it in light of modern theory on learning and memory, and concluded that within- and between-session habituation is unnecessary for clinically significant improvement at the end of a course of exposure (Craske et al., 2008). Instead of habituation, they proposed that *inhibitory learning* (cf. Bouton, 1993) is a central mechanism of change that can account for exposure's effectiveness. From an inhibitory learning standpoint, clients remain in contact with feared situations and stimuli until their expectations for worst-case outcomes are violated. That is, when a person has prolonged contact with a feared stimulus or situation, she learns that the dreaded outcomes that she expects to occur do not happen. She learns that being the presence of a feared stimulus or situation is not as bad as she would have expected. She learns that she can indeed cope effectively and tolerate her anxiety. The original learned pathway between the feared situation or stimulus and anxiety or fear still exists, but a new pathway is formed that is shaped by the learning that occurs during exposure trials. Thus, the goal of the inhibitory learning approach in the treatment of anxiety disorders "is to maximize the likelihood that non-threat associations inhibit access and retrieval of threat associations" (Arch & Craske, 2011, p. 310). Moreover, rather than aiming to experience a significant reduction in anxiety, exposure therapists now regard the main purpose of exposure as being an opportunity for clients to learn to tolerate the distress that accompanies exposure (Abramowitz & Arch, 2014; Craske et al., 2008). Indeed, evidence suggests that efforts to avoid, suppress, control, or escape aversive emotions is associated with an increased severity of fear during an encounter with a feared situation or stimulus (e.g., Karekla, Forsyth, & Kelly, 2004).

Exposure is a different behavioral treatment for anxiety than the affective coping skills. Whereas clients use affective coping skills to *decrease* their anxiety, clients who undertake exposure can expect to experience a temporary *increase* in anxiety due to the prolonged contact with feared stimuli and situations before experiencing some benefit. Even across the course of several exposure trials, clients may continue to experience high levels of anxiety. This often makes therapists hesitant to deliver exposure to their anxious clients, and nowhere is this more evident than with therapists who work with perinatal women, who often feel called to nurture and take care of perinatal women who are hurting and scared.

Here we encourage readers to remember that CBT is a collaborative endeavor, meaning that both the therapist and the client must contribute to and be in agreement about the treatment plan. Cognitive behavioral therapists do not force their clients to engage in any activities for which they believe they are not ready. Many perinatal women are in acute distress when they present for treatment, and they benefit first from the establishment of a trusting therapeutic relationship, psychoeducation to normalize their experiences, (perhaps) referral for a medication consultation, and practice of cognitive and behavioral strategies that will give them some immediate relief from their emotional distress so that they can attend to the basic needs of their child or children. As the acute distress subsides, they and their therapists can more clearly conceptualize the aspects of their clinical presentation, such as avoidance, that are persisting and that are in need of a systematic and strategic intervention. It is at that point that they are in a place where they can begin to implement exposure. They can then embrace the adage stated by Abramowitz et al. (2011): "Invest anxiety now for a calmer future."

Implementing Exposure

Functional Assessment

The first step in implementing exposure is usually to conduct a *functional assessment*, which Abramowitz et al. (2011, p. 51) defined as "the gathering of patient-specific information about the factors that control anxiety or fear." In other words, therapists use functional assessment to identify the *antecedents*, or triggers of anxiety, as well as the *consequences* of anxiety, which are often avoidance and escape. The information from the functional assessment points to the specific targets that therapists and clients work toward in exposure therapy.

One way to collect the information needed for a functional assessment is through a *self-monitoring form*, such as that displayed in Figure 8.2. In this sample self-monitoring form, clients are asked to record instances in which they notice a spike in their anxiety (i.e., the trigger, or the antecedent), their maximum level of fear, feared consequences of contact with the trigger (which can be targeted using cognitive restructuring), avoidance

Trigger	Maximum Fear (0 = low; 10 = high)	Feared Consequences of Having Contact with Trigger	Avoidance and Ritualistic Behaviors to Prevent Anxiety	Beliefs about the Effects of Avoidance and Ritualistic Behaviors

Figure 8.2 Self-Monitoring Form.

141

and ritualistic behaviors to reduce anxiety, and beliefs about the effects of ritualistic and avoidance behaviors (cf. Abramowitz & Arch, 2014). At times, mental health professionals add additional columns to the self-monitoring form, such as physiological reactions and adaptive coping strategies that they used to managed the distress associated with the trigger. Typically, clients will complete a self-monitoring form in between the initial evaluation with the therapist and their next visit, with the idea that they will return to their second visit with several days' worth of "data" that can be used for treatment planning.

Perinatal women have the potential to experience the same sorts of problems with completing the self-monitoring form as they encounter when they complete an activity monitoring form, described in Chapter 7. They are tired, overwhelmed, and consumed with caring for a newborn. They have difficulty finding time to take a shower, let alone completing a form that requires focused attention several times a day. In instances in which perinatal women have difficulty completing a self-monitoring form in between sessions, the therapist can reserve time for specific questioning of recent instances in which the client was triggered and the associated emotional, cognitive, and avoidance or ritualistic behavioral responses. Assessment can continue in a formal or informal manner after the client has begun to implement exposure.

Fear Hierarchy

A *fear hierarchy* is an ordered sequence of feared stimuli and situations with which the client plans to have prolonged contact in order to overcome avoidance. The information from the self-monitoring exercise (or from the targeted questioning that the therapist does in the event that the client does not complete a self-monitoring form) is used to begin to develop the hierarchy. In session, clients work with their therapist to generate a comprehensive pool of feared stimuli and situations. As the process unfolds, clients begin to think of additional items for their hierarchy that were not included on their self-monitoring forms or identified in guided questioning. When a sufficient pool has been generated (i.e., around 10 items, although there could be more), clients assign a Subjective Units of Discomfort (SUDs) rating to each item (0 = little or no anxiety; 10 = the most anxiety one could experience). They then order the list according to the SUDs ratings, with the lowest-rated item on top, and the highest-rated item at the end of the list.

It is important to be as specific as is possible when listing the items on the hierarchy. The goal is for clients to be able to conduct the exposure on their own outside of sessions, so they need to know exactly what to do and how to do it. An item that is vague (e.g., "call a friend and ask her out to lunch") for a socially anxious client will likely leave her with too many decisions to be able to execute the exposure in any one moment—who, exactly, would she call? Where, exactly, would she suggest that they go for lunch? In addition, in many instances, the SUDs rating assigned is tied to the nature of the details. For example, calling a best friend from childhood to go to lunch at a diner would likely be associated with a lower SUDs rating than calling an acquaintance who the client finds intimidating to have lunch at a five-star restaurant.

Because these details so intricately affect SUDs ratings, it is often the case that, as the course of exposure proceeds, clients identify different variations of the same general type of exposure that would associated with different SUDs ratings. In these cases, additional items are added to the hierarchy. It is even conceivable that clients change their minds about the previous SUDs ratings that they have assigned once they begin exposure and identify additional manifestations of the exposures written on their hierarchy. For this reason, it is helpful to list the hierarchy items in Microsoft Word or Excel table format, rather than recording them longhand on a sheet of paper, in order to keep the hierarchy as organized and readable as is possible.

In many instances, clients have difficulty assigning SUDs ratings and comment that their ratings seem arbitrary, almost as if they are choosing a number out of the air. Thus, it is the responsibility of the therapist to spend time defining each of the 10 SUDs anchors so that clients have a clear idea of the types of experiences that would warrant each rating. For example, a rating of 10 might be reserved only for instances in which clients had a full-blown panic attack. Clients can then consult their anchors as a guide in rating the items on their hierarchy, as well as reporting the levels of anxiety that they experience during exposures. This exercise is especially helpful for perinatal women, who often report being foggy-headed and unable to attend to precise details.

Conducting Exposure Trials

After clients have developed their hierarchies, they are in a position to begin their exposures. Traditionally, exposure interventions proceeded by encouraging clients to engage in exposures sequentially, as they are listed in the hierarchy. The idea behind this procedure is that once clients have mastered contact with a lower-rated feared situation or stimulus, then they are ready to face a higher-rated feared situation or stimulus. However, as is described later in this section, this exposure need not always proceed in this manner, and there is some evidence that exposure to hierarchy items at random locations in the order maximizes outcome.

It is optimal to use in-session time to complete an exposure and then encourage the client to do the same type of exposure for homework in between sessions (Wenzel, 2013). Implementing this model, however, might require forethought and creativity. Session time will be devoted to a few activities in addition to the exposure exercise, including addressing any issues that the client believes is important to put on the agenda, the review of her previous homework, debriefing after the exposure, and development of new homework. There needs to be sufficient time for the client to fully immerse herself in the exposure. Thus, many cognitive behavioral therapists reserve longer session times (e.g., 90 minutes or 2 hours) when they have planned to do exposure with a client, as well as scheduling more than one session per week (see Abramowitz, Foa, & Franklin, 2003, for an example). Such intensive scheduling may or may not work with the demanding schedule of a new mother.

Figure 8.3 displays a recording form for clients to write down the exposures that they have practiced, as well as their peak and ending SUDs ratings. On the one hand, perinatal clients will likely encounter the same obstacles that they encounter with the completion of any of the forms described in this book, such that the demands on their time will make

Date	Exposure Description	Practice #	Peak/Ending SUDs (0–10)
			/
			/
			/
			/
			/
			/
			/
			/
			/
			/
			/
			/

Figure 8.3 Exposure Recording Form.

it difficult for them to give systematic attention to implementing and recording their work. On the other hand, this is one recording form for which we believe quite strongly that it is important to devise a creative way to make this recording work in light of the multiple demands that perinatal women face. It is important to know: (a) how much and what types of exposure clients are doing outside of session, as that information will guide the development of new homework in the subsequent session; and (b) the degree to which exposure practice is associated with a reduction in anxiety. It is true that research conducted by cognitive psychologists who study learning and memory suggests that performance during one learning trial (in this case, reduction in anxiety) is a poor predictor of ultimate outcome (Bjork & Bjork, 2006). Nevertheless, from a clinical perspective, decreasing levels of anxiety can build a sense of self-efficacy that, while also unrelated to ultimate outcome (Bjork, 2004), nevertheless can serve as motivation to comply with the schedule of exposures and remain in treatment.

Perhaps the more frequent question asked by cognitive behavioral therapists is how long the exposure must last in order to achieve therapeutic gains. Those who practice exposure from the traditional habituation model recommend that the client remains in contact with the feared situation or stimulus until her anxiety decreases by at least half and is associated with no more than mild anxiety (Abramowitz et al., 2011). Therapists know when this occurs by obtaining SUDs ratings at periodic intervals throughout the exposure trial. However, authors of recent research that tests various aspects of the inhibitory learning model have indicated that the client must remain in contact with the feared stimulus or situation until her expectations for the occurrence of a catastrophic outcome are violated. According to Michelle Craske and her colleagues, "extinction is posited to follow from a mismatch between the expectancy of an aversive event and the absence of its occurrence" (Craske et al., 2008, p. 13; see also Arch & Craske, 2011). This means that durations of exposures that surpass the time in which aversive events are expected to occur would provide potent mismatches to form the basis of new learning. Thus, lengthier exposures provide more opportunity for clients to learn that aversive outcomes will not occur. Arch and Craske (2011) suggested that therapists can track clients' expectancies throughout the exposure to provide evidence that the expected aversive outcomes do not occur, rather than tracking SUDs ratings.

In addition to considering the preferred length of time that clients remain in contact with a feared situation or stimulus, cognitive behavioral therapists also consider the frequency with which clients participate in exposure. When clients first begin to participate in exposure, it is recommended that they do some exposure every day. As stated previously, it can be helpful to have two or three exposure sessions a week in order to give the client massed practice and achieve meaningful reductions in anxiety. However, cognitive psychologists who study learning have also found that spacing out learning trials allows for the consolidation of learning. On the basis of this research, exposure experts recommend an "expanding spaced" schedule of exposures in order to capitalize on the benefits of both massed practice as well as spaced practice (Abramowitz & Arch, 2014; Abramowitz et al., 2011; Arch & Craske, 2011; Craske et al., 2008). This means that exposure sessions are held more frequently early in the course of exposure (e.g., two or three times a week), and then they can be spread out later in the course of exposure (e.g., biweekly, monthly).

In addition to the guidelines described to this point, recent theoretical and empirical work based on the inhibitory learning model points to several other tips for maximizing the effectiveness of exposure. They are as follows:

- Exposure to multiple stimuli or situations simultaneously has the potential to result in greater learning than exposure to a single stimulus or situation (Craske et al., 2008). For example, a client can engage in imaginal exposure to an intrusive thought of contamination while simultaneously having in vivo contact with a place that is typically avoided for fear of contamination, such as a public restroom. A client can engage in interoceptive exposure to a feared bodily sensation while simultaneously remaining in a situation for which escape would be difficult if she were to have a panic attack.
- Therapists should include variability in exposures. One way to introduce variability is to choose random items on the hierarchy to subject to exposure, rather than proceeding through the hierarchy systematically from the lowest-rated items to the highest-rated items (Lang & Craske, 2000). In addition, exposures should also be practiced in a variety of environments and circumstances in order to increase the durability of learning by establishing many cues that were present during the learning, thereby increasing generalization (Arch & Craske, 2011). For example, clients who practice imaginal exposure can do so in different rooms of the house.
- Therapists should be alert for "safety signals" that diminish the potency of the exposure. When clients engage in exposure in the presence of a safety signal, the absence of an aversive outcome is attributed to the safety signal. This scenario creates an untestable hypothesis, such that clients do not have the opportunity for clients to learn on their own that the aversive outcome will not occur. Examples of safety signals include the presence of another person and the easy availability of medication. It is the responsibility of therapists to be alert for the possibility that some CBT strategies might be functioning as safety signals during exposure. For example, psychoeducation

about the low likelihood of aversive outcomes occurring could serve as reassurance, reducing the amount of anxiety that the client experiences during the exposure and depriving the client of learning on her own that a feared outcome might occur (Arch & Craske, 2011). Even the application of standard affective coping tools, such as breathing and relaxation, might distract clients from fully experiencing anxiety during exposure and give them the message that they otherwise would be unable to tolerate the increase in anxiety that accompanies exposure (Abramowitz et al., 2011; Arch & Craske, 2011; Craske et al., 2008). Here, therapists are mindful that the goal of exposure is for clients to learn that they can tolerate anxiety, not that they are guaranteed to experience a reduction in anxiety.

- In a similar vein, cognitive behavioral therapists are also alert for ritualistic behavior in which clients engage in order to neutralize anxiety. Ritualistic behavior serves the same purpose as do safety signals—it neutralizes the anxiety (Rachman & Hodgson, 1980) by reducing the client's perceived uncertainty regarding the occurrence of an aversive outcome, as well as by preventing the natural lessening of anxiety that would eventually occur when enough time passes (Abramowitz & Arch, 2014). In addition, rituals can increase the frequency of intrusive thoughts because they serve as cues that are associated with the thought (Abramowitz & Arch, 2014). Although the disorder that most frequently comes to mind when one mentions ritualistic behavior is OCD (e.g., hand washing, checking), it is now accepted that clients with a wide range of anxiety, obsessive compulsive, and traumatic stress disorders engage in ritualistic behavior (e.g., Schut, Castonguay, & Borkovec, 2001). It is also important to recognize that, in many instances, ritualistic behavior is not easily observed; it can come in the form of a mental ritual like counting, reassurance seeking of others, and Internet searching. Thus, *response prevention* is often paired with exposure, which means that anxious clients refrain from engaging in ritualistic behavior when they experience a surge of anxiety.
- Cognitive restructuring is often used in conjunction with exposure (Abramowitz et al., 2011). However, on the basis of the recent theoretical and empirical work on inhibitory learning, it is important to use it in a way that facilitates long-term learning, rather than promoting short-term anxiety reduction. Cognitive restructuring that is solely focused on the low likelihood of aversive outcomes occurring from the exposure can provide reassurance, reducing a client's anxiety during an exposure trial. However, there may be long-term detriments to this approach, as clients do not learn to tolerate their anxiety and accept uncertain outcomes. Thus, Abramowitz and Arch (2014) recommended that cognitive restructuring target false beliefs that clients hold about their inability to tolerate distress and uncertainty.

Special Considerations with Perinatal Women

Exposure has rarely been tested with perinatal women, as they are excluded from RCTs examining exposure's efficacy. According to Arch, Dimidjian, and Chessick (2012), this exclusion has its basis in untested assumptions that exposure is dangerous because it increases clients' stress and anxiety, which some believe could, in turn, harm the fetus. However, Arch et al. (2012) have brought to the forefront an additional consideration—that the risk of a chronic, untreated anxiety disorder far outweighs the risk that exposure confers, particularly in light of research demonstrating that many people who undergo exposure report no more than moderate levels of anxiety (Grayson, Foa, & Steketee, 1982). In addition, results from other studies show that pregnant women have lowered responses to stress on measures such as heart rate, blood pressure, and cortisol, relative to people who are not pregnant (Kammerer, Adams, Castelberg, & Glover, 2002; Matthews & Rodin, 1992). Thus, when conducting exposure with a pregnant client, it is important to test one's own assumptions about the procedure before uniformly rejecting it. As mentioned in Chapter 3, Lilliecreutz et al. (2010) indeed implemented exposure with pregnant women who had a specific phobia of injections. There were no adverse effects, and no participants dropped out of the study, demonstrating exposure's safety and tolerability.

In their important article on exposure therapy in perinatal women, Arch et al. (2012) made specific recommendations for the conduct of exposure with this population. First, despite the fact that Lilliecreutz et al. (2010) found exposure to be safe in pregnant women, at times, the provocation of anxiety will be particularly uncomfortable in pregnant women who are already experiencing similar symptoms (e.g., nausea, increased heart rate after the first trimester). Arch et al. (2012) recommended a "gentler, graduated exposure model" in these cases. Second, they recommended that cognitive behavioral therapists measure and regard heart rate as a proxy for physiological reactivity, as it is easy and inexpensive to monitor, and use exercise guidelines for pregnancy to determine safe levels of reactivity. Such guidelines consider the woman's average resting heart rate, age, body mass index, and fitness level in order to calculate her maximum heart rate in bpms. If the women's heart rate exceeds the maximum, then a sitting rest procedure can be implemented, such that she remains sitting until her heart rate returns well below the maximum and then reenters the exposure, which is not problematic unless the person does not return to the exposure.

The type of exposure that often evokes the greatest amount of hesitation among cognitive behavioral therapists who work with perinatal women is interoceptive exposure. Although there is no evidence that interoceptive exposure during pregnancy has harmed a woman or her fetus, L. S. Cohen, Rosenbaum, and Heller (1989) described the case of a woman who had a panic attack near the end of her pregnancy that was followed by vaginal bleeding and placental abruption, prompting a cesarean section. The authors speculated that increased blood pressure and sympathetic arousal associated with her anxiety symptoms were responsible for the placental abruption. There is no causal evidence that supports this speculation, but it suggests that panic-like symptoms experienced in late pregnancy should be monitored carefully.

We recommend that cognitive behavioral therapists consult with clients' obstetricians before conducting interoceptive exposure with pregnant women. Not only will this allow the therapist to have medical clearance for conducting the exercises, it also will alert him or her to any other medical conditions of note that could affect the course of treatment. In addition, it will promote a spirit of collaboration among the client's team of care providers. Cognitive behavioral therapists who receive medical clearance to implement interoceptive exposure with their pregnant clients can follow the guidelines described by Arch et al. (2012) to ensure that they are reasonable. As stated previously, spinning in one place is an interoceptive exposure exercise that is commonly used to simulate dizziness. Arch et al. recommended that pregnant women spin while sitting in a swivel chair, rather than standing upright, in order to avoid falling. As stated previously, heart rate can be monitored, and exposures can be stopped if the heart rate exceeds the maximum level for safety.

Case Demonstration

This section describes how exposure was conducted with Donna, whose longstanding OCD manifested when she presented for treatment as intrusive thoughts about having postpartum psychosis. When she first presented for treatment, she agreed to complete a self-monitoring form in order to understand the triggers of her intrusive thoughts, the amount of fear she experienced when she had an intrusive thought, and the behaviors in which she engaged in response to the intrusive thoughts. Figure 8.4 displays an excerpt from Donna's self-monitoring form. Upon review of the things that Donna recorded on this form, she and her therapist concluded that uncomfortable and foreign bodily sensations triggered fears that she was experiencing postpartum psychosis or otherwise going crazy. When she experienced these fears, she engaged in behaviors to try to suppress the thought (e.g., distraction) or to obtain reassurance and support from others (e.g., asking her mother to come over, asking her husband to leave work early). On occasion, she was triggered by an external, rather than internal stressor, such as her 6-week follow-up visit with her obstetrician. Because she had had a negative experience with her obstetrician during delivery, she expected to experience increased anxiety

Trigger	Maximum Fear (0 = low; 10 = high)	Feared Consequences of Having Contact with Trigger	Avoidance and Ritualistic Behaviors to Prevent Anxiety	Beliefs about the Effects of Avoidance and Ritualistic Behaviors
Feeling of unreality	9	I have postpartum psychosis.	Distract with feeding the baby	If I don't find something to occupy my mind, I will go crazy.
Overwhelmed, tired	7	Something is really wrong with me.	Called Mom and asked her to come over	My mom will be here is a back-up in case I really lose it.
Looking at Ellie and not believing she is my daughter	8	I have postpartum psychosis.	Tried to get rid of the thought	If I keep thinking this, then it will be true.
Dizziness	9	My postpartum psychosis is spreading into other symptoms.	Asked my husband to come home from work	If I'm not alone, then I won't be alone with these thoughts, and they won't spiral out of control.
Getting ready for my 6-week follow-up visit with my obstetrician	9	I wont be able to take it; I'll break down.	Cancelled appointment	This prevented me from having a full-blown psychotic episode.

Figure 8.4 Sample Self-Monitoring Form.

in her presence, as well as a lack of understanding of her postpartum experience. Thus, she responded with avoidance behavior by cancelling the appointment.

On the basis of these data, Donna's therapist reasoned that three types of exposure would be appropriate. First, imaginal exposure could be used to fully experience distress associated with the idea that Donna might be suffering from postpartum psychosis. We say "might," rather than "is," in order to maximize the degree of uncertainty associated with the exposure exercise. Second, interoceptive exposure could be used to have contact with some of the physiological sensations that prompted concerns that she was suffering from postpartum psychosis. Third, in vivo exposure could be used to have contact with stimuli and situations that she was avoiding (e.g., obstetrician, driving by the hospital where she delivered). Donna's therapist worked with her to develop the full pool of targets for the exposure. Donna assigned SUDs ratings to each of them, and they were assembled into a fear hierarchy (see Figure 8.5). For homework, Donna agreed to type her hierarchy items and their corresponding SUDs ratings into a notes application on her smartphone so that she could consult them as a guide when she engaged in exposure in between sessions.

At the time of the next session, Donna agreed to repeat several times out loud "I might have postpartum psychosis." Prior to engaging in the exposure, her therapist asked her what she expected would happen if she were to engage in this activity. Donna indicated that she believed that

Target	SUDs
Saying out loud, "I might have postpartum psychosis"	3
Calling obstetrician	3.5
Spinning in swivel chair	4.5
Seeing obstetrician in person (in office away from hospital)	5
Driving by hospital	5
Walking in hospital	7
Staring at spot on wall	7.5
Staring at eyes in mirror	8.5
Imagining having a psychotic episode at home	9
Imagining being in the psych ward at the hospital	10

Figure 8.5 Sample Fear Hierarchy.

she would have a postpartum psychotic episode by repeating this statement, and when her therapist asked her to give a rating of how much she believed it, she gave a rating of 5 on a 10-point Likert scale (0 = do not believe feared outcome will occur; 10 = believe 100% that feared outcome will occur). In addition, her therapist asked her to define what a postpartum psychotic episode would look like so that they could determine whether she was having one during or after the exposure. Donna indicated that she would know she is having a postpartum psychotic episode if she cried hysterically, pounded her fists on the wall or ground, began to have hallucinations, and was unable to be brought back down.

Donna's therapist then encouraged her to begin repeating the phrase, "I might have postpartum psychosis." After every fifth time that Donna repeated the phrase, her therapist assessed the belief that she was having a psychotic episode on the 10-point Likert-type scale. After repeating the phrase 15 times, Donna gave a rating of "0," indicating that she no longer believed that just stating this phrase would make her have a psychotic break. The following dialogue demonstrates the debriefing that occurred after the exposure.

Therapist:	Tell me what you learned from this exercise.
Donna:	[sighs] I guess that just saying it out loud does not mean that it's going to happen. That it won't make me psychotic.
Therapist:	How uncomfortable were you during this exercise? With 0 being no discomfort, and 10 being the most discomfort that you could imagine?
Donna:	Oh, very uncomfortable. I was an 8 or 9 the whole way through. [shudders] I just hate that I feel like this.
Therapist:	But you tolerated it. You were able to get through it.
Donna:	Yeah. I guess I did.
Therapist:	That's a big step for you, Donna. I know it took a lot for you to do this.
Donna:	Thanks. I can't believe I did it. It feels good.
Therapist:	What does this tell you about the next time you start to feel very uncomfortable and wonder if you are psychotic?
Donna:	I think that I can ride it through.
Therapist:	Yes, what you're saying is consistent with my experience. No one can absolutely guarantee an outcome like becoming psychotic. But you taught yourself a valuable lesson—that you can get through the uncertainty and discomfort, even if it doesn't feel good.
Donna:	[eyes brighten] I guess this is the same idea as our work together those times when I thought I might have run someone over with a car. That it probably didn't happen, but that I might not know for sure. And that I have to learn to live with that.

152

Therapist: Exactly. What do you think of this for homework—each day in between sessions, would you be willing to repeat out loud "I might have postpartum psychosis."

Donna: Just like in here? Sure.

Therapist: And just like I asked you to do in here, every five times you repeat it, rate the degree to which you believe that you'll actually have a psychotic episode. Continue with the exposure until your rating is "0."

Donna: OK, I can do that.

Therapist: Would you be willing to record your work on this exposure recording form?

Donna: Can I record in my phone instead?

Therapist: Sure, whatever will work best for you.

As the dialogue progressed, Donna's therapist continued to work with her to plan the specifics of her exposures in between sessions. In order to increase generalizability, her therapist encouraged her to repeat "I might have postpartum psychosis" in every room in her house, as well as places outside of her home (e.g., in the yard, in the park, while on a walk). She also encouraged Donna to vary other variables, such as the time of day at which the exposure was conducted and whether there was anyone else in the house. Finally, Donna's therapist asked her to estimate the likelihood that she would follow through with daily exposures. Donna estimated that there was a 100% likelihood that she would follow through, as she valued the learning experience that she had in session.

A few points about the dialogue deserve note. First, Donna's therapist asked questions that allowed Donna to consolidate her learning. She asked questions like "Tell me what you learned from this exercise" so that Donna could put her own words on to the psychological principles that accounted for her experience in the exposure exercise. Doing this allowed Donna to take ownership over her success, which has the potential to increase the likelihood that she follows through with exposure in between sessions. Second, the therapist framed Donna's success from the perspective of her ability to tolerate discomfort and uncertainty, rather than on the degree to which her discomfort decreased in keeping with the inhibitory learning approach. Third, her therapist took care to acknowledge Donna's efforts, which enhanced the therapeutic relationship by demonstrating her support of Donna and recognition that exposure of this nature is difficult for her. Finally, Donna's therapist tried not to simply "assign" more exposure for homework. Instead, she was collaborative, asking Donna what she thought of similar exposures for homework and asking her if she would be willing to record her progress on a recording form. Notice that her therapist was highly responsive when Donna suggested an alternate format for recording her exposure.

Donna continued to participate in exposure for an additional ten sessions. Rather than going through the items on the hierarchy systematically, from the lowest rated SUDs items to the highest rated SUDs items, Donna agreed to participate in exposure to each item on the hierarchy on a random basis. For all of the imaginal and interoceptive exposures, she first completed them with her therapist in the therapist's office, and then she practiced them outside of session for homework, taking care to vary the environments in which she practiced them in order to achieve generalizability. In contrast, she practiced the in vivo exposures (i.e., calling her obstetrician, seeing her obstetrician in her office, driving by the hospital, walking in the hospital) on her own. However, in each of these instances, Donna conducted imaginal rehearsal, such that she walked herself through the manner in which she would do each of these exposures on her own. Because two of the in vivo exposures were ones that did not lend themselves to multiple repetitions (i.e., calling her obstetrician, seeing the obstetrician in her office), Donna was sure to engage in other exposures during the time in between sessions to maintain her momentum. After ten sessions, she decreased the frequency of her visits to biweekly appointments for the next four sessions, and then monthly appointments for an additional two sessions.

The strength of the new learning that she acquired was demonstrated when Donna was faced with two OCD-related challenges during the time in which she had tapered down her sessions. First, she had begun to have intrusive thoughts about causing harm to her baby, such as drowning her baby in the bathtub and dropping her baby down the stairs. However, she recognized them as intrusive thoughts, rather than as guarantees that she would act on them, and without the help of her therapist, she began to engage in imaginal and in vivo exposure to tolerate the discomfort associated with these thoughts. Second, she experienced hypnagogic hallucinations when she woke up one night when she was in a hotel during a beach weekend getaway with her husband and baby. Her first reaction was that she was finally having hallucinations associated with postpartum psychosis. However, because she practiced imaginal and interoceptive exposure to thoughts of and sensations associated with postpartum psychosis in a variety of settings, she was able to tolerate the discomfort of this experience and remain present with it until she realized that she was not having a full-blown psychotic episode.

Conclusion

Behavioral strategies to target anxiety in CBT fall into two domains. The aim of affective copings skills, like controlled breathing and muscle relaxation, is to reduce acute symptoms of anxiety and agitation so that the client is more centered, grounded, and able to think clearly to address her life problems. The rationale that underlies the implementation of these tools is that they promote a sense of controllability over physiological manifestations of anxiety, as well as an overall sense of relaxation. They often give clients the confidence that they are able to manage their distress in any one moment, especially when their distress feels overwhelming or all-encompassing. However, it should be recognized that these are short-term strategies that clients use in order to survive moments of acute emotional distress, and that their long-term application might prolong anxiety because it deprives clients of learning the powerful lesson that they can indeed tolerate distress.

Exposure is prolonged contact with feared stimuli and situations. It is not a tool that is implemented in any one moment in order to feel better; many clients report a temporary increase in anxiety because they are facing a fear that makes them quite uncomfortable. Thus, exposure is not a behavioral coping strategy, but a systematic program for achieving new learning that the aversive outcomes expected when one has contact with a feared stimulus or situation are unlikely to occur, and more importantly, can be tolerated.

Some therapists are hesitant to implement exposure because of their own discomfort with it. They often have beliefs that they will damage the therapeutic relationship, or drive their client away, or even harm their client. Fortunately, scholarly work published by leading exposure experts indicates that this is not true (Foa, Zoellner, Feeny, Hembree, & Alvarez-Conrad, 2002; Olatunji, Deacon, & Abramowitz, 2009). It is true that contact with the most highly rated feared situations or stimuli facilitate an increase in anxiety, but it is hardly re-traumatization. The effects are transient, relatively small, and not associated with ultimate outcome in treatment (Arch et al., 2012). Thus, it is important for therapists who implement any cognitive behavioral strategy, and especially exposure, to carefully examine their own automatic thoughts and determine whether any of their automatic thoughts have the potential to dilute the commitment with which they implement the intervention. If such automatic thoughts are detected, therapists can consult the literature for factual information on the delivery of exposure and use the cognitive restructuring tools described in Chapter 5 to ensure that they are approaching their treatment plan as accurately and as helpfully as is possible.

9

PROBLEM SOLVING TRAINING

Problems are inevitable in life, and they are especially common in times of transition, such as the transition to parenthood. Perinatal women often describe a host of problems that they are facing, such how to decide what arrangements to make for their baby when they go back to work, how to deal with a mother-in-law who parents very differently than they do, and what to do with a baby that is not latching properly. They are often overwhelmed and do not know where to begin. They are desperate to find the "right" solutions to their problems because they are fearful that they are not a "good mother."

Cognitive behavioral therapists do not solve their clients' problems for them. Doing so would be inconsistent with many fundamental tenets of CBT, such as its collaborative nature and its reliance on guided discovery to give clients the space to grapple with their problems and draw their own conclusions. Instead, cognitive behavioral therapists help their clients to acquire problem solving skills, commit to a solution to one or more problems to enact in between sessions, and restructure any negative thoughts about problems or their own problem solving skills that have the potential to interfere with the execution of problem solving. In this way, clients can leave the session with a solution to a problem over which they can take ownership, a plan for implementing that solution, and hints for generalizing their newly acquired skills to address other current problems, as well as problems that might arise in the future.

Over the past four decades, much empirical research has been devoted to understand how people solve problems, how problem solving contributes to and exacerbates psychopathology, and how best to help clients acquire skill in problem solving. Much of this research was translated into a specific CBT that is focused on problem solving (D'Zurilla & Nezu, 2007). In this chapter, we describe D'Zurilla and Nezu's (2007) four steps to problem solving. In addition, we discuss obstacles that can interfere with the effective execution of problem solving and ways to overcome those obstacles.

Acquisition of Problem Solving Skills

According to Bell and D'Zurilla (2009, p. 349), "a rational problem-solving style involves the deliberate and systematic application of four major problem-solving skills: (1) problem definition and formulation; (2) generation of alternative solutions; (3) decision making; and (4) solution implementation and verification." Each of these skills is described in this section, with discussion of the manner in which they aid in the cognitive behavioral treatment of perinatal distress.

Problem Definition and Formulation

Many clients, especially perinatal women, present for treatment with a host of problems that leaves them feeling overwhelmed and unable to determine where to begin. Simply defining the scope of each problem can be a tremendous asset in helping the therapist and client know exactly what needs to be addressed. Although seeing a full problem list has the potential to be discouraging for clients when they see the number of problems they are facing, doing so will ultimately transform the problems from being vague and abstract to being concrete, tangible, and ripe for action.

When multiple problems are identified, cognitive behavioral therapists work with their clients to prioritize them, with the idea that the highest priority problem will be addressed before lower priority problems (Wenzel, 2013). At times it can be difficult to know which problems to prioritize first. It is logical to start with the most important problems. However, in many instances, the most important problems are ones that are complex and require much time and effort to address. As a result, it could be several sessions before the problem is solved, meaning that it could be several sessions before the client notices a meaningful change in her mood state. Instead, at times therapists and clients collaboratively decide to prioritize a smaller problem that is addressed more easily, with the idea that the skills acquired in addressing this problem can then be honed and generalized to address the larger problem. In still other instances, one particular problem takes precedence either because it must be solved within a specific time frame or because it must be solved before another problem can be addressed. If any problems are life-threatening, then those problems are considered the highest priority and are addressed before the other problems on the problem list (Wenzel, Brown, & Beck, 2009).

Consider this dialogue with Tara and her therapist, which took place early in the course of her treatment (i.e., third session) when Tara was reporting difficulties adjusting to being a stay-at-home mother.

157

Tara: I think I'm starting to feel better. I really do, between what we're doing in here, and the meds. But it just still seems like this isn't my life. Like I'm in somebody else's shoes. It's all very surreal to me.

Therapist: Is this sense of your life being surreal upsetting to you?

Tara: Yes, kind of. I just don't know what to do with myself. I go through the motions of taking care of Thomas. I know I love him. But there are so many things that I need to figure out and that I'm just putting off.

Therapist: I wonder if it would be helpful to very specifically identify the things that you need to figure out, that you've been putting off, so that we can choose one and see if we can make some headway?

Tara: OK. Right now, they're all like mush in my head.

Therapist: Do you mind if I write these down? [Tara nods her head] I find that when we write down the full pool of problems that need to be addressed, it ensures that we keep them straight and don't forget anything as we decide where to direct our focus.

Tara: That makes sense. I can't even keep two things in my mind at once right now.

Therapist: That's perfectly understandable. So tell me one thing that you believe you need to figure out.

Tara: Well, I have to get out of the house more. Thomas and I have been cooped up for over two months now. We're going stir crazy.

Therapist: [writes "getting out of the house"]

Tara: And I also think that Alex and I need to get wills done. I'm so worried that something will happen to one of us, and that the one who's still around won't have enough to live.

Therapist: [writes "wills" and also makes a mental note that this concern could represent another manifestation of Tara's anxiety, which could be a treatment target in subsequent sessions.] OK, so far we have getting out of the house and wills. What else has been on your mind that you think you need to address?

Tara: Ugh, the holidays are coming up. I've been dreading talking to my mom and Alex's mom about this. Both mothers want us to spend all of our time with them, which is impossible. There are going to be hurt feelings either way . . . And then there are big things. As soon as we find out which location my husband will be assigned to, we'll have to get ready to put our house on the market, find a new house, arrange for movers, and probably a whole bunch of things I can't think of. It will all have to happen so quickly. How awful would it be to have to move to a new location and not have a place to live? We'll have to live in a hotel! [beginning to escalate]

Therapist: [gently leans in] When you know which location your husband will be assigned to, we can certainly come up with a plan for dealing with the move. But since you won't find out that information for a few weeks yet, I wonder if we can focus on one of the problems on which we *can* start making some headway?

Tara: You're right, I think that's a good plan. See where my mind goes? Always the worst-case scenario. I know, really, that we won't have to live in a hotel. In reality, my husband's post-doc ends three months before his job starts, so we'll have some breathing space.

Therapist: Exactly. And what we're focusing on here are actual problems that you can take some steps to address right now. What do you think would be the benefit of solving one of these actual problems?

Tara: It will make me feel so much better. Like I have more control over my life.

Therapist: Let's go about prioritizing the problems for which you *can* do something about right now. Which one do you think is the most important?

[Tara and her therapist proceeded to prioritize her problems, considering the importance of the problems, the problems that were most easily addressed, and the problems that would make the greatest immediate impact.]

Therapist: On the basis of this discussion, which one do you think we should tackle first?

Donna: Well, the wills are a big deal, but it's not like I can address those immediately. And I can't even really make a decision about what to do about them. I need to talk to Alex. So either getting out of the house, or figuring out how to handle the holidays. [pauses] Actually, I'd like to work on getting out of the house first because that's something that I can do soon, maybe even today.

Therapist: That sounds reasonable. Perhaps today, we can work on solving the problem of getting out of the house more, and next time, we can keep the momentum going by addressing the grandma time during the holidays?

Tara: That sounds perfect.

Generation of Alternative Solutions

Once the therapist and client have agreed on the problem to be addressed, the client is encouraged to identify potential solutions to the problem. This process is called *brainstorming*, and the key to brainstorming is that clients generate a wide range of solutions without attaching judgment or preconceived notions. Too often, clients begin to identify solutions but easily dismiss them, saying "yeah but this would be too expensive," or "yeah but I could never do this." The instant dismissal of potential solutions runs the risk that viable solutions are not given adequate consideration. Quite often, the solutions that are ultimately decided on are ones (or combinations of ones) that otherwise would have been overlooked.

As was seen with the problem list, it is important to record potential solutions on a piece of paper or a white board. Doing so allows clients to keep the full pool of potential solutions within their visual field, which will be of use when they begin to evaluate each potential solution in order to move toward the next phase of problem solving, decision making. In the following dialogue, Tara works with her therapist to generate potential solutions to the problem of getting out of the house more often with her baby.

Therapist:	Can we think of some options?
Tara:	Sure [pauses] But what? That's the problem, I don't really know what we can do. I think that's why we've stayed cooped up.
Therapist:	Do you know anyone else with a newborn?
Tara:	Just a couple of people. I'm one of the first of my friends to have a baby, and my sisters don't have kids yet.
Therapist:	Of the couple of friends who do have children, can you think of what they do?
Tara:	I don't really know. Both of them work, so their kids are in day care all day. I'm gonna stay at home instead.
Therapist:	Where do you imagine new mothers might go with their infants?
Tara:	Maybe for a walk?
Therapist:	Sure! [writes "go for a walk."]
Tara:	But that's the thing, I can't do that, we live on a busy road, and there are no sidewalks.
Therapist:	OK, it sounds like there might be some obstacles to walking around the neighborhood. Is it OK, though, if we leave this on the list? We might be able to figure out some other ways to take a walk that don't involve walking on the busy street you live on.

Tara:	Oh, OK.
Therapist:	Where else would you imagine that new mothers would go with their infants?
Tara:	I don't know. Maybe to the store?
Therapist:	Sure, it's nice to socialize the little ones into getting out and being in public. [writes "go to the store"] Tara, I'm sensing that you're really struggling with coming up with some places that you can take Thomas to get out of the house.
Tara:	Yes, I really am. I don't know why, this isn't rocket science. I should be able to figure this out.
Therapist:	[ignoring, for the moment, Tara's "should" statement] Would you like me to share some other ideas that I have from my years of work with new mothers?
Tara:	[looking relieved] Yes, that would be really helpful.
Therapist:	Well, for example, many of my clients take their babies to "Mommy and Me" classes at their local branch library.
Tara:	[face brightens up] Oh, that sounds like a good idea. The library is only ten minutes from my house. I can check that out.

[Therapist goes on to provide a few more suggestions.]

Therapist:	It looks like we have a lot of options here to evaluate. Tell me, if we hadn't had this session today, but you were trying to solve this problem, how would you have gone about generating these options?
Tara:	I guess I could have called my mom to see if she had any ideas. [pauses] Or I could have also gone on some parenting web sites on the Internet while I was nursing. I bet there would be discussion about this kind of thing among other new moms.
Therapist:	Bingo. Those are great ideas. You're going to be faced with other problems at times when we don't necessarily have a session scheduled, so it's important for you to know what resources you have.
Tara:	Yes, exactly.

Note that, at first, Tara did not readily have ideas of where to go to get out of the house. After some prompts (e.g., "Where do your friends go?"), her therapist reluctantly gave her some suggestions. There are times when perinatal women are too tired and overwhelmed to generate solutions to their problems. When cognitive behavioral therapists supply some suggestions, they follow up in the manner that Tara's therapist did, such that they help clients to locate resources to consult when they are faced with generating solutions outside of the therapist's office.

Decision Making

Once clients have generated a pool of potential solutions, they evaluate them in order to decide on one or more that they will pursue. As with the generation of potential solutions, it is important to be systematic with the evaluation of these solutions. To facilitate the evaluation process, cognitive behavioral therapists often use an *advantages-disadvantages analysis*. Although an advantages-disadvantages analysis can take many forms, when it is used in conjunction with problem solving, therapists often construct three columns: one to list the various options, one to list advantages, and one to list disadvantages. Figure 9.1 is an example of Tara's advantages-disadvantages analysis that she developed to decide on a solution that would help her get out of the house more often with her son.

Note that some of the items that Tara listed on her advantages-disadvantages analysis are factual (e.g., the fact that there are no side-walks on the street on which she lives), whereas other items listed on the advantages-disadvantages analysis were outcomes that may or may not happen (e.g., the possibility of meeting other new mothers through some of the activities). In many cases, it is difficult to avoid listing possible outcomes that have not yet occurred, as the client has not yet implemented the solution. When the possible outcomes are positive, it can be helpful to talk further with clients to determine how they would make those positive outcomes occur in order to maximize the success of the implemented solution. When the possible outcomes are negative, it can be helpful to frame them as predictions to be tested (much like a behavioral experiment), and then talk further with clients about ways to cope with those negative outcomes if they occur.

On the basis of the advantages-disadvantages analysis, Tara decided that all of the solutions other than walking along the busy street on which she lived were viable. She remarked that she could envision implementing all of them at some time or another. However, in order to ensure that Tara did not become overwhelmed, she chose two solutions to implement in the time in between her weekly sessions. Specifically, she decided that she would brave the cold, bundle up herself and her son, and go for a walk in the park at least once during the week. Second, she committed to looking into a Mommy and Me class at the library and attend the next class that worked with her son's sleeping schedule.

	Advantages	*Disadvantages*
Go for a walk around neighborhood.	• Can do whenever I feel like it	• No sidewalks—dangerous • Noisy, not soothing • A little cold right now
Go for a walk at the park.	• Can do whenever I feel like it	• A little cold right now • Park is 15 minutes away
Go to the grocery store.	• Can do whenever I feel like it • Often find that I need little things during the day	• A lot of effort for not much payoff
Attend Mommy and Me class at the library	• Would be fun for both of us • Structured activity that might be enriching for Thomas • Might meet other new moms • Library is a calm, soothing place	• None, other than I need to make the effort to find a class
Find a local play group	• Would be fun for both of us • Will meet other new moms • Might get lots of good ideas from other new moms • Might even make a friend who is in a similar situation	• Need to put in the effort to find a group • Anxiety over whether they are taking new members, whether I would fit in
Attend a breastfeeding support group	• Might meet other new moms • Would get valuable information about breastfeeding, can get my questions answered • Already have the information about it from Dr. Wenzel	• Kind of far from my house (30 mins)
Go to a Mom & Baby yoga class	• Would be fun for both of us • Might help both of us to relax • Might meet other new moms	• Alex might not like that I'm spending this money • Parking by the studio might be stressful

Figure 9.1 Tara's Advantages–Disadvantages Analysis.

Solution Implementation and Verification

A logical homework exercise for clients to implement in between sessions is the solution or combination of solutions that they identified during the session's focus on problem solving. As mentioned above, in order to maximize the likelihood of success, therapists can spend time with their clients practicing the skills needed to implement the solution, as well as coping tools for managing disappointment or other obstacles. Therapists can also utilize the technique of *imaginal rehearsal*, such that clients vividly imagine implementing the solution and walk their therapist through the details in a step-by-step fashion. This exercise increases clients' confidence that they can enact the solution, and it gives them another opportunity to identify any part of the solution implementation for which they might need to practice skills or identify ways to overcome obstacles.

As has been stated previously, it is vitally important to spend time during the subsequent session reviewing clients' homework and consolidating learning, and in no instance is this more important than in problem solving. Review of solution implementation allows the client to solidify the problem solving skills that she obtained, identify additional skills to be developed and practiced, and examine the manner in which solution implementation increased her self-confidence. Thus, discussion of solution implementation is usually the first item on the agenda at the time of the subsequent session, barring any immediate needs that must be addressed.

It is important to approach discussion of solution implementation from a "win-win" perspective; it is heartening when the solution that the client implements is successful. However, in many cases, the implemented solution is not successful, or only partially successful. When this occurs, it is easy for clients to fall into an all-or-nothing pattern of thinking, judging the exercise as pointless and becoming discouraged. When solution implementation is framed from a "win-win" perspective, clients gain benefit either because their problem has been solved, or because they have learned something valuable from attempting to implement the solution. There are several types of learning that can occur. For example, the client could learn that there are more pieces of the problem than she had realized and for which she needs to prepare to address. She could learn that she needs to develop additional problem solving or communication skills.

This occurred for Tara as she began to engage in some of the activities that would address the problem of being isolated. She went on walks, went to the park, and joined a Mommy and Me class at the library. Although she enjoyed getting out of the house, she felt uncomfortable around the other mothers and perceived that she had little to add to the conversation. Her therapist regarded this as valuable information and proposed that they devote some time in session to interpersonal effectiveness in order to form relationships with other mothers. Some of the communication tools that they practiced are described in the next chapter.

Overcoming Barriers to Problem Solving

Many of our clients are, in actuality, strong problem solvers, but they are experiencing barriers associated with depression and anxiety when they attempt to use their problem solving skills. Perhaps the biggest culprit is a *negative problem orientation*. A problem orientation is the cognitive set that people bring as they address the problems that they are facing. According to Bell and D'Zurilla (2009, p. 349), "a positive problem orientation consists of a general disposition to: (a) appraise a problem as a 'challenge' or an opportunity for benefit; (b) believe that problems are solvable; (c) believe in one's own ability to solve problems effectively; and (d) recognize and accept the fact that problem solving takes time and effort." When a problem orientation is negative, the person has unhelpful beliefs about problems themselves, the likelihood that problems can be solved, and their ability to solve problems. Some people who have a negative problem orientation even believe that they are bad or defective because they are experiencing problems in their lives.

Fortunately, the cognitive restructuring strategies described in Chapter 5 can be used to modify unhelpful beliefs about problems that might be interfering with the successful application of problem solving skills. Consider this dialogue with Lyla, who was faced with transitioning her son from the bassinet in her bedroom to the crib in his bedroom. She reported that he was inconsolable in his crib, and as a result, that she would eventually "give in" and being him back into her bedroom. She expressed disappointment in herself and wondered whether she would ever be able to get him to sleep in his own room.

Lyla: Just one more thing that I'm supposed to be doing as a mom, and one more thing that I'm failing at. [puts head in hands] I'll never be able to do this. Why does motherhood have to be so hard?

Therapist: I can tell you're really discouraged right now.

Lyla: You bet I am.

Therapist: I'm curious, Lyla. In the past, have you faced problems that seemed insurmountable, but for which you ultimately found a solution?

Lyla: [begrudgingly] Yeah, I guess so.

Therapist: Tell me about one in particular.

Lyla: Well . . . I found out second semester of my senior year that I needed a required class to graduate. I didn't even know it was required. By the time I figured it out, it was too late. The class was full. I thought I was going to have to wait to graduate in the summer or fall.

Therapist: What was the outcome?

Lyla: It all worked out. I graduated on time.

Therapist: Sounds like that *was* a big problem that you eventually addressed. How did you do that?

Lyla: First, I went to the professor to see if she would squeeze me in. That didn't get me anywhere. She said there was a big waiting list.

Therapist: So what did you do next?

Lyla: Then I went to the Dean to see if there was another way to meet the class requirement. She said that I could do an independent study under the same professor if she would take me on.

Therapist: Hmm, an independent study. How did you make that work?

Lyla: It was a ton of work. The professor said she would take me on, but she didn't have time to develop a curriculum for me. So I had to go through the book and her syllabus and basically design my own course.

Therapist: Sounds impressive. What did you learn from that experience?

Lyla: [sighs] That if I put my mind to something, that if I really need to get it done, then I can do it.

Therapist: What gets in the way of applying the same principle to sleep training?

Lyla: I'm just so tired. I don't know if I can do it. Being a mother is not supposed to be this hard!

Therapist: I wonder if you had a similar reaction when you first learned that you couldn't get into the required class. That graduating from college is not supposed to be this hard?

Lyla: [looks surprised] I did! That's exactly what I thought!

Therapist: So the fact that this has come up at least twice in your life, what does that tell you?

Lyla: I guess that problems are inevitable.

Therapist: Do they mean you're a failure?

Lyla: No, I guess not.

Therapist: When you have ideas like, I'm a failure as a mom, I can't do this, and motherhood isn't supposed to be this hard, what happens to your motivation and ability to stick with sleep training?

Lyla: Oh, it affects it a lot. I just give up and bring him right back in his bassinet. Which only makes the problem worse.

Therapist: What might be a more balanced way of viewing the problems associated with sleep training, or associated with being

Lyla: a parent in general, that would increase the likelihood that you'd stick with it?

Lyla: Um, I could say that all mothers have to go through times like this. And that I've faced tough times in the past, and that I've always figured out a way to make things work.

Therapist: How much do you believe that?

Lyla: I do. I believe it. 100%.

Therapist: At the beginning of this conversation, I sensed that you were quite down about the whole thing. On our scale of 0–10, with 0 being no depression and 10 being the most depression you've ever experienced, how down are you feeling?

Lyla: Much better. I'm down to a 5.

In this dialogue, Lyla's therapist helped her to recognize two unhelpful beliefs about problems—that one "should not" have problems, and that she was a failure and therefore unable to solve her problems. However, when her therapist called her attention to a seemingly insurmountable problem that she had faced in the past, she realized that she had been quite creative and resourceful in addressing that issue. In addition, her therapist used careful observation and guided questioning to help Lyla realize that her typical response to problems is that "life should not be this hard," and Lyla was quickly able to recognize that problems are a part of life and do not mean that she is doing anything wrong.

There are times when clients are faced with problems, and despite their best efforts to solve them, there are extraneous factors out of their control that preclude a solution to the problem. When clients find themselves in this position, it is easy for them to ruminate on these factors or on their perception of injustice or unfairness. In these cases, therapists can work with their clients to either change their environments altogether or accept the aspects of the problem that they cannot control.

Conclusion

Although problem solving might seem like a straightforward cognitive behavioral strategy, it involves several specific steps, as well as a recognition of skills deficits and unhelpful cognitions that have the potential to interfere with the execution of solutions. Cognitive behavioral therapists give their clients space to brainstorm potential solutions to their problems, evaluate the advantages and disadvantages of those solutions, and decide on the solution (or combination of solutions) that best fits their needs. As much as is possible, therapists create the context for a "win-win" situation, such that either clients' problems get solved, or they learn something valuable that can continue to be a focus of therapy.

At times, perinatal women are in such distress that they simply want to be cared for. If a client is decompensating and does not have the ability to enact the steps of problem solving on her own, then the therapist will take the lead in developing a plan to address her immediate needs. A general rule of thumb is that, over time in CBT, clients take more and more ownership over the work that is done in session. Translated to problem solving, this means that, over time, clients take an increasingly significant lead in applying the steps of problem solving and determining the best solution on their own.

10

COMMUNICATION SKILLS TRAINING

The transition to parenthood can feel like a time of great isolation. New mothers have gone through an experience that has wreaked havoc on their bodies, and it is possible that no one else around them is going through the same type of physical adjustment. They are likely to be the primary caregiver for a newborn that is dependent on them for nourishment, which requires that they tend to their newborn around the clock. They are up in the middle of the night when everyone else in the household is sleeping. They have yet to settle into a routine, when everyone else around them seems to be going about their days. In the first several days, they may not even have left the home. In many instances, they need help, but may do not know how to ask.

Qualitative research suggests that interpersonal problems are even more central in understanding the clinical presentations of clients with perinatal distress than non-perinatal clients who struggle with depression and anxiety (O'Mahen et al., 2012). For example, a large body of literature has examined the relation between postpartum depression and anxiety and *social support*, or the sense that one is a part of a caring network of close others who provide assistance when needed. As long as 30 years ago, Cutrona (1984) demonstrated that a low level of social support accounted for significant variance in postpartum depression 8 weeks after delivery. Perhaps the greatest type of social support needed by perinatal women is *instrumental support*, or direct, tangible assistance from others, to help them complete household chores and engage in personal self-care (Negron, Martin, Almog, Balbierz, & Howell, 2013). However, when the type of social support that perinatal women receive does not match what they perceive that they need, or when they experience it as intrusive or unhelpful, then emotional distress often increases (Haugen, 2003).

On the basis of this research, it is not difficult to conclude that psychotherapy could provide the ideal forum to help perinatal women maximize the effectiveness of their social support network. Cognitive restructuring, described in Chapter 6, could be used to ensure that perinatal women have accurate expectations for their social support network. However, it is also logical that perinatal women might need assistance in the acquisition of effective communication skills to make requests of their social support network, as well as to draw appropriate boundaries and negotiate differences of opinion. The remainder of this chapter is devoted to strategies for developing effective communication skills in two domains: assertiveness and building close relationships.

Assertiveness Skills

Assertiveness is a communication style that is used when a person must make requests of others, say no to others, or express a difference of opinion. When people are assertive, they advocate for their own needs while, at the same time, hearing and respecting the needs of others. They are confident in their own requests while, at the same time, demonstrating the ability to put themselves in the shoes of the other person. As a result, assertive people are open to negotiation and compromise in order to arrive upon a solution that works for all parties involved.

The assertive communication style can be contrasted with three other, less helpful communication styles. People who are *aggressive* confidently request that their own needs be met, but they do so in a manner suggesting that they are disregarding the needs and rights of the other parties involved. An aggressive communication style is often associated with a cognitive orientation of entitlement. People who are *passive* usually do not make requests to meet their own needs and instead, often go out of their way to take care of the needs of others at the expense of their own well being. A passive communication style is often associated with a cognitive orientation of being undeserving or not good enough. People who are *passive aggressive* go "behind the scenes" to get their needs met in a way that is not above-board to the other parties involved. In other words, they often do not make direct requests and might even appear as if they are acquiescing to the needs of others, but they engage in subtle behaviors that contradict the stance they have communicated to the other parties involved.

Although most clients agree that assertiveness seems sensible, they sometimes report that they have difficulty imagining themselves using assertive communication skills. An entirely different communication style might have been modeled for them during their formative years, and they cannot imagine their family members responding to a communication style that is foreign to them. Female clients sometimes express concern that their voices will crack or that they will become tearful in their attempts to be assertive. Other clients predict that they will get derailed the first instance in which the other party expresses discontent or says something unexpected. Many of these concerns are automatic thoughts that can be evaluated and modified using cognitive restructuring.

Regardless of whether clients' assumptions about assertiveness are or are not accurate, it is likely that they will need some help in acquiring these skills. The list of specific assertiveness skills that can be practiced is endless. Several books have been written that describe the cognitive behavioral application of communication skills for specific psychiatric disorders, such as depression (Becker, Heimberg, & Bellack, 1987), borderline personality disorder (Linehan, 1993a, 1993b), and schizophrenia (Bellack, Mueser, Gingrich, & Agresta, 2004). Many of the communication skills described in these books are general enough that they cut across diagnostic categories and would be useful to consider implementing with many clients, including clients with perinatal distress.

In general, communication skills training typically focuses on three domains. First, therapists work with clients to hone their *verbal skills* to ensure that clients are communicating clearly, accurately, and effectively. Therapists who work with clients to acquire verbal skills might focus on the specific contents of what the client hopes to address. Doing this helps clients to clarify the main points that they would like to communicate to another party. However, therapists might also focus more generally on their clients' style. Many cognitive behavioral therapists who work with their clients to acquire skill in assertiveness encourage their clients to: (a) open their communication on a positive note so that the other party is not put on the defensive; (b) then make their request; set their boundary, or express a differing opinion; and (c) then end their communication on another positive note, such as by expressing appreciation for the other's willingness to compromise or by communicating that the relationship is an important one to them. In other words, clients are taught a skillful approach to communicating something that the other party might not want to hear in a way that maximizes the likelihood that the other party will be open-minded and receptive.

Recall, in Chapter 5, that Lyla was upset when her husband left for work without saying goodbye. Although she was able to use cognitive restructuring to see that this was not necessarily an indication that her husband was fed up with her, she continued to be hurt and wanted to talk directly with him about this so that it did not happen again. The following is her rendition of what happened when she brought her concerns to his attention.

Lyla: How could you just leave this morning without saying goodbye? It's like you don't care one bit.

Husband: [taken aback] I just tried to leave quietly because I thought you were sleeping. I didn't want to wake you.

Lyla: Oh yeah right. You could be a little more thoughtful, you know.

Husband: [throws his hands in his air and mutters] Geez, nothing I do is right lately.

In the above example, Lyla comes across in a manner that is accusatory and even aggressive. When her husband tried to explain himself, she continued to point out ways that he had fallen short. After Lyla relayed this interaction to her therapist, her therapist taught her about the importance of communicating more precisely what it is that she wants, as well as about the importance of beginning and ending assertive requests on positive notes and refraining from statements that could be taken as an accusation. On the basis of this therapeutic work, Lyla revisited the issue with her husband the following week.

Lyla: [starting on a positive note] It really means a lot to me to see you at the beginning of the day. It always starts my day off on a positive note.

Husband: Good, I'm glad to hear that.

Lyla: [making her request] I'd love it if you could come in to say goodbye before you leave for work, even if it means that you have to wake me up.

Husband: Sure, honey, of course. I didn't realize that you'd rather be woken up than sleep when I am ready to leave for work.

Lyla: This is great. Thank you. I will always look forward to my mornings.

Notice that, as a result of using the communication skills that she had practiced in session, the conversation remained calm, positive, and productive, that Lyla achieved her desired outcome, and that, more generally, Lyla left the conversation feeling cared for by her husband.

Another verbal process that is often practiced as clients acquire assertiveness skills is the use of "I" language. The rationale behind encouraging clients to use "I" language is that they take ownership over their own viewpoints and feelings, rather than accusing others of behaving inappropriately or claiming that the other person made them feel a certain way. The use of "I" language is another technique that decreases the likelihood that the party on the receiving end of the communication feels defensive. Compare and contrast these two styles of communication, with and without the use of "I" language, when Lyla talked to her husband about his leaving for work without saying goodbye.

Lyla: You make me feel like you don't care, like I'm some sort of burden on the family.

Husband: What? I'm not sure what you are talking about.

Lyla: In the mornings. When you leave the house. You can't even take the time to check in on me.

Husband: [exasperated] You're ridiculous. I can't even have a conversation with you. [leaves the room]

In the above example, Lyla makes "you" statements that sound accusatory and put him on the defensive. Not surprisingly, the conversation does not go well; her husband leaves the room frustrated, and Lyla views the interaction as providing further evidence that her husband does not care. In the next excerpt, Lyla uses "I" language, and the outcome of the conversation is more favorable.

Lyla: When you left for work this morning without saying good-bye, I felt hurt.

Husband: Really? I didn't realize that you felt hurt. I just tried to leave quietly so that I wouldn't wake you.

Lyla: [looks relieved] Oh, that was the reason? I thought it was because you didn't care.

Husband: [gives her a hug] That, my dear, couldn't be further from the truth. I know you've been having trouble at night, so I thought you could use your rest.

Through Lyla's use of "I" language, her husband was able to hear her concerns and see that her communication came from a place of hurt, not from a place of criticism. He remained calm and supportive during the interaction, which decreased her emotional upset and reinforced the notion that he does, indeed, care for her.

The training of verbal communication skills is not limited to these two techniques; there is an infinite array of verbal skills that can be taught depending on the nature of the client's clinical presentation and the unique interpersonal challenges that she faces in her life. In addition, therapists often work with their clients on the tone through which they deliver their verbal communication, such as loudness of their voice, the speed at which they utter their words, and the inflection of certain words. The experiment in session, such that they state a message with two different tones of voice and ask their clients the messages that they received from each statement. Such demonstrations provide valuable experiential learning on which clients can rely when they deliver various assertive statements in their own lives. Therapists are encouraged to use their own knowledge of communication skills, as well as resources like those that were described earlier in the chapter, in order to target the specific needs of the client.

Verbal communication skills are only one domain that is considered in communication skills training. A second domain consists of *nonverbal communication skills*. Nonverbal communication skills include behaviors such as head nods, eye contact, fidgeting, smiles, touching, and gestures. It is thought that moderate use of many of these nonverbal skills communicates interest in and understanding of what the other is saying. Using too few of these nonverbal skills can communicate disinterest or aloofness; using too many of these nonverbal skills can communicate overeagerness or can be experienced as intrusive. Lyla, for example, often received feedback from others that her closed postural stance and lack of eye contact communicated that she was uninterested in talking to others, when these behaviors actually indicated that she was socially anxious and feared rejection by others. As she did with her verbal communication skills, Lyla practiced communicating with effective nonverbal communication skills with her therapist in session and then observed, in her own environment, how they affected others' responses toward her. An additional consideration is that it is important for nonverbal communication skills to match verbal communication skills, as the other party might take away an unintended message if there is a mismatch.

Finally, a third domain of communication skills that is often consider in communication training is *listening*. During interpersonal conflict, all too often people are busy plotting the next part of their argument without truly hearing what the other person is saying. Therapists can help their clients acquire listening skills by teaching them: (a) to be present-focused and mindful when the other person is speaking so that they truly absorb what the other person is saying; and (b) to repeat back the main points of what the other person has said to ensure accurate understanding. Therapists also encourage their clients to refrain from taking assumptions about the other person's intentions as fact, but instead to check out those assumptions before drawing a conclusion. This skill is demonstrated in the next excerpt between Lyla and her husband, which occurred after Lyla's therapist worked with her to acquire listening skills and verify her assumptions about her husband's intentions.

Lyla: Did you know that you left this morning without saying goodbye?

Husband: [looking up from the article he was reading on his tablet device] What? Really? [looking back down at his tablet] Oh, you know I didn't mean anything by it.

Lyla: [pauses and takes a breath] I hear that you didn't mean it. When you say that at the same time you are reading an article on your tablet, though, I assume that you're just trying to placate me so that we don't get in a big fight. Is that what's going on?

Husband: [looks up and puts tablet on the coffee table] I'm sorry, hon, I didn't mean to give you that impression. I was just really wrapped up in the scores from last night.

Tips for Maximizing Effectiveness

There are many ways to maximize the effectiveness of communication skills training. The most important point to remember is that adequate time must be devoted for the client to truly understand the rationale for the communication skill under consideration, practice the skill, and anticipate how she will use the skill in interactions outside of the session (Wenzel, 2013). Thus, communication skills training is much more than a simple suggestion made by the therapist to say something differently; instead, it provides an opportunity for psychoeducation, practice, and the consolidation of new learning.

In order to begin communication skills training, therapists ask their clients to state, verbatim, what they hope to communicate to another person. This exercise provides "data" about clients' communication skill level and allows for careful and collaborative evaluation of the strengths and weaknesses of clients' communication style. After this evaluation, the therapist and client agree on one or more specific communication skills to be practiced. This process is illustrated with Wendy, who perceived that her mother was being critical of her overprotectiveness with her children. During the session, she hoped to work with her therapist to develop an effective approach for asking her mother to communicate her concerns in a softer manner, or perhaps not communicate them at all.

Wendy: It's just so frustrating. It's like, yeah mom, I get it. I know that I'm overprotective with the kids. That's why I'm going to therapy. But criticizing me for it just rubs salt in the wounds. I'd just really like her to stop.

Therapist: Have you talked to her about this?

Wendy: No, not really. I'd like to, but she just gets all defensive and upset, and it's just one more person to take care of on top of the kids.

Therapist: I wonder if we could put our heads together and figure out an effective but gentle way to communicate your concerns and your request that she refrain from what you experience as criticism?

Wendy: I would be thrilled if we could do that.

Therapist: Let's role-play for a moment. I'll play your mom, and you play yourself. I'll criticize you, and you respond with your concerns and a request to refrain from criticism. Sound OK?

Wendy: OK.

Therapist: [assuming role of Wendy's mother] Geez, Wendy, you're so overprotective. You don't let the kids do anything. They're gonna grow up to be scared of everything.

Wendy: [snaps] Mom, stop it, just stop it. You're only making it worse.

Therapist: Well, it's true, whether you want to face it or not.

Wendy: You've been like this ever since I remember. All you ever do is criticize. It's a miracle that I'm not more messed up than I am.

Therapist: [out of role play] Was that an accurate depiction of what sometimes transpires between the two of you?

175

Wendy:	Yes, very.
Therapist:	Let's evaluate your communication style. What do you think worked, and what do you think needs more attention?
Wendy:	[hesitates] Well . . . I was honest with her. That's a good thing. At least I don't roll over and take it.
Therapist:	Fair enough. What about the other side of the coin? Anything to work on?
Wendy:	Well, when you think about it, nothing changes. She keeps doing the same thing. So something must not be working.
Therapist:	Can you put yourself in your mom's shoes for a moment?
Wendy:	OK.
Therapist:	I'm going to repeat back what you said. "Mom, stop it, just stop it. You're only making it worse. You've been like this ever since I remember. All you ever do is criticize. It's a miracle that I'm not more messed up than I am." What do you notice, being on the receiving end of that?
Wendy:	Oh yikes, it sounds kind of harsh.
Therapist:	You experienced it as harsh.
Wendy:	Yeah. I guess it sounds like a lot of finger pointing. She kind of deserves it. But, of course, she won't see it that way. She'll just get defensive.
Therapist:	That was my reaction precisely. I often find that even when a person believes she has the right to be harsh and forthcoming with another person, it isn't always the most effective route to go.
Wendy:	Exactly. I just want her to stop criticizing me.
Therapist:	How's this for an idea? First, let's clarify exactly what you want to communicate to her. Then, I can share some skills that might make your communication more effective.
Wendy:	[looks relieved] Yes, that would be great.

Wendy decided that she wanted to communicate her experience of hurt when her mother makes critical comments and request that her mother either ask permission to share her opinion or not make the comment at all. Wendy's therapist taught her about beginning and ending requests with positives, as well as using "I" language and staying with the topic at hand, rather than dragging in incidents from the past.

After educating their clients about specific communication skills, cognitive behavioral therapists ensure that their clients have space to practice the skills. Role play is a key technique that is used for practicing communication skills. It is often most effective for the therapist first to model the communication skill, such that he or she takes the role of the client, and the client takes the role of the person with whom she hopes to apply the communication skills, and next switch roles, such that the client plays herself, and the therapist takes the role of the person with whom she hopes to apply the communication skills. This approach allows the client to learn by modeling her therapist's behavior and also learn by doing. During the first role play, the therapist asks the client what it feels like to be on the receiving end of the effective communication skill, and during the second role play, the therapist asks the client what it feels like to be delivering the effective communication skill. At times, multiple role plays are conducted in order to hone the client's skill acquisition.

As stated previously, cognitive restructuring is used in conjunction with communication skills training because clients often report negative, unhelpful thoughts that interfere with their ability to apply effective communication skills. In the ensuring dialogue, Wendy's therapist helps her to identify and restructure a central idea that has prevented her from talking with her mother directly about her mother's criticism of her. This dialogue occurred immediately after a role play in which Wendy practiced using the communication skills that she had acquired in session.

Therapist:	Tell me about your experience in using these new communication skills.
Wendy:	They're really helpful. I think I can use them in a lot of different situations, not just with my mother. But . . . [voice trails off]
Therapist:	Ah, there's a "but." You have some doubts, at least doubts about using these skills with your mother.
Wendy:	That's just it, it's my mother. I think these skills would be pretty straightforward to use with other people. But my mom, she's just so irrational. And then she makes me feel guilty, that I'm ungrateful for all that she does for me.
Therapist:	I'm ungrateful is a powerful belief. Does that run through your mind when you picture yourself expressing your concerns to your mother?
Wendy:	Definitely. I mean, I'm not grateful *enough*. Maybe I should just put up with the bad sides of her.
Therapist:	Well, let's evaluate this idea that you're ungrateful. What makes you conclude this?
Wendy:	I'm short with her a lot. I think she can tell that she gets on my nerves.
Therapist:	Do you say things to her that suggest you are ungrateful?
Wendy:	Oh no. If anything, I probably thank her too much.
Therapist:	Is saying thank you an expression of gratitude?
Wendy:	Yes, I guess it is.
Therapist:	What other expressions of gratitude do you show?
Wendy:	[thinking] I bought her a gift card to a spa as a way to thank her for all of the work she has done. And when my husband

brings home take-out for dinner, we almost always ask her to stay and eat with us so that she doesn't have to go home and fix a meal after a long, exhausting day with the kids.

Therapist: Let me make sure that I've heard you correctly. On the one hand, you're short with her, and you wonder whether she knows that she gets on your nerves. But on the other hand, you thank her profusely, you bought her the gift card to the spa, and you frequently ask her to stay for dinner. What conclusion do you draw from this evidence?

Wendy: [sighs] OK, I know I'm not ungrateful.

Therapist: I wonder if we can formulate this into a balanced response that you can remember the next time you want to say something to your mother, but the idea that you're ungrateful pops into your mind?

Wendy: I can list all of the things I have done to show my mom that I am grateful for her help.

Therapist: I think that would be a terrific idea. Would it be helpful to write these reasons down on a coping card and glance at the coping card to remind yourself of these reasons before you initiate a hard conversation with her?

Wendy: [nods emphatically, grabs a pen and a card, and writes the reasons]

Therapist: Let me play devil's advocate for a moment. Let's say you start to express your concerns to your mother, and, despite using these effective communication skills, she accuses you of being ungrateful. How will you handle that?

Wendy: That's a good question because I can see that happening. I can remember the things I've done to be grateful, and I can say to her in a non-defensive way, "Mom, I don't think that is true. I've shown a lot of appreciation for everything that you've done."

Therapist: If you had a friend in this situation, would you say that your friend is allowed to set boundaries and address concerns even if her mother is doing a lot to help out with her three children?

Wendy: Yes, definitely. So I have to remember that I'm allowed, too.

Therapist: Exactly.

A logical homework exercise for clients is to enact the effective communication skills and have the conversation that they had been practicing in session. Much as has been discussed previously in the book regarding behavioral experiments, it is important to follow up with the homework at the time of the subsequent session and evaluate what went well, what did not, and what additional skills would be helpful to practice.

The acquisition of effective communication skills is an ongoing process, and clients are not expected to perfect an assertive communication style on one occasion. Thus, ongoing assessment, practice, and refinement are usually necessary.

When communication skills-based homework is reviewed, therapists often find that clients continue to report many negative automatic thoughts. For example, they fixate on a point in the conversation in which they could have responded differently. They might ruminate on concerns about what the other person thinks of them. They run through the conversation play-by-play, evaluating themselves negatively at many junctures. This cognitive style is called *post-event processing* (Brozovich & Heimberg, 2008). Simply educating clients about this tendency can often be helpful, as many clients quickly recognize they fall prey to post-event processing and can then catch themselves more quickly the next time it occurs. However, cognitive restructuring can also be used to evaluate the accuracy and helpfulness of cognitions associated with post-event processing. When possible, clients are encouraged to solicit feedback from others with whom they used assertiveness skills in order to verify their perception that they performed poorly or that the other person now thinks negatively of them.

Relationship Challenges

In some instances, communication-based therapeutic work focuses less on what precisely to say, or how precisely to get a message across, and instead is directed more broadly on how to repair or build relationships. The perinatal period can be a time in which there is dispute about roles, disappointment about support given or received, and little time for fostering a connection. In this section, we describe some of the common interpersonal issues that are typically reported by perinatal women in therapy and ways to address them using communication skills training and other CBT strategies.

Overcoming Distance From Spouse or Partner

It is well established that marital satisfaction declines after the birth of a child (Doss, Rhoads, Stanley, & Markman, 2009; Lawrence, Nylen, & Cobb, 2007; Lawrence, Rothman, Cobb, Rothman, & Bradbury, 2008). When people are consumed with the demands of caring for a newborn, it is logical that there is little time remaining to attend to the partner relationship. The connection between partners seems to disappear (Kleiman & Wenzel, 2014). It is not difficult to imagine that misinterpretation, resentment, and conflict are frequent in the absence of a sense of connection.

In addition to the general communication skills that have been described to this point in the chapter, there are many specific communication skills that cognitive behavioral experts have identified as being particularly important in negotiating marital distress and distance. In his ground-breaking book, *Why Marriages Succeed or Fail*, renowned scholar John Gottman (1994) identified four problematic communication styles—termed the Four Horsemen of the Apocalypse—that predict divorce. *Criticism* occurs when one spouse attacks the other's personality or character, usually in overarching generalizations, rather than expressing upset with one specific behavior. For example, spouses can be taught to move away from a criticism like, "You never listen to me," to a specific complaint like, "It didn't seem to me that you were paying attention when I was telling you about my stressful day." *Contempt* takes criticism one step further, such that one spouse intentionally tries to insult the other spouse. Contempt is manifested in name calling, humiliation, hostile humor, mockery, and dismissing body language like eye rolls and sneers. *Defensiveness* occurs when spouses deny responsibility, make excuses, cross-complain (i.e., respond to the spouse's complaint with a complaint about him or her without stopping to think about what the spouse is saying), respond with a "yes but" that negates the spouse's concern, whine, or assume a closed bodily posture. Finally, *stonewalling* occurs when one partner does not respond to what the other is saying, and in the extreme form, when a spouse shuts down the conversation (e.g., by walking away).

Cognitive behavioral therapists can educate their clients about these four communication barriers. They can use role play with their clients to identify alternative ways to engage in dialogue about differences of opinion with their spouses. Often, one or more conjoint sessions are held with the spouse so that the spouse can also learn ways to avoid falling into one or more of these communication traps. As clients begin to adopt different approaches to communicating concerns to their spouse as a result of this training, they can then observe how their sense of connection to their spouse has improved.

Other cognitive behavioral strategies can be used to overcome distance between spouses or partners and restore their connection, as well. For example, a program of research that is over two decades old demonstrated that the tendency to make malicious attributions for a spouse's behavior is associated with less effective interpersonal problem solving, negative behaviors enacted toward the other, and marital dissatisfaction (e.g., Bradbury & Fincham, 1992). The cognitive restructuring tools described in Chapter 6 can be used to help examine those malicious attributions in the same way as one would evaluate automatic thoughts. Clients can be taught to examine the evidence supporting their maladaptive attribution (e.g., "My husband just doesn't care enough about me") and consider other explanations for their spouse's behavior in order to construct a more benign way of viewing the upsetting interaction (e.g., "My husband is just as sleep-deprived as I am, plus he's juggling the demands of a high-pressure job"). When clients shift toward adopting more benign attributions for their spouse or partner's behavior, their emotional distress usually decreases, and they are in a better position to use the communication skills that have been described in this chapter.

Other clients find that they simply need to spend more time with their spouse or partner. Although it is important to have realistic expectations for the amount of time that a newborn will allow them to have "alone" time, perinatal clients often find that, with some creativity, they are able to increase the amount of quality time that they spend with their spouse or partner. The problem solving skills described in Chapter 9 allow clients space to brainstorm ways to find time to spend with their spouse or partner. If it is impossible to find time away from the children, clients can use problem solving to identify family activities that facilitate a sense of connection, rather than devoting free time solely to mundane tasks such as chores and errands. When clients implement quality time either alone with their spouse or partners, or with their spouse and children in the context of a family activity, they are encouraged to be mindful and savor the connection that they are nurturing in order to vary over the positive effects from the activity, making it more likely that they will use effective communication skills with their partner when they must make decisions about coparenting and running the household.

Overcoming Tension with Other Family Members

Many perinatal women express frustration with other family members during the transition to parenthood. At times, these frustrations stem from events that trigger reactions associated with previous hurts and disappointments. At other times, these frustrations occur when perinatal women expect to receive a certain type of support from certain family members, and they are disappointed when they do not get it. Other perinatal women experience their in-laws as intrusive and as imposing a different type of family culture than the one in which they were raised. These scenarios often fuel anger, resentment, and disappointment, exacerbating the emotional distress that perinatal women report.

At times, perinatal women will find it helpful if they apply the assertiveness skills described earlier in the chapter to draw boundaries and set limits with others. Well-meaning grandparents can give unsolicited advice or approach childcare in an outdated manner that is inconsistent with the practices that the new mother hopes to establish. Perinatal clients can practice clear communication about how they want things done while, simultaneously, acknowledging that they appreciate the effort that these family members are trying to give and respect that they successfully reared their own children. When there is a difference of opinion with a family member about child care, it can be helpful for perinatal clients to first discuss their concerns with their spouse or partner so that they have a united stance and can support one another when they address the issue with other family members.

Cognitive behavioral therapists work with their clients to proactively communicate boundaries and expectations to others in order to ensure that all family members are "on the same page" in the days and weeks following childbirth. Others can only be responsive if they know what is expected of them. Thus, therapists use the communication techniques and practice approaches described in the chapter to this point in order to coach clients in using effective communication skills to make their requests known.

Many clients remark that these communication skills seem effective, in theory, but that single instances of disagreements about boundaries or expectations reflect larger, more engrained interactional patterns that have developed over a long period of time. They doubt that their family member will respond to these communication approaches because of the history of tension that has built up gradually between them. In these instances, cognitive behavioral therapists can educate their clients about two principles. The first is the principle of *shaping*, such that clients are encouraged to gradually enact behaviors that will change the response of another person over successive trials. Because of long-standing unhelpful interactional patterns, family members might not necessarily respond as expected the first time the client uses effective communication skills to make a request or establish a boundary. However, when effective communication skills are delivered on several occasions over time, the message that they send becomes that much stronger, and it is hoped that the person on the receiving end gradually begins to recognize and respond favorably.

A second principle that therapists often consider in session is the focus on communication *process*, rather than *content*. When clients report that they repeatedly fall into the same unhelpful pattern when they introduce concerns to a particular family member, then therapists can help them clarify their observations of the aspects of the communication pattern that seem not to achieve their aims and initiate a conversation with the other person to come to an agreement about ways to handle conversations differently in the future. Consider this dialogue that Wendy had with her mother, which she implemented after a session devoted to communication skills practice.

Wendy's Mother:	I really wish you'd let me take the two older kids to the amusement park on the Boardwalk. Nothing bad is going to happen. You're always so overprotective.
Wendy:	[takes a breath before beginning] Mom, is it OK to talk for a minute about something I've noticed?
Wendy's Mother:	[hesitant] Well, OK. Go on.

Wendy:	Well, I've noticed that something happens when we talk about the things I let the kids do. You and I have different views of what is safe and what is not safe. It seems to me that when your opinion differs than mine, you speak up, and I experience that as criticism. In turn, I lash out, probably in a way that is a bit unfair, and then you seem to be hurt and say that I am ungrateful. It seems to get us in trouble, and it takes away from the close relationship that we had. Do you see the same pattern?
Wendy's Mother:	[exasperated] Honestly, Wendy, I'm just trying to help and make sure that those kids are well-adjusted as they get older.
Wendy:	[attempting to use a calm, gentle voice] See, Mom, this is where I think we get off track. [acknowledging a positive] I know you mean well and that you love your grandkids more than anything. And when you say things like you just want them to be well-adjusted, I take that as criticism, as if you are saying that the way I am parenting is going to make them poorly-adjusted.
Wendy's Mother:	I never said they were going to be poorly-adjusted. I do think, though, that you're going to give them a complex or something.
Wendy:	Well, Mom, I think this is an area in which we will have to agree to disagree. At this point, I know where you stand. I even agree with you to some extent, which is why I'm getting some help through therapy. I wonder, though, from now on if you'd agree to keep your opinion to yourself? I ask because I want to make sure that our relationship remains as strong as it ever was.
Wendy's Mother:	I can try. You know that I'm an opinionated old woman, though. I'm not going to be perfect.
Wendy:	I will acknowledge that you are trying. If you do say something that I'm taking as criticism, I'd like to be able to point that out in a nice way without you interpreting it as being ungrateful. Because that couldn't be further from the truth. All of us are so grateful for the help you give us.
Wendy's Mother:	[looks down] I know you're grateful. I think I react like that when you start to imply that I meddle all the time.
Wendy:	Then I will be aware that I can come across like that and try to express my concerns in a way that doesn't give that message.

[Wendy and her mother hug.]

This dialogue illustrates a number of different communication techniques that cognitive behavioral therapists can practice with their clients. First, notice that Wendy asked her mother's permission to talk about something she noticed. This is a collaborative approach that brings the other person on board, rather than one that immediately puts the other on the defensive. Wendy's words, "something I've noticed happening," are neutral as opposed to "loaded" language like "something that you always do" or "something that really irritates me." Second, when Wendy elaborated on the communication pattern that she had noticed, she continued to use balanced, non-accusatory language, taking care to state her observations as factually as possible and identify anything that might have been an interpretation (e.g., "it seems that . . ."). Third, when it appeared that her mother was going to say something else that could be taken as criticism, Wendy remained calm, refraining from raising her voice and instead using it as an example of the point that she was attempting to illustrate. Then she followed up with making a request of her mother to refrain from making such statements, but not before acknowledging something positive (i.e., that her mother was trying to help and loves her grandchildren very much). Finally, as they were negotiating an agreement for handling similar interactions in the future, Wendy took responsibility for the role that she played in the communication pattern and agreed to make her own changes.

The importance of making benign attributions, discussed in the previous section, is equally as relevant to negotiating conflict with family members as it is to negotiating conflict with one's significant other. Focusing on the good intentions of the other, rather than inferring malicious intentions, can help clients approach sensitive topics with an adaptive cognitive orientation that allows them to focus on using language that is effective, rather than getting their point across at all costs or being vindictive. This cognitive orientation brings a spirit of collaboration and respect to interactions in which one must address differences of opinion with a close other.

Communication with the Baby

As stated in Chapter 1, research shows that postpartum depression is associated with a host of negative infant and child outcomes, such as poor cognitive functioning, insecure attachment, and emotional and social maladjustment (see Murray & Cooper, 2003, for a comprehensive review). On the basis of this research, it has been suggested that the mother-infant relationship should be targeted in treatment in addition to maternal depressive symptoms (e.g., Cooper et al., 2003).

There is nothing that would preclude therapists from focusing on the mother-infant relationship in CBT if it is clear from the cognitive case conceptualization that the client's cognitive behavioral style is associated with significant infant sequelae. Psychoeducation and therapeutic interventions could target constructs such as responding to the infant's cues, recognizing affective states, sustaining infants' attention, and providing opportunities for infants to explore their environments. As clients have success experiences with these behaviors, they experience interactions with their infants as more enjoyable and satisfying, thereby increasing the likelihood that they continue to implement positive parenting behaviors and decreasing their depressed mood (cf. R. Clark, Tluczek, & Brown, 2008).

This is an example of the fact that inclusion of interventions that might not be prototypical for a standard course of CBT for depression is warranted. However, the key to their inclusion is that they are incorporated in a theoretically coherent manner, such that they target constructs that are conceptualized as central to causing, maintaining, or exacerbating the client's emotional distress or that are serious consequences of the client's emotional distress. Moreover, standard cognitive behavioral techniques can be used to facilitate their delivery, including: (a) cognitive restructuring to reframe any negative cognitions that would interfere with their execution; and (b) problem solving and role play to optimize their execution. After setting up and practicing a particular parenting skill, cognitive behavioral therapists ask their clients to anticipate how its use in between sessions will improve their interactions with their infants, as well as reduce their emotional distress. Doing this reinforces the rationale for the intervention and provides a clear understanding of the pathway by which the intervention will achieve its desired effects. As women implement these interventions across the course of several sessions, they are encouraged to carefully observe the effects on their relationship with their infants and their mood in order to make further adjustment as needed.

Maintaining Existing Friendships

It is not uncommon for perinatal women to report a disconnect from some of their friends, especially friends without children, following childbirth. In these cases, women are left to deal with the emotional consequences of feeling distant from these friends, as well as the charge of reestablishing, and perhaps redefining, these relationships. Cognitive restructuring can help to: (a) form reasonable expectations for these relationships going forward; and (b) keep any hurts and disappointments in perspective, utilizing the concept of considering all explanations for their friends' behavior that may feel offputting or distant and attributing those behaviors to benign intentions. Communication skills training can focus on approaches to the open discussion of tension or distance in the relationship and on ways to enhance the relationship in light of the significant transition through which the client is undergoing. Often, the focus of this work is on achieving a balance between feeling comfortable sharing the details of the transition to parenthood with friends while, at the same time, showing interest in things going on in their friends' lives and engaging in discussion of nonchildbearing-related topics that had been enjoyable in the past.

Developing New Relationships

New mothers, especially those who have given birth to their first child, often report a great deal of social isolation because their life circumstances have changed dramatically and abruptly. They may perceive that they are without a community of women at a similar place in life who would understand what they are going through. Qualitative research indicates that women perceive that a major benefit of group treatment for perinatal distress is the establishment of such a community (O'Mahen et al., 2012). Thus, even when a therapist is providing individual psychotherapy, a reasonable goal of treatment would be to help build a community of women who are undergoing a similar life transition.

As was illustrated in Chapter 9 with Tara, many cognitive behavioral therapists who work with perinatal clients create space for them to brainstorm ways to connect with other new mothers, such as by joining mothers' groups, attending Mommy and Me classes at the local library or gym, or even going to the park. Some clients are able to run with these potential solutions, and in a short period of time, they report developing new friendships with women who have children of a similar age as their own child. In our clinical experience, success in developing relationships with new mothers provides perinatal clients with hope, optimism, and a sense of belonging.

However, other perinatal clients report a great deal of anxiety and trepidation about forming new relationships. In Chapter 1, we indicated that a small subset of postpartum women report clinical significant symptoms of social anxiety, which is associated with dissatisfaction with the size of their social support network and depression. These women report that they do not know what to say and that they worry that other new mothers will not like them (Wenzel, 2011). As we have seen in the other sections on relationship challenges, cognitive restructuring can be used to identify, evaluate, and modify cognitions that would prevent women from approaching interactions with others in an effective, healthy manner. However, communication skills training can be used to help clients acquire and practice skills that would increase the likelihood of developing meaningful friendships.

When perinatal clients hope to develop new relationships and see a need to develop communication skills, several different content areas can be addressed. Some women benefit from practicing ways from making small talk with other new mothers. Other women benefit from considering strategies for asking other new mothers to get together for an event like a play date. Still others struggle with self-disclosure and benefit from consideration of socially appropriate information to share when getting to know another person. Cognitive behavioral therapists use the cognitive case conceptualization, particularly the client's history of relationships and interactions with others, as a guide for determining appropriate points of intervention on an individualized basis.

Conclusion

Quality close relationships are essential for perinatal women. They provide an array of social supports, including emotional support and, perhaps most importantly, tangible support as they recover from childbirth and negotiate the transition to parenthood. When there is conflict, tension, or disconnection in close relationships, it can be especially devastating for perinatal women.

Perinatal women often need assertiveness skills now, more than any time in their lives. They need to communicate effectively and efficiently to meet the constantly changing demands of a new child. There is much less time than they had before having children to deal with the aftereffects of misinterpretation and miscommunication. The principles and practice of assertiveness, as described in this chapter, can help perinatal women to set boundaries, make requests, say no to requests, and express their opinion more proactively and confidently than they may have been able to do in the past. This skill set can generalize to a wide array of relationship contexts, including the relationship with the partner, extended family members, friends, and other new mothers.

The acquisition of effective communication skills takes practice. It is a complex process that requires the development of skills along with effective problem solving and cognitive restructuring to address unhelpful thoughts that impede the delivery of strategic communication. Early on, many clients become discouraged that their attempts at effective communication did not go as planned, either because the person on the receiving end did not respond as they had hoped, or because they were caught off guard by something the other said and had difficulty regaining their footing. Communication skills training requires patience and an openness to feedback from others in order to hone one's ability to use these skills. Each success experience builds confidence in perinatal clients that they can rely on as they approach increasingly sensitive and difficult interactions.

11

RELAPSE PREVENTION AND THE COMPLETION OF TREATMENT

Clients begin CBT with the understanding that there is an end to treatment. The idea is for them to become their own cognitive behavioral therapist so that they do not need to continue to attend psychotherapy sessions on a regular basis. Many clients, like Lyla in Chapter 5, express relief that there is an end to treatment because with young children, regular attendance in psychotherapy requires a great deal of energy and coordination. Thus, eventually clients will move from the middle phase of treatment, in which they are actively developing cognitive and behavioral strategies to understand and address their life problems, to the late phase of treatment.

The main focus of the late phase of treatment is on *relapse prevention*, which we define as the process by which clients consolidate their learning; demonstrate how they can apply it to future challenges, stressors, and disappointments, and recognize when they are experiencing a recurrence of emotional distress and when resumption of professional treatment might be warranted. In this chapter, we consider the ways therapists know when movement into the late phase of treatment is indicated, strategies to achieve the aims of relapse prevention, and ways to wind down the course of treatment.

When is Movement into the Late Phase of Treatment Indicated?

Cognitive behavioral therapists do not unilaterally move the client into the late phase of treatment. Instead, it is a collaborative decision between the therapist and client. Nevertheless, therapists likely have a better sense of when movement toward the late phase of treatment is indicated on the basis of the data collected in treatment (e.g., from the brief mood check), as well as from their clinical experience.

A quantitative indicator that the client is ready to move into the late phase of treatment is sustained low scores obtained during the brief mood check. There is no hard-and-fast rule-of-thumb as to a precise score that a client must report in order to move into the late stage of treatment. Therapists typically base this decision not only on the absolute scores that are obtained, but also on the degree to which low scores are sustained. For example, the therapist and clients can consider moving into the late stage of treatment when depression and anxiety scores move into the low range (e.g., no higher than a 3 on the 0–10 likert scale) and when those scores are sustained for at least three weeks. However, it is important to recognize that some clients who report chronic depression and anxiety might have benefited a great deal from treatment and are ready to move toward the end of treatment, but still report mood ratings of at least moderate severity. An alternative indicator of improvement in these cases is the degree to which functioning has improved in a number of domains (e.g., parenting, occupational, interpersonal).

Another indicator of the degree to which clients are ready to move into the late phase of treatment is the rate of successful homework completion. Most clients who are ready to move into the late phase of treatment have been actively using cognitive and behavioral strategies in their lives between sessions, and they are noticing positive changes in their lives as a result of doing so. Thus, clients who move into the late stage of CBT have acquired many CBT skills and know when and how to use them on their own, without the presence of their therapist.

A more subtle indicator that the client is ready to move into the late stage of treatment is when she has little to offer for the agenda. When clients report to sessions reporting that "things have been going well" and that they "don't have anything pressing that needs to be addressed," it is a sign that the acute issue that brought them into treatment has subsided and that they are moving back to their baseline level of functioning. When this occurs, therapists can ask permission to place review of the treatment plan on the agenda. Then, collaboratively with their client, they assess the degree to which goals have been met. If all goals have been met, and there are no additional goals to add to the treatment plan, then the client is ready to move into the late phase of treatment.

Relapse Prevention

As stated previously, the major aim of the late phase of treatment is relapse prevention, in which the client reviews all that she has learned in treatment and demonstrates to herself and the therapist that she can apply these skills when needed. The three major components of relapse prevention are the: (a) consolidation of learning; (b) application of skills to future stressors, challenges, and disappointments; and (c) development of a Relapse Prevention Plan.

Consolidation of Learning

The consolidation of learning refers to the process by which clients articulate the skills that they have acquired and the cognitive behavioral principles that underlie the rationale for the use. In other words, clients not only review what they have taken away from their course of CBT, but they are able to put words to why these strategies have worked for them. When clients can put words onto these psychological principles, they have increased the likelihood that they will be able to remember and generalize these principles to new situations that occur after treatment has ended. To prepare for this relapse prevention exercise, clients often agree, for homework, to review any worksheets and notes that have accumulated before the subsequent session.

Application of Skills

Proactively thinking ahead about how clients can apply the cognitive behavioral strategies they have acquired gives clients and therapists, alike, confidence that these strategies will be able to be relied upon on the future. A systematic way to achieve this aim is to have clients engage in a series of guided imagery exercises in which they depict the way in which they could apply cognitive behavioral tools to manage distress associated with stressors, challenges, and disappointments (cf. Wenzel et al., 2009). For example, they can first close their eyes and remember the events that prompted the acute crisis that brought them into treatment. As they describe their experiences in vivid detail, they can indicate the tools that they would use to manage emotional distress as it escalates. In the following vignette, Donna engages in this exercise to indicate how she would apply what she has learned in therapy to manage her fear that she was becoming psychotic.

Therapist: Donna, would you be willing to close your eyes and describe, in great detail, the events leading up to the point at which you decided to call me and make an appointment to come in?

Donna: Yes, I can do that.

Therapist: And as you do this, I will prompt you to indicate how you would apply what you've been learning in treatment to manage the emotional distress as your concerns accumulated. And if I haven't prompted you, but you can think of a place where you would use your skills, would you be sure to speak up and show how you would do that?

Donna: Yes, definitely. [leaning her head back on the chair and closing her eyes]

Therapist: Why don't you start when you really started to notice your concerns? If you can, speak in the present tense, as if it is happening again.

Donna: OK. I'm home alone with Ellie. She is perfectly content. But I'm feeling weird. I haven't taken a shower in days, and I feel really grubby. I feel sleep-deprived even though she is sleeping pretty decently. And, then I start to feel surreal, like everything around me is a dream. I'm asking myself, "Is this really me? Is this my life? Is this even my daughter?" And I start to really freak out.

Therapist: Tell me how you would use what you've learned in therapy to deal with this experience, in the present tense, as if you're actually applying your tools.

Donna: I remember what you told me, that it's not abnormal for postpartum women to feel like they're in a dream, and that it is happening to someone else, due to the fact that they're overwhelmed by the whole transition.

Therapist: Keep going. Tell me how that works, in the present tense.

Donna: I feel a little bit better, but I'm still bothered by this nagging feeling that something is really wrong. I still wonder whether I have postpartum psychosis.

Therapist: Describe how you feel when you're wondering whether you have postpartum psychosis.

Donna: I'm uncomfortable. I start to wonder whether my husband ever should have married me. I start to wonder whether Ellie would be better off with someone else as her mother. Ick. I start to feel creepy crawlies all over me. I just want to jump out of my own skin.

Therapist: How do you cope with these uncomfortable sensations?

Donna: I just experience them, not trying to push them away. I know that my mind is running wild and these thoughts are not facts. I try to breathe into them, rather than push them away, because when I push them away, I know they will just get stronger.

Therapist: And what happens, as you are sitting with them?

Donna: They hold less power over me. [breathes in] OK, I'm better now. This is just the way my OCD is showing myself right now.

In addition to encouraging clients to walk through how they would use their cognitive behavioral strategies to manage emotional distress associated with the events that led them to present for treatment, therapists also ask their clients to do the same exercise for a reasonable future challenge, stressor, disappointment, or crisis. The procedure is the same—clients close their eyes, vividly imaging the scenario, describe it in the present tense as if it were currently happening, and describe the cognitive behavioral tools that they would use to intervene. Consider how

Wendy's therapist conducted this exercise when Wendy was in the late phase of treatment.

Therapist: Is it OK if we do the same exercise, but this time applying it to a challenge that you can reasonably expect to experience in the future?

Wendy: I think that would be a good idea. I've come a long way. But this is winter now. In the summer, there are a lot more activities that the kids are going to want to do. And our annual vacation to the shore. I still get nervous thinking about that because there are so many ways for the kids to get hurt. Being unsupervised near the water. The amusement rides on the boardwalk. Et cetera, et cetera.

Therapist: That's a perfect example for us to focus on. Are you willing to close your eyes and describe the scene to me in the present tense?

Wendy: [takes a deep breath] OK, here we go. [closes eyes] We're at the shore. The little one has just turned 1 and is toddling around. All of my attention goes to him. The older ones, my gosh, they're 3½ and 5, and they're ecstatic to be at the beach. They can't wait to get in the water.

Therapist: What is running through your mind?

Wendy: My husband needs to be right on top of them, or one of them will get sucked out by the current.

Therapist: What is the effect of focusing on that thought?

Wendy: I snap at my husband, get on his case for not being attentive enough. I'm trying to be present with the little one, but I keep looking up to make sure my husband is watching the older ones. I'm getting more and more nervous, and I'm not feeling like this is a vacation at all.

Therapist: Show me how our work will influence the manner in which you handle your anxiety from this point on.

Wendy: [takes a deep breath] First of all, I know I am falling into the trap of emotional reasoning. I'm always a bit on edge when I take the kids to an unfamiliar place. But, because I'm on edge, I'm taking that as an indication that something bad will happen.

Therapist: How do you feel after you acknowledge that?

Wendy: Still pretty wound up, actually.

Therapist: Fair enough. Keep going.

Wendy: OK. Every time I look up, I see that my husband is with them. Maybe he lets them run a little bit further away from him than I would, but he's on top of it. It's not like he's lying on the beach, just sipping a piña colada and getting a suntan.

192

He's never let anything bad happen to them before. Plus, the beach is packed, so if something happened, surely some other adult would see what is going on and come to their rescue [pauses] And, also, this is the third summer we've gone to the shore. [laughs sarcastically] No one in the family has drowned in the ocean yet.

Therapist: On our 0–10 scale, with 10 being the most anxiety you've ever experienced, how much anxiety are you experiencing as a result of applying your thought modification tools?

Wendy: It's definitely down. Like a 4. But I don't know if I'll ever get to a 0.

Therapist: And what would you tell a friend about that if she gave you the same rating?

Wendy: [sighs] That it's good to have some anxiety. We will never totally rid ourselves of anxiety. It's best to use our anxiety as a signal to make whatever adjustments we need to make, and know that we can still go on with our lives, doing whatever it is that we value, in spite of the anxiety.

Therapist: Do you continue to snap at your husband and watch him like a hawk?

Wendy: No, I'm relaxing a bit and enjoying watching the little guy experience the beach for the first time in his life.

Cognitive behavioral therapists always ask clients' permission to engage in these exercises before beginning them. Although most clients are readily agreeable to engaging in the exercise, at times, clients have a negative reaction to the guided imagery exercise and would prefer not to participate in it. Although this can be indicative of avoidance behavior, cognitive behavioral therapists do not force the guided imagery exercise on their clients. It is always administered in a collaborative manner.

In addition, cognitive behavioral therapists leave time at the end of guided imagery exercises for debriefing. Debriefing consists of: (a) conducting another brief mood check to ensure that the client is not leaving the session in a high state of negative affect; and (b) asking questions to facilitate the consolidation of learning, such as encouraging the client to articulate what she learned from this exercise and what she will remember about it when she is faced with a stressor or disappointment in the future. If the acute crisis that brought the client into treatment involved suicidal ideation, the therapist assesses for suicidal ideation following the completion of guided imagery exercises and addresses it before she leaves the session. At times, clients benefit from a breathing or relaxation exercise before leaving the session in order to manage any residual negative affect and achieve a sense of groundedness.

Relapse Prevention Plan

In addition to articulating the way in which they will apply the tools that they have learned in treatment, clients also compose a written document, called the *Relapse Prevention Plan*, that summarizes this information in a single place. Not only does the act of writing a Relapse Prevention Plan facilitate the consolidation of learning, it also ensures that clients have a resource that they can consult quickly when they experience emotional distress after therapy has been completed. The rationale behind the Relapse Prevention Plan is that it is a user-friendly resource that prompts clients to remember the highlights of therapy so that they can continue to cope effectively with stress and disappointment.

Figure 11.1 is an example of a Relapse Prevention Plan. It consists of five sections. In the first section, clients list warning signs that raise the possibility that they might be headed for a relapse in symptoms. These warning signs can be behavioral (e.g., drinking too much), cognitive (e.g., thoughts racing through my mind), or emotional (e.g., very depressed) in nature. Some clients list observations from concerned others (e.g., my mother comments that I'm not taking care of myself). It is hoped that clients notice these warning signs before they are overcome with a significant relapse in depression or anxiety, so that they can take skillful action to center themselves and continue to use psychologically healthy habits. Figure 11.2 displays Lyla's Relapse Prevention Plan. The warning signs that she recorded were the four most salient symptoms of the depression that prompted her to seek treatment.

Second, clients list tools and coping strategies that they can practice on their own when they notice one or more of the warning signs. Most of these tools and strategies will be ones that were introduced and practiced in therapy. Here, the client is able to identify and reflect on the tools and coping strategies that were the most useful for her in managing her emotional distress. Clients are encouraged to be detailed in their description of the coping strategies so that they can obtain maximal benefit just by reading the Relapse Prevention Plan. For example, writing "Use thought modification" has the potential to be less helpful than writing "Use thought modification: Step 1 = identify unhelpful thought that is running through my mind, Step 2 = examine the evidence that supports and refutes that thought, Step 3 = construct a balanced response to that thought on the basis of my questioning." Clients can be as creative as they would like to be when developing their list of effective coping strategies. For example, some clients refer to this part of the Relapse Prevention Plan as a "Top 5" or "Top 10" list. On her Relapse Prevention Plan, Lyla included the steps for cognitive restructuring as well as some conclusions that she had drawn on the basis of the behavioral activation and sleep hygiene work that she had done earlier in the course of treatment.

RELAPSE PREVENTION PLAN
Warning signs that tell me I might be experiencing a relapse:
How to cope with the warning signs on my own:
People I can call for support:
How I know when professional help is needed:
Names and contact information for professional help:

Figure 11.1 Relapse Prevention Plan.

RELAPSE PREVENTION PLAN
Warning signs that tell me I might be experiencing a relapse: • Napping during the day • Staying up all night • Inactivity • Persistent worries that others are judging me or that I will get in trouble
How to cope with the warning signs on my own: • Remember that activity makes me feel better and gives me more energy. Take Jack to the park or to the Y. • Don't nap, even if I am tired. Remember that this will help me to feel pressure to sleep that night. • Use my thought modification tools: STEP 1 = Identify an unhelpful automatic thought; STEP 2 = Ask myself whether there is evidence to support the thought and whether there are any other explanations; STEP 3 = Develop a more balanced thought by answering those questions.
People I can call for support: • Luanne (333-333-3333) • Rita (444-444-4444) • Ally (555-555-5555)
How I know when professional help is needed: • When I decide to sleep instead of using my CBT tools • When I can't control my crying • When I know I'm not making the best decisions for Jack
Names and contact information for professional help: • Therapist: Dr. Wenzel (267-746-0566) • Support Group: The Postpartum Stress Center (610.525.7527) • Psychiatrist: Dr. Goldman (777-777-7777)

Figure 11.2 Sample Relapse Prevention Plan.

Third, clients list the names and phone numbers of people who they can contact for support. Inclusion of phone numbers is crucial in order to have access to contact information in the event of a technological problem, such as a cell phone being without battery power. Some clients express discomfort in contacting others to disclose that they are struggling or in a crisis. In these instances, clients can be educated about the importance of interpersonal relationships in buffering them from emotional distress (see Chapter 10) and simply contact one or more of these individuals for the purpose of experiencing a connection, rather than obtaining specific help in addressing the warning signs that they had noticed. Simply having a conversation with a close friend or a family member facilitates a sense of belonging and of being cared for, even if that person is not providing specific assistance with a stress or crisis. Lyla listed three people in this section of her relapse prevention plan: (a) her sister, (b) a close friend from childhood, and (c) a mother whom she met at the park and to whom she was feeling increasingly close. Although Lyla indicated that she would only feel comfortable disclosing her emotional distress to her sister, she recognized that her sister might not always be available to talk when Lyla needs her, and that interacting with one or both of her other friends would give her a sense of acceptance that could serve as a buffer against depression.

In the fourth section of the Relapse Prevention Plan, clients list the indicators that suggest it is time to contact a healthcare professional. Clients are encouraged to refrain from all-or-nothing thinking in the event that they observe these signs and resume treatment, as it does not necessarily mean that they have experienced a full-fledged relapse and are back to "square one." In fact, part of a balanced response to automatic thoughts associated with the discouragement of relapse is that recognizing when to seek help is an indicator of strength and wisdom. In addition, clients can be helped to recognize that seeking professional help is not necessarily equivalent to having to undertaking another full course of CBT. It could be that they simply need a few "booster" sessions (described below), in which they obtain support from their therapist and review the tools and strategies that had been helpful for them in the past. Lyla identified the point at which she would resume professional services as one in which she stopped making sound choices for herself and for her son. She also identifying "crying all the time" as an indicator, as she often experienced a sense of uncontrollability associated with frequent crying bouts that correlated with the severity of her depression.

Finally, at the bottom of the Relapse Prevention Plan, clients write the names and contact information of the professionals that they would contact if they decide that additional professional help is warranted. These contacts might include the cognitive behavioral therapist, the psychiatrist, and other mental health professionals who provided services (e.g., group facilitator). In addition, clients can list numbers for hotlines and crisis services, such as the National Suicide Prevention Hotline (1–800–273-TALK [8255]).

In addition to the completion of the Relapse Prevention Plan, therapists work with clients to decide the best location in which to keep it.

The Relapse Prevention Plan will only be helpful if clients are able to use them in times of need. Some clients keep it with their other therapy materials; others keep it in a readily accessible location, such as in the drawer of a nightstand or in the glove compartment of the car. Many clients keep important information in their smartphones, so they type the components of the Relapse Prevention Plan into the notes function of their devices.

Completion of Treatment

As the late phase continues, therapists work with clients to prepare for the completion of treatment. The completion of treatment can mean many things. Many women believe that they received ample benefit from a course of CBT that is between 12 and 16 sessions long. Other women present for treatment in crisis with issues that require immediate attention (e.g., suicidal ideation, decompensation). However, during the course of treatment they acknowledge longer-standing issues (e.g., marital discord) that provided a context for the crisis to emerge during the transition to parenthood. In these cases, they move from an "acute" phase of treatment to a "continuation" phase of treatment in order to address these contextual difficulties (cf. Wenzel et al., 2009). For example, the continuation phase could involve the cognitive behavioral treatment of traumatic stress associated with childhood sexual abuse, couple's therapy, or family therapy to address issues with older children. Still other women have longstanding difficulties (e.g., chronic medical illness, Axis II pathology) that are not easily resolved within 12 to 16 sessions and that require ongoing treatment. For these women, CBT may continue for many months and even years in order to address longstanding, and sometimes contradictory, core beliefs that perpetuate emotional distress (A. T. Beck, Freeman, Davis, & Associates, 2004). After the acute phase of treatment, they may meet with their therapist on an occasional basis (e.g., monthly, every six weeks) for maintenance.

Tapering

CBT does not typically end abruptly; clients agree to taper their sessions near the end of the middle phase of treatment or during the late phase of treatment. For example, a client might be seen on a weekly basis for 12 weeks, then be seen on a biweekly basis for another 4 sessions, and then be seen on a monthly basis for the last 2 sessions. There is no specific rule-of-thumb to follow when tapering sessions; the decision is guided by the client's individualized cognitive case conceptualization and the feasibility of regular attendance on the basis of her life circumstances, and it is made collaboratively between the therapist and client.

Consider the four cases that have been followed throughout this book. Tara, whose longstanding generalized anxiety had escalated to panic attacks and who suffered from postpartum depression, attended 12 weekly sessions and 8 biweekly sessions until she moved out of the area. Lyla, who had chronic depression that had persisted throughout pregnancy and the postpartum period as well as social anxiety disorder and many Axis II features, attended 24 weekly sessions, 12 biweekly sessions, and 8 sessions separated by 4 to 6 weeks. Donna, who had longstanding OCD, and had participated in CBT in the past, attended 10 weekly sessions, 4 biweekly sessions, and 2 monthly sessions. Wendy, who experienced an exacerbation of GAD during pregnancy that persisted into the postpartum period, attended 8 CBT sessions separated by 1 to 2 weeks during pregnancy and resumed occasional sessions when she was 2 months postpartum.

Booster Sessions

Many clients like to know that there is an opportunity to reconnect with their therapist following the completion of treatment and update their therapist on their lives. *Booster sessions* allow the opportunity for such a reconnection. They are typically scheduled 3 or 6 months after the last session in the course of treatment. The typical agenda for a booster session is the client's description of successes that she has achieved, especially using the tools and strategies that she learned in treatment, as well as how she coped with any stressors, challenges, and disappointments that occurred since her final CBT session. At the booster session, the therapist and client can evaluate the degree to which gains made in treatment have been maintained. They also assess the need for any continued services. Some clients who continue to report emotional distress opt to re-initiate a short course of CBT (e.g., 4 sessions) as a "tune-up" and review of the work that they had done during the full course of CBT.

The option of scheduling a booster session was presented to all four of the perinatal women who have been followed in this book. It was not feasible for Tara to schedule a booster session because her husband got a job out of state, and they moved out of the area. However, she was invited to contact her therapist to inform her of any successes, as well as to contact her therapist if she recognized warning signs indicative of the need for additional professional help. Tara indeed initiated contact with her therapist on one occasion a year and a half after the completion of treatment to inform her that she was pregnant with her second child. At that time, she indicated that she had experienced minimal anxiety and depression and was continuing to use the tools and strategies that she had learned in treatment.

Lyla scheduled a booster session three months after the completion of her treatment. Her life circumstances were very different at the time of that visit than they were when she initiated treatment, as she had gone back to work full-time, and she was pregnant with her second child. She reported that she noticed some automatic thoughts about her coworkers that were indicative of her old patterns of thinking (e.g., "The other person on my shift doesn't like me and wishes someone else was working with her"). However, she recognized that these were thoughts, not necessarily facts, and she was able to apply cognitive restructuring to view her work situation in an adaptive manner so that she did not react in a manner that would create tension or conflict. Because Lyla had a long history of depression and had discontinued her antidepressant medication due to the pregnancy, she and her therapist decided to initiate a maintenance course of CBT during pregnancy and the first few months postpartum with monthly visits.

Donna opted not to schedule a booster session for three reasons: (a) she lived a significant distance from her therapist; (b) finances were tight; and (c) due to the chronic nature of her OCD, she expected that she would probably experience another stressor in her life that would prompt the recurrence of OCD-like thoughts and behaviors that would then require a CBT "tune-up." Donna's therapist recommended several contemporary CBT books written for consumers and invited her to provide occasional updates on her status. Donna emailed her therapist approximately every other month, indicating that she was getting a great deal out of the reading and that she and her husband were planning to try for another child.

As stated previously, Wendy took a break from therapy around the time she had her baby and resumed treatment at 2 months postpartum. She had an additional 4 biweekly sessions. At that time, she believed that she needed some time on her own to implement the tools to achieve the cognitive and behavioral changes that she hoped to make. She scheduled a booster session for six months later but cancelled it, indicating that she was feeling good and that CBT had made a significant difference in her life.

Referral for Other Services

At times, cognitive behavioral therapists make referrals for other services. In some instances, clients need a higher level of care, so they are referred to intensive programs such as residential treatment, partial hospitalization, or day treatment. Other clients are dealing with specialized problems (e.g., alcohol or drug use disorders, eating disorders), and they are referred to programs to address those issues before they return for CBT for depression and anxiety. If conjoint therapy is needed, and the cognitive behavioral therapist does not specialize in couple's and family therapy, then clients can be referred to other therapists for these purposes.

Conclusion

CBT is a treatment that is characterized by three distinct phases: an early phase, a middle phase, and a late phase. Clients enter into the late phase of treatment when: (a) their mood ratings have decreased to a level of no more than mild distress (and have been sustained for a period of time); (b) they have met their treatment goals; and (c) they have demonstrated the ability to successfully apply cognitive and behavioral tools and strategies to problems and challenges that they encounter between sessions. The late phase of treatment assumes a relapse prevention focus, such that clients consolidate the learning that they have acquired, use guided imagery to demonstrate how they would apply cognitive and behavioral tools and strategies to previous and future stressors, and develop a Relapse Prevention Plan that they can consult when they experience an increase in emotional distress after treatment has ended.

The decision to move toward the completion of treatment is one that is made collaboratively by the therapist and client. When clients enter into CBT, they know that it was developed as a time-sensitive treatment and that there will eventually be an end to treatment. Nevertheless, therapists do not abruptly end treatment without the clients' involvement in determining the specific way in which treatment will end. When therapists examine the data that have been collected across the course of treatment and see that clients' depression and anxiety have decreased significantly, they ask clients' permission to introduce these observations as an agenda item and discuss their implications with the clients. If clients agree that they have achieved what they had hoped to achieve in treatment, then they work with their therapist toward developing a plan for tapering the frequency of sessions.

Not all clients want to end treatment. Many perinatal clients view their hour in therapy as sacred, away from the chaos of small children, demanding jobs, and their household responsibilities. They have a close connection with their therapist that might be unlike any other connection in their current lives. Many perinatal women experience a loss of their sense of self, as it was before they had children, and losing the therapeutic relationship can feel like another manifestation of this loss.

In these instances, it is important to critically examine the function that the therapeutic relationship plays and whether there are any disadvantages associated with continuing with treatment. In most cases, the disadvantages are minimal, although it is important therapists revisit the treatment plan with their clients and ensure that they are working toward a well-articulated aim. For example, some clients who complete a course of CBT for depression and anxiety view themselves as having gotten back to their usual level of functioning. However, they begin to realize that their usual level of functioning is nevertheless below their potential, or inconsistent with the hopes and dreams that they have for their lives. Continuing into another phase of treatment allows clients to redefine what is meant by usual functioning and mobilize their cognitive and behavioral skills to achieve quality of life and fulfillment (Frisch, 2006). In addition, many clients find it useful to go through a course of mindfulness-based cognitive therapy (Segal, Williams, & Teasdale, 2013), a relapse prevention program that helps clients to adopt a lifestyle in which they live intentionally, in the moment, and without judgment.

It may be detrimental to continue with therapy when the client demonstrates a great deal of dependence on the therapist, or when it is clear that the support she receives from the therapeutic relationship interferes with her ability to obtain support from others in her social support network. Even in these instances, the therapist does not unilaterally end treatment, but instead understands this behavior in light of the client's cognitive case conceptualization and uses cognitive behavioral strategies to address them. For example, clients might have inaccurate, exaggerated, or otherwise unhelpful thoughts about the end of treatment, and cognitive restructuring can be used to evaluate and modify them so that they are more balanced. Therapists can also use a behavioral experiment, such that they schedule more time than usual between sessions in order for the client to test her ability to use cognitive and behavioral tools without the direct coaching of the therapist. In other words, cognitive behavioral therapists are cognizant of the function of therapist and client behaviors within the therapeutic relationship, understand them in light of the cognitive case conceptualization, and set up strategic interventions aimed to facilitate a corrective learning experience. All of this is done in a sensitive supportive manner that maintains the therapeutic relationship.

12

SPECIAL CONSIDERATIONS AND FUTURE DIRECTIONS

Increasingly, there is interest in and demand for CBT for perinatal distress. CBT's problem-focused, time-sensitive nature is attractive for perinatal clients who want immediate relief, as well as for insurance companies who reimburse for a limited number of sessions. Perinatal women who complete a course of CBT develop skills that will extend far beyond the transition to parenthood. By modeling healthy approaches to coping with stress and disappointment, perinatal women who have received a course of CBT have the potential to mitigate any adverse effects of depression and anxiety on their children. They can show their children how to tolerate emotional distress. They can demonstrate to their children how to cope with ambiguity when life does not go as planned. They can model tools for solving problems effectively.

As described in Chapter 3, although a large body of literature supports the efficacy and effectiveness of CBT for depressed and anxious adults in general, the evidence-based for the efficacy and effectiveness of CBT for perinatal distress is mixed. The majority of the studies examining CBT for perinatal distress have examined versions of CBT that are of a prescribed number of sessions (e.g., eight sessions), that have a defined curriculum describing topics to be covered in each session, and that focus mainly on specific techniques. There is a heavy emphasis on psychoeducation and behavioral skills training in these protocols, and many are delivered in a group format. Although cognitive restructuring is usually included in these protocols, it is not the central feature, nor is it applied across several sessions to underlying beliefs about the self, others, and motherhood. Results from these studies raise the possibility that the approaches that have been evaluated in the literature thus far, while logical, intuitive, and attractive on many levels, might not include the elements that perinatal women need in excess of routine care.

What we have described in this book is a Beckian cognitive behavioral approach to the treatment of perinatal distress. As we stated earlier, Aaron T. Beck is regarded as the "father" of cognitive therapy (now regarded as synonymous with CBT). Although he incorporated many skills-based techniques into cognitive therapy, even more foundational to his approach was the cognitive case conceptualization. Using conceptualization-driven CBT, information about clients' presenting problems and psychosocial histories is used to develop an intricate understanding of the development, maintenance, and exacerbation of the client's clinical presentations in light of cognitive behavioral theory. This conceptualization, in turn, drives the specific strategic interventions that the therapist proposes to the client. What this means is that the Beckian approach to CBT is individualized to each client on the basis of the cognitive case conceptualization, so that every course of CBT looks a bit different. It is anything but a "one size fits all" approach. We believe that this approach is ideal for perinatal women, who present for treatment with their powerful and unique beliefs about the meaning of motherhood, best parenting practices, and family roles. As with any client, conceptualization-driven CBT is molded to the needs, strengths, and challenges associated with each clinical presentation. The effects of strategic interventions are carefully tracked across sessions to ensure that clients are benefitting from them. It could be the case that the centrality of the cognitive case conceptualization was missing from the CBT protocols that have been evaluated in the literature thus far.

It also is surprising that many of the group CBT protocols did not fare better relative to routine care, in light of qualitative research emphasizing women's perception that group therapy confers unique benefits by providing a sense of community and social support to women with perinatal distress (O'Mahen et al., 2012). Another hypothesis to explain the mixed empirical findings evaluating the effectiveness of CBT for perinatal samples is that the skills-based group treatments did not foster a strong enough therapeutic alliance to facilitate change above and beyond routine care. Perinatal psychology experts have long emphasized the key role that the therapeutic relationship plays in the healing of women with postpartum depression (e.g., Kleiman, 2009). The more cognitive behavioral groups feel like a "class," the less opportunity there is to attend to the therapeutic relationship with individual clients. Fortunately, individual psychotherapy maximizes the opportunity to nurture the therapeutic relationship. The development of the therapeutic alliance is an important component of Beckian CBT, especially when the cognitive case conceptualization suggests that a client who has had formative experiences that contributed to the development of unhelpful beliefs about relationships with others.

From Theory and Research to Practice

A conceptualization-driven approach to CBT for perinatal distress has yet to be evaluated in the literature. A rigorous randomized controlled trial comparing conceptualization-driven CBT and routine care would be a welcome addition to the body of research on CBT for perinatal distress. However, the absence of such a study does not mean that conceptualization-based CBT cannot be implemented with perinatal women, nor does it mean that its delivery is not informed by evidence. There is no reason to believe that the literature on CBT for adults in general cannot be generalized to perinatal women, as perinatal women share many of the same characteristics as the people who comprised the samples recruited for these studies. A significant reason pregnant women are sometimes excluded from studies examining CBT for adults with emotional distress has nothing to do with the non-applicability of CBT to this population, but rather the logistical facts that therapy could be interrupted by the birth of a child, which is not ideal for a clinical trial, or that therapy is being compared to medication.

Delivering conceptualization-based CBT in an evidence-based manner also does not require that a therapist must deliver any specific CBT technique in a specific way or at a specific time. It requires that the therapist begin developing a cognitive case conceptualization from the first visit and then revise it, collaboratively, over time (Kuyken et al., 2009). In addition, it requires that the therapist think critically about strategic interventions that follow logically from the conceptualization, identify their function and mechanism of change, and implement them collaboratively and in their entirety (Wenzel, 2013). Therapists who deliver conceptualization-driven CBT are aware of clients' cognitions that might be exacerbating emotional distress or interfering with progress in treatment, even if they are not addressed using a tool like the thought records. They are aware of behavioral patterns that might be maintaining emotional distress even if they are not addressed using a tool like an activity log. Conceptualization-driven CBT captures the spirit of CBT without being mechanistic or rigid overly relying on techniques. In other words, there is nothing that says that the therapist *must* use a tool like a thought record, or that homework *must* be done in a certain way. Throughout the course of treatment, an equal balance is maintained between strategic and flexible cognitive behavioral intervention and the nurturing of a supportive therapeutic relationship (Wenzel et al., 2011).

Above all, cognitive behavioral therapists function as true practitioner-scientists. This means that they: (a) have a working knowledge of the literature on psychotherapy efficacy, effectiveness, and mechanisms of change and are able to translate that knowledge in a an understandable and meaningful way to clients; (b) monitor the implementation of strategic interventions to know whether they are achieving their desired aims; and (c) gather objective data throughout the course of treatment to monitor progress and revise or amend strategic interventions. In other words, they take an empirical approach to their therapeutic work. Thus, until the Beckian approach to CBT has been evaluated in the literature, practitioner-scientists will collect their own "data" from their clients across the course of treatment and use those data to make informed clinical decisions in collaboration with their clients.

Special Issues

The CBT strategies described in this book are those that are commonly used to treat depression and anxiety in adult clients, adapted slightly in some cases to meet the demands of new motherhood. Many therapists who treat perinatal clients find that additional issues arise that require attention. Three common issues include clients' struggle over whether or not to take psychotropic medication, the ruling out of postpartum psychosis, and the need to address suicidal ideation. Each of these topics is addressed in this section.

To Medicate or Not To Medicate

Perinatal clients with depression and/or anxiety are often faced with the decision of whether or not to take psychotropic medication. The official guidelines from the American College of Obstetrics and Gynecology are that psychotherapy should be the first-line treatment for symptoms of mild severity and that psychotropic medications should be used, either alone or in conjunction with psychotherapy, for symptoms of moderate to severe severity (Yonkers et al., 2009). Although the "gut reaction" of many women is that they want to avoid at all costs taking medications during pregnancy or while breastfeeding, the decision is a complex one that requires careful thought. The value of pharmacotherapy cannot be overstated in certain cases.

It is true that psychotropic medications cross the placenta and can be detected in breast milk, meaning that the fetus or infant will be exposed to the medication that his or her mother is taking. However, many of these medications are categorized by the Food and Drug Administration (FDA) as Category C, meaning that there *may* be a risk of adverse effects in a fetus that is exposed to a medication, but there are no well-designed studies with human subjects that have demonstrated this, and the benefits of taking the medication may outweigh the risks. Even medications that are labeled as Category D, meaning that research has indeed shown that there are adverse effects on the fetus, might still be indicated during pregnancy if the benefit of taking them outweigh the risks of not taking them. The term "adverse effects" has many meanings, and adverse effects need not be those that last indefinitely, that affect the long-term prognosis of the infant, or that are life-threatening. The US government has not published an official guide to categorize risk of taking medications while breastfeeding, so many practitioners heed the guide developed by the renowned professor of pediatrics Dr. Thomas Hale (2012), which includes five categories ranging from "safer" to take while nursing to "contraindicated." Most of the medications used to treat depression and anxiety fall in the third category, "moderately safe," meaning either that there are no studies that have examined adverse effects in nursing infants or that studies have shown that adverse effects are minimal and non-threatening.

A vast literature has documented the effects of medications to treat depression and anxiety in perinatal women, and it is generally concluded that many of the antidepressants that have been developed over the past 25 years (e.g., serotonin reuptake inhibitors [SRIs]), which are typically used to treat depression and anxiety, are safe to take during both pregnancy and the postpartum period (Wenzel & Stuart, 2011). If studies indeed find differences in the infants that were and were not exposed to antidepressants during pregnancy, the differences are small, and the averages for the babies exposed to antidepressants are usually still in the healthy range (Nonacs, Cohen, Viguera, & Mogielnicki, 2005). These are broad generalizations, and there are some exceptions; for example, some (but not all) studies have found a slight increase in the rate of cardiovascular defects in infants exposed to paroxetine during pregnancy (e.g., Cole, Ephoss, Cosmatos, & Walker, 2007), which led to the FDA reclassifying this medication as Category D rather than Category C. Thus, practitioners and consumers, alike, should be encouraged to read about the latest research on any particular medication under consideration and educate themselves about the safety profiles of newer medicines that have not yet been evaluated in rigorous empirical research. The point we make here is that the decision to use medications during pregnancy or the postpartum period should be made on the basis of factual information (e.g., data from research studies, pharmacokinetics of the particular medication under consideration), rather than on fears that are unfounded. Perinatal women should work closely with a prescribing professional (e.g., a psychiatrist) to evaluate this factual information and determine what is right for them, given their clinical presentation, personal and family psychiatric history, response to previous courses of treatment, and preferences (Wenzel & Stuart, 2011; Yonkers et al., 2009).

Safety considerations are only one part of the equation when evaluating whether or not to take psychotropic medications. Women and their healthcare providers must also consider the results from research examining the efficacy of medications in treating perinatal distress—and, surprisingly, this literature is quite small. Sharma and Sommerdyk (2013) recently conducted a meta-analysis of six randomized controlled trials (RCTs), three of which were placebo-controlled, in the treatment of postpartum depression. Results indicated that only one of the three placebo-controlled study demonstrated superior efficacy of antidepressants and that adding antidepressant medication to psychotherapy did not enhance efficacy. Attrition rates were higher than in large RCTs examining anti-depressant medication for adults in general (e.g., Warden et al., 2007). There are a number of reasons that could account for these findings, such as that fact that, in most of the studies, women received only a low dos-age of the medication. Moreover, postpartum depression is often accom-panied by significant anxiety, and research has shown that comorbid depressive and anxious clinical presentations take longer to treatment with antidepressants (Hendrick, Altshuler, & Strouse, 2000). In all, no firm conclusions can be drawn from this small literature that is in its infancy, but the present state of this research suggests that psychotropic medications for perinatal distress are far from a panacea and that psycho-therapy will continue to play a central role in its treatment.

Many therapists who practice CBT are not prescribing profession-als; thus, referrals are often in order. However, non-prescribing cogni-tive behavioral therapists can nevertheless play an important role as perinatal women decide whether to take medication for their emotional distress. For example, therapists can help these clients to identify, eval-uate, and modify automatic thoughts about medication that are either inaccurate (e.g., "My baby will be deformed") or unhelpful (e.g., "I'm weak because I have to take medicine" or "Why bother to try medicine? It won't work"). They can work with clients to engage in a systematic advantages-disadvantages analysis of taking medications once factual information about adverse effects has been identified. They can encour-age effective problem solving to optimize medication use in light of their current life circumstances (e.g., pumping breast milk at times in which there is the lowest dosage of the medication in one's system). They can use a strong therapeutic relationship to provide support and empathy to women who find themselves in a position in which they choose to take medication despite the fact that they do not want to do so. In addition, therapists can maintain close contact with the prescribing professional to achieve a collaborative "teamwork" approach to optimize care for the client.

Postpartum Psychosis

As was stated in Chapter 1, postpartum psychosis is a serious condition that occurs in approximately 1 out of every 1,000 births (Jones & Craddock, 2001). It is characterized by bizarre and out-of-character behavior, con-fusional states, and mood swings (both elation and depression). Postpar-tum psychosis is considered a psychiatric emergency, and hospitalization is indicated (Robertson Blackmore, Heron, & Jones, 2015). Thus, out-patient cognitive behavioral therapists will typically not be working with women with active postpartum psychosis. However, they may be in a posi-tion in which they are the first professional who would detect postpartum psychosis and intervene so that the woman can get the appropriate level of care. It follows that cognitive behavioral therapists should have knowledge of the signs of postpartum psychosis and be able to differentiate it from other manifestations of postpartum emotional distress.

As stated previously, many perinatal women admit to their therapist that they are having "scary thoughts" (Kleiman & Wenzel, 2011). It is common for these scary thoughts to take the form of the mother enacting intentional or unintentional harm to her newborn (e.g., stabbing her baby with a knife; drowning her baby in the bathtub). The most important question that therapists use to differentiate whether these thoughts are consistent with postpartum psychosis versus consistent with postpartum obsessive compulsive symptoms (or disorder) is "Are these thoughts ego-syntonic, or are these thoughts ego-dystonic?" An *ego-syntonic* thought is one that is not viewed as alarming or bizarre by the person experiencing them; in fact, the thought might seem quite logical and consistent with her character. In contrast, when a thought is *ego-dystonic*, the person is alarmed, and even mortified, that she has the thought. She often believes that something is quite wrong with her and afraid that she will do something to act on the thought. Thus, if a perinatal woman expresses significant distress at having a thought of harm to her child, then she likely is not suffering from postpartum psychosis.

In addition, therapists consider other factors when ruling out a diagnosis of postpartum psychosis. For example, research suggests that postpartum psychosis typically has its onset in the first few weeks postpartum (Heron, Robertson Blackmore, McGuinness, Craddock, & Jones, 2007), whereas other manifestations of postpartum emotional distress can occur as many as 12 months following the birth of a child. If a new mother with scary thoughts presents for treatment when her newborn is several months old, it is unlikely that she is struggling with postpartum psychosis. Furthermore, because postpartum psychosis is likely to be a manifestation of bipolar disorder, an indicator that the new mother might be experiencing postpartum psychosis is a personal or family history of bipolar disorder (Robertson Blackmore et al., 2015). Finally, therapists can also be alert for other indicators of psychosis, such as hallucinations, delusions, and disorganized thinking.

Cognitive behavioral therapists might also work with women who have been released from the hospital after an episode of postpartum psychosis and are reintegrating themselves back into their families. CBT strategies such as cognitive restructuring, behavioral activation, problem solving, and communication skills training have the potential to be essential in helping these women transition back into their previous roles, as well as the new role of being a mother. CBT can also target areas of self-care to ensure that women develop good mental hygiene to avoid future decompensation. Conjoint sessions with the spouse or partner might be particularly indicated in order to clarify roles and expectations and ensure that the woman has ongoing support.

Suicidal Clients

One of the strongest protective factors against suicidal behavior is a reason to live (Linehan, Goodstein, Nielsen, & Chiles, 1983), and one of the most frequently cited reason to live by suicidal clients is one's children. Research using vital statistics data has shown that the rate of completed suicide is lower in pregnant and postpartum women, relative to non-pregnant and non-postpartum women (Samandari et al., 2011), perhaps for this reason. Nevertheless, some new mothers believe that their children would be better off without them, before they have time to cause significant damage to their child's emotional well being, and research has found that between 5.7% and 11.1% of women who had given birth within the previous three months reported thoughts of death or self-harm (Pinheiro, Da Silva, Magalhães, Horta, & Pinheiro, 2008). Thus, it behooves cognitive behavioral therapists who work with perinatal women to know how to conduct efficient and effective suicide risk assessments, how to determine whether a higher level of care is indicated, and how to apply CBT with a focus on suicide prevention.

Suicide Risk Assessment

Figure 12.1 displays risk and protective factors for suicidal acts. Although this is a summary of factors that affect the risk of suicidal behavior in adults in general, there is no reason why this cannot be applied to perinatal women. Therapists who suspect that a client is suicidal ask about frequency, duration, and intensity of suicidal thoughts (i.e., suicidal ideation). At times, suicidal ideation comes in the form of violent images or urges instead of thoughts expressed with words, so therapists should be alert for these various manifestations. In addition, therapists assess for the degree to which the client has specific intent to hurt herself. If she reports intent to hurt herself, therapists determine whether she has a specific plan to do so. The more intent that a client reports, and the more specific the plan she has to cause harm to herself, the more she is at risk of engaging in suicidal behavior (Harriss & Hawton, 2005; Harriss, Hawton, & Zahl, 2005).

Perhaps the most potent factor that predicts risk of suicidal behavior is a history of suicidal behavior (Joiner et al., 2005). According to suicidologist Thomas Joiner (2005), this is true because it demonstrates an acquired ability to enact lethal self-harm. Because human beings' self-preservation instinct is so engrained, previous experience with self-harm provides an opportunity for the person to habituate to pain and the fear of death. Even if the person has a history of non-suicidal self-injury without intent to die, she has still acquired the ability to enact lethal self-harm. This ability becomes more potent with each suicidal act (Van Orden, Witte, Gordon, Bender, & Joiner, 2008), which accounts for the

Risk Factor	Protective Factor
Previous suicide attempt (especially multiple previous suicide attempts)	Reasons for living
Suicidal ideation	Strong social support network
Suicidal intent	Participation in religious activities
Specific plan	Sense of spirituality
History of self-injurious behavior	Active participation in mental health treatment
Greater wish to die than wish to live	
Regrets failure of previous attempt	
Access to lethal means	
Family history of suicide attempts	
Major depressive disorder	
Bipolar disorder	
Alcohol or substance use disorder	
Axis II personality disorder	
Chronic medical illness	
Perceived burdensomeness	
Low belongingness	
Hopelessness	
Impulsivity	
Problem solving deficits	
Perfectionism	
History of childhood physical or sexual abuse	
Noncompliance with treatment	
Intimate partner violence (IPV)	

Figure 12.1 Risk and Protective Factors for Suicidal Acts.

fact that people who have a history of multiple suicide attempts have the highest risk for suicidal behavior, relative to people who made a single attempt or had no suicide attempt history at all (Oquendo et al., 2007).

Although the variables described to this point are perhaps the most directly related to suicidal behavior, there are a number of other risk factors that therapists can consider when they are conducting a suicide risk assessment. Nearly every mental health disorder is associated with increased suicide risk (Harris & Barraclough, 1997), as is chronic medical illness (Hughes & Kleespies, 2001). In addition, therapists can be alert for a number of psychological variables that have been demonstrated to increase the likelihood of psychological variables. For example, *low belongingness* (i.e., the perception that one is alienated from others or is not part of a group) and *perceived burdensomeness* (i.e., the perception that one is a burden on their loved ones) are associated with the sense that one will not be missed if she is dead, or even that her death is worth more to others than her life (Van Orden, Lynam, Hollar, & Joiner, 2006; Van Orden, Witte, James, et al., 2008). *Hopelessness*, or the idea that things will not improve in the future, increases the risk of eventual suicide threefold (McMillan, Gilbody, Beresford, & Neilly, 2007), especially when it is stable over the course of time (Young et al., 1996). Suicidologists have also linked impulsivity (Mann, Waternaux, Haas, & Malone, 1999), problem solving deficits (Reinecke, 2006), and perfectionism (Hewitt, Flett, Sherry, & Caelian, 2006) with suicidal ideation and behavior. Historical variables, such as a history of childhood physical or sexual abuse (Brodsky & Stanley, 2008), and current behavior, such as non-compliance with treatment, also serve as indicators of increased suicide risk.

Very little research has been conducted to identify risk factors for suicidal behavior in perinatal women. In one exception, Gold, Singh, Marcus, and Palladino (2012) compared characteristics of people who died by suicide as a function of pregnant/postpartum and non-pregnant/non-postpartum status using data from the United States National Violent Death Reporting System. Variables that were highly prevalent in all women who died by suicide were the presence of a mental health disorder, substance abuse, and some sort of crisis in the two weeks preceding the suicide. Depressed mood was elevated in the postpartum women, relative to the pregnant and non-pregnant/non-postpartum women who died by suicide. Moreover, both pregnant and postpartum women who died by suicide were characterized by higher rates of intimate partner violence (IPV) than the non-pregnant/non-postpartum women who died by suicide, which underscores our point from Chapter 1 that it is important for therapists who work with perinatal clients to assess for IPV.

Therapists who conduct suicide risk assessments are mindful not only of the variables that put people at risk of suicidal behavior, but also of variables that decrease the likelihood that a person will engage in suicidal behavior, or *protective factors*. Although there is a much smaller research literature on protective factors than there is on risk factors, the variables most frequently identified by suicidologists are conferring protection against suicidal behavior are reasons for living, a strong social support network, participation in religious services, a sense of spirituality, and active participation in mental health treatment (Nock et al., 2013). Being part of a group, whether through family, a circle of friends, or a spiritual community, guards against a sense of low belongingness. Moreover, people who are religious or spiritual often report that they would not engage in suicidal behavior because it is inconsistent with their beliefs.

It can be overwhelming to make sense of the vast array of data gathered during a suicide risk assessment, and there is no standard heuristic that yields precise estimates of suicide risk. In fact, researchers have attempted to create algorithms to predict suicide risk, only to find that they were unable to predict even one suicide (Goldstein, Black, Nasrallah, & Winokur, 1991). From a general standpoint, risk of suicidal behavior increases as the weight of a client's risk factors outweighs the weight of her protective factors (Wenzel et al., 2009). Therapists can also use their cognitive case conceptualization to aid them in determining their client's level of suicide risk. For example, a client whose core beliefs reflect chronic hopelessness, failed belongingness, or perceived burdensomeness would be regarded as someone who is at risk of suicidal behavior.

Many therapists identify three levels of suicide risk: none, moderate, or imminent (Rudd, Joiner, & Rajab, 2001). *Imminent risk* is typically defined as risk for suicidal behavior occurring in the next 24 to 48 hours and requires hospitalization. *Moderate risk*, in contrast, means that the client will be monitored for an increase in risk factor, suicidal thoughts, and suicidal behavior, and that she might need more support than weekly psychotherapy sessions. Contrary to concerns reported by many clients, moderate risk does not necessarily mean that hospitalization is required, nor does it guarantee that they will be viewed as unfit mothers. Options for managing clients at moderate risk for engaging in suicidal behavior include (but are not limited to): (a) increasing the frequency of outpatient psychotherapy sessions; (b) scheduling a telephone check-in in between sessions; or (c) informing the spouse or partner or another family member of her moderate level of risk so that they can monitor and provide support in between sessions. When therapists see their clients at moderate risk, they continue to monitor suicidal ideation and intent during the brief mood check and target their therapeutic interventions toward reducing suicide risk, as described in the next section.

CBT for Suicide Prevention

The cognitive model of suicide regards suicidal thoughts and behaviors as the primary clinical issue, rather than a symptom of another condition.

Thus, cognitive behavioral therapists who work with suicidal clients target suicide risk during an *acute* phase of treatment until it resolves, allowing them to move onto a *continuation* phase of treatment that will address other issues that are associated with poor adjustment and functional impairment (Wenzel et al., 2009). A full description of CBT for suicide prevention is beyond the scope of this book; interested readers are encouraged to consult Wenzel et al. (2009). Here, we highlight two features of the protocol that can be used with suicidal perinatal women.

A *safety plan* is a written list of prioritized coping strategies and resources that they agree to use during times of increased risk of engaging in suicidal behavior (i.e., a suicidal crisis; Stanley & Brown, 2012; Wenzel et al., 2009; see Figure 12.2). Its format is similar to the Relapse Prevention Plan described in Chapter 11. It contains six steps, with the idea that clients will move to subsequent steps on the Safety Plan if previous steps do not provide appropriate resolution. The first step is the identification of warning signs, as the Safety Plan is only effective if a client knows when to use it. Warning signs can be cognitions (e.g., "Thinking things will never get better"), emotions (e.g., "severe depression"), behaviors (e.g., "staying in bed all day"), or others' observations. Step 2 contains coping strategies that clients can do on their own to self-soothe, such as controlled breathing or muscle relaxation. Both Steps 3 and 4 list names and contact information for people to which the client can reach out. The difference is that the purpose of contacting the people listed in Step 3 is for a sense of connectedness and for a shift in the focus of attention to something pleasing and helpful, whereas the purpose of contacting the people listed in Step 4 is for specific help in managing the suicidal crisis. Clients typically include only very close friends and family in Step 4. Step 5 lists the contact information for professionals who can assist (e.g., therapist, psychiatrist), names and addresses of hospital with emergency departments, and suicide prevention crisis lines. Finally, Step 6 outlines a specific plan for safeguarding the client's environment by removing access to lethal means.

After completing the suicide risk assessment, therapists work with clients who are at elevated risk of suicidal behavior to complete a Safety Plan. If the client is in the midst of treatment, then many of the cognitive and behavioral coping strategies that she has developed can be included on the safety plan. If the client is new to the practice, she and her therapist can list some basic coping skills and then continue to add to the safety plan as she acquires additional cognitive and behavioral skills across the course of treatment. The therapist encourages the client to think ahead as to where she will keep the Safety Plan so that it is readily available when she needs it. At the time of the subsequent session, the therapist inquires as to whether the Safety Plan was used and the clients' perception of whether it was effective. If the client experienced suicidal ideation

SAFETY PLAN
STEP 1: Warning signs that I need to use the safety plan
STEP 2: Ways to cope on my own
STEP 3: People I can talk to
STEP 4: People who can help
STEP 5: Professionals who can help
STEP 6: Safeguarding my environment

Figure 12.2 Safety Plan.

Note: Compiled on the basis of guidelines put forth by Stanley & Brown (2012).

but did not consult the Safety Plan, the therapist uses problem solving to ensure that she will use it in the future. If the client experienced suicidal ideation and consulted the Safety Plan, but found it to be unhelpful, then the therapist works with the client to modify it.

All of the strategies that have been described in this book can be applied to CBT for suicide prevention. Cognitive restructuring can be used to reframe unhelpful cognitions, such as those associated with hopelessness, perceived burdensomeness, and failed belongingness. Behavioral activation can be used to ensure that the client is engaging in meaningful and valued activity, which can readily supply reasons for living. Many cognitive behavioral therapists who work with suicidal clients encourage their clients to develop a Hope Kit, or a compilation of reminders of reasons to live, such as photographs of close others, verses from religious texts, and inspirational quotations. In perinatal women, items such as ultrasound pictures, birth announcements, baby booties, and rattles can be included in the Hope Kit. Problem solving and communication skills strategies can be used to improve clients' interactions with their social support network and to improve adherence to other medical and mental health treatments that they may be receiving. The most comprehensive study examining the efficacy of this protocol found that it reduced the rate of suicide attempts by approximately 50% in a sample of clients who presented to the emergency department following a suicide attempt (Brown et al., 2005). Thus, when a therapist determines that a perinatal client is at moderate to high risk for suicidal behavior, suicidality is addressed directly in an acute phase of treatment, rather than assuming that it will decrease as a function of treating other mental health concerns.

Future Directions

Clearly, the literature on CBT for perinatal distress is still in its infancy, as a large-scale RCT examining the efficacy of individual conceptualization-driven CBT relative to routine care has yet to be conducted. In addition, there is compelling evidence for the use of interpersonal psychotherapy (IPT) in the treatment of perinatal depression (e.g., O'Hara et al., 2000). Research comparing the two treatments, as well as the characteristics of clients who are particularly responsive to each treatment, would significantly advance the literature. Admittedly, most RCTs that compare two active evidence-based treatments usually find few differences among treatments (e.g., Luty et al., 2007); nevertheless, such a direct comparison would provide further data confirming that both CBT and IPT are evidence-based treatments for perinatal distress, and it would allow attention to be shifted to more sophisticated research designs examining components of these treatments that can be enhanced to maximize success.

Moreover, in the larger CBT literature, calls have been made to move beyond comparing CBT to routine care or other types of psychotherapy in RCTs and to instead examine mechanisms associated with change in CBT (Kazdin, 2007). By isolating the mechanisms of change, therapists will be able to hone in on CBT strategies that maximize those factors during the course of treatment. To take but one example, over ten years ago, Hofmann (2004) determined that reductions in estimated social cost mediated change pre- and post-treatment in socially anxious clients. Estimated social cost is the expectation that making a social error will have catastrophic consequences. At its heart, estimated social cost is a cognition that can be addressed directly using cognitive restructuring. It is sensible, then, that cognitive behavioral therapists would assess each of their socially anxious clients for the degree to which the estimate exaggerated social costs and target this construct in treatment. Therapists should be aware of the mechanisms of change literature, and as additional constructs are identified as central targets for the treatments of different types of clients with emotional distress, they can assume a central focus with perinatal and non-perinatal clients, alike. Moreover, we encourage scholars who examine CBT specifically for perinatal distress to also move toward examining mechanisms of change, as it is possible that some unique constructs will be identified that are especially relevant to this population (e.g., unrealistic expectations for parenting).

In addition, researchers must examine the impact on special perinatal circumstances and the way in which CBT can be adapted. Most studies examining psychotherapy for women with perinatal distress exclude women who did not have live births or who experienced significant pregnancy complications. It is the women who experienced perinatal losses and pregnancy complications who might be most in need of evidence-based treatment for emotional distress. In fact, research shows that women who experience miscarriages show more depression, anxiety, and somatization six months following the loss, relative to women in the six months following a live birth (Janseen, Cusinier, Hoogduin, & de Graauw, 1996). Women who experience infertility also constitute a special population of perinatal women who experience emotional distress and even crisis in their confidence in strongly held core beliefs about parenthood, family, and even competence (Greil, Schmidt, & Peterson, 2015). One of us (AW) has put forth suggestions for using cognitive and behavioral strategies for coping with and making meaning of pregnancy loss and infertility (Wenzel, 2014b). However, a full CBT package for this population has yet to be evaluated in the research literature.

Most studies examining the course of and treatment for perinatal distress follow women across the course of one year. However, few women have another child within the first year following childbirth. Thus, there is a lack of understanding of how an episode of perinatal distress affects women's experience during pregnancy and the postpartum period with a subsequent child, as well as how successful intervention prevents future episodes of perinatal distress. CBT is described as a psychotherapy that gives clients skills to manage stressors and challenges that will be effective even when they are no longer actively attending sessions (Wenzel, 2013), and research shows that many people who have received cognitive behavioral therapy demonstrate enduring effects, meaning that they continue not to meet diagnostic criteria for depression and anxiety disorders and might even report continued improvement in symptoms (Hollon et al., 2006). Thus, another avenue for research is to examine the degree to which a CBT for perinatal distress has a preventive effect against additional episodes of perinatal distress in future pregnancies, relative to routine care.

Finally, we call for researchers to continue to examine treatments for perinatal distress in ethnically and culturally diverse samples. We applaud researchers who have already adapted cognitive behavioral treatment and prevention packages for low-income women (Swanson, 2010) and high risk Latinas (Le et al., 2011; Muñoz et al., 2007) in the United States, as well as in other countries where there are a limited number of mental health professionals (Rahman et al., 2008). Nevertheless, much additional work in this area needs to be done, as research shows that there is great variation in the prevalence of postpartum depression depending on the particular country under consideration, which suggests that there are unique cross-cultural psychological variables, reporting styles, experiences of stigma, and environmental variables that affect the phenomenology of emotional distress associated with childbirth (Halbreich & Karkun, 2006). Therapists who work with perinatal clients from a range of ethnic and cultural backgrounds must be cognizant of variables such as (but not limited to) traditionally accepted gender roles, the role of extended family in child rearing, and the role of family members in treatment participation. Research examining the manner in which these factors impact perinatal distress and the efficacy of specific interventions that account for these variables would provide welcomed guidance to therapists who work with perinatal clients.

A Hopeful Note

The good news is that women who struggle with perinatal distress have options. Perinatal distress has received a great deal of attention in the media, and although not all of the media depictions are accurate or have been helpful, they have shed light on something that affects more than 10% of all childbearing women. Legislation has been passed by the United States Senate (i.e., the Melanie Blocker Stokes MOTHERS Act) that recognizes the need for treatment of perinatal distress and funding to further elucidate the causes, diagnosis, and treatment of perinatal distress. Efforts are increasingly being implemented to encourage obstetricians to be on the lookout for perinatal distress and make referrals for mental health treatment.

Much attention has been devoted to the adaptations of evidence-based treatments for depression and anxiety to the perinatal population. IPT can be regarded as an empirically supported treatment for perinatal depression because its efficacy has been established relative to a credible control condition by at least two independent research groups (cf. Chambless & Ollendick, 2001). The drawback with IPT is that there is a paucity of therapists in the community who have received training and achieved competency to deliver this modality of treatment.

A surge of research on CBT for perinatal distress has been conducted in the past 15 years. Although our reading of this literature suggest that adapted CBTs for perinatal distress cannot yet be regarded as empirically supported, it is important to remember that there is a vast literature on the efficacy and effectiveness of CBT for adult populations (e.g., Butler et al., 2006), and there is nothing to suggest that this literature cannot be generalized to perinatal women. Thus, we regard CBT, in general, as an empirically supported treatment for emotional distress, and we look forward to further empirical support of specific adaptations that are tailored to this population. Moreover, leading CBT scholars and clinicians have made great efforts to disseminate CBT to community agencies that treat large numbers of clients (e.g., Stirman et al., 2009; Wenzel et al., 2011). The CBT community is working diligently to ensure that quality CBT meeting a standard of excellence is readily available in the community. We expect that perinatal women can look forward to increasing access to cognitive behavioral therapists when they need them.

The transition to parenthood is one of the more significant times in a woman's life. Adjustment difficulties and emotional distress can be devastating to new mothers who experience them. Perinatal women who struggle often express a profound sense of failure, as well as disappointment that the transition to parenthood did not go as they had hoped it would go. Conceptualization-based CBT has the potential to significantly curb the episode of emotional distress that brings these women to treatment, provide women with skills to manage the continued stress and uncertainty associated with child rearing, and allow them to gain wisdom and growth from their experience.

REFERENCES

Abramowitz, J. S., & Arch, J. J. (2014). Strategies for improving long-term outcomes in cognitive behavioral therapy for obsessive-compulsive disorder: Insights from learning theory. *Cognitive and Behavioral Practice, 21,* 20–31.

Abramowitz, J. S., Deacon, B. J., & Whiteside, S. P. H. (2011). *Exposure therapy for anxiety: Principles and practice.* New York, NY: Guilford Press.

Abramowitz, J. S., Foa, E. B., & Franklin, M. E. (2003). Exposure and ritual prevention for obsessive-compulsive disorder: Effects of intensive versus twice-weekly sessions. *Journal of Consulting and Clinical Psychology, 71,* 394–398.

Abramowitz, J. S., Schwartz, S. A., & Moore, M. K. (2003). Obsessional thoughts in postpartum females and their partners: Content, severity, and relationship with depression. *Journal of Clinical Psychology in Medical Settings, 10,* 157–164.

Abramowitz, J. S., Nelson, C. A., Rygwall, R., & Khandker, M. (2007). The cognitive mediation of obsessive compulsive symptoms: A longitudinal study. *Journal of Anxiety Disorders, 21,* 91–104.

Abramowitz, J. S., Schwartz, S. A., Moore, K. M., & Luenzmann, K. R. (2003). Obsessive compulsive symptoms in pregnancy and the puerperium: A review of the literature. *Journal of Anxiety Disorders, 17,* 461–478.

Abramowitz, J. S., Khandker, M., Nelson, C. A., Deacon, B. J., & Rygwall, R. (2006). The role of cognitive factors in obsessive compulsive symptoms: A prospective study. *Behaviour Research and Therapy, 44,* 1361–1374.

Abramowitz, J., Moore, K., Carmin, C., Wiegartz, P. S., & Purdon, C. (2001). Acute onset of obsessive compulsive disorder in males following childbirth. *Psychosomatics, 42,* 429–431.

Addis, M. E., & Martell, C. R. (2004). *Overcoming depression one step at a time: The new behavioral activation approach to getting your life back.* Oakland, CA: New Harbinger.

Adewuya, A. O., Ola, B. A., Aloba, O. O., & Mapayi, B. M. (2006). Anxiety disorders among Nigerian women in late pregnancy: A controlled study. *Archives of Women's Mental Health, 9,* 325–328.

Altemus, M. (2001). Obsessive compulsive disorder during pregnancy and postpartum. In K. Yonkers & B. Little (Eds.), *Management of psychiatric disorders in pregnancy* (pp. 149–163). New York, NY: Oxford University Press.

American Psychiatric Association (2013). *Diagnostic and statistical manual of mental disorders (5th ed.).* Washington, DC: Author.

Applby, L., Warner, R., Whitton, A., & Faragher, B. (1997). A controlled study of fluoxetine and cognitive-behavioural counselling in the treatment of ostnatal depression. *British Medical Journal, 314,* 932–936.

Arch, J. J., & Craske, M. G. (2011). Addressing relapse in cognitive behavioral therapy for panic disorder: Methods for optimizing long-term treatment options. *Cognitive and Behavioral Practice, 19,* 306–315.

Arch, J. J., Dimidjian, S., & Chessick, C. (2012). Are exposure-based cognitive behavioral therapies safe during pregnancy? *Archives of Women's Mental Health, 15,* 445–457.

Austin, M.-P, Frilingos, M., Lumley, J., Hadzi-Pavlovic, D., Roncolato, W., . . ., & Parker, G. (2008). Brief antenatal cognitive behaviour therapy group intervention for the prevention of postnatal depression and anxiety: A randomised controlled trial. *Journal of Affective Disorders, 105,* 35–44.

Avan, B., Richter, L. M., Ramchandani, P. G., Norris, S. A., & Stein, A. (2010). Maternal postnatal depression and children's growth and behaviour during the early years of life: Exploring the interaction between physical and mental health. *Archives of Disease in Childhood, 95,* 690–695.

Barlow, D. H., & Craske, M. G. (2007). *Mastery of your anxiety and panic (4th ed.).* New York, NY: Oxford University Press.

Battle, C. L., & Salisbury, A. L., Schofield, C. A., & Ortiz-Hernandez, S. (2013). Perinatal antidepressant use: Understanding women's preferences and concerns. *Journal of Psychiatric Practice, 19,* 443–453.

Beck, A. T., Freeman, A., Davis, D. D., & Associates (2004). *Cognitive therapy of personality disorders (2nd ed.).* New York, NY: Guilford Press.

Beck, A. T., Rush, A. J., Shaw, B. F., & Emery, G. (1979). *Cognitive therapy of depression.* New York, NY: Guilford Press.

Beck, C. T. (2001). Predictors of postpartum depression: An update. *Nursing Research, 50,* 275–285.

Beck, C. T., & Driscoll, J. W. (2006). *Postpartum mood and anxiety disorders: A clinician's guide.* Boston, MA: Jones and Bartlett.

Beck, J. S. (2011). *Cognitive behavior therapy: Basics and beyond (2nd ed.).* New York, NY: Guilford Press.

Becker, R. E., Heimberg, R. G., & Bellack, A. S. (1987). *Social skills training for depression.* New York, NY: Pergamon Press.

Beebe, B., Jaffe, J., Buck, K., Chen, H., Cohen, P., . . ., & Andrews, H. (2008). Six-week postpartum maternal depressive symptoms and 4-month mother-infant self- and interactive contingency. *Infant Mental Health Journal, 29,* 442–471.

Bell, A. C., & D'Zurilla, T. J. (2009). Problem-solving therapy for depression: A meta-analysis. *Clinical Psychology Review, 29,* 348–353.

Bellack, A. S., Mueser, K. T., Gingrich, S., & Agresta, J. (2004). *Social skills training for schizophrenia: A step-by-step guide (2nd ed.).* New York, NY: Guilford Press.

Bernstein, D. A., Borkovec, T. D., & Hazlett-Stevens, H. (2000). *New directions in progressive relaxation training: A guidebook for helping professionals.* Westport, CT: Praeger Press.

Beydoun, H. A., Beydoun, M. A., Kaufman, J. S., Lo, B., & Zonderman, A. B. (2012). Intimate partner violence against adult women and its association with major depressive disorder, depressive symptoms, and postpartum depression: A systematic review and meta-analysis. *Social Science & Medicine, 75,* 959–975.

Bisson, J. I., Ehlers, A., Matthews, R., Pilling, S., Richards, D., & Turner, S. (2007). Psychological treatments for chronic post-traumatic stress disorder: Systematic review and meta-analysis. *British Journal of Psychiatry, 190,* 97–104.

Bjork, R. A. (2004). Memory and metaconsiderations in the training of human beings. In J. Metcalfe & A. Shimamura (Eds.), *Metacognition: Knowing about knowing* (pp. 185–205). Cambridge, MA: MIT Press.

Bjork, R. A., & Bjork, E. L. (2006). Optimizing treatment and instruction: Implications of a new theory of disuse. In L.-G. Nilsson & N. Ohta (Eds.), *Memory and society: Psychological perspectives* (pp. 116–140). New York, NY: Psychology Press.

Bloch, M., Schmidt, P. J., Danaceau, M., Murphy, J., Nieman, L., & Rubinow, D. R. (2000). Effects of gonadal steroids in women with a history of postpartum depression. *American Journal of Psychiatry, 157,* 924–930.

Bohart, A. C., Elliott, R. E., Greenberg, L. S., & Watson, J. C. (2002). Empathy. In J. C. Norcross (Ed.), *Psychotherapy relationships that work: Therapist contributions and responsiveness to patients* (pp. 89–108). New York, NY: Oxford University Press.

Bordin, E. S. (1979). The generalizability of the psychoanalytic concept of the working alliance. *Psychotherapy: Theory, Research, & Practice, 16,* 252–260.

Bouton, M. E. (1993). Context, time, and memory retrieval in the interference paradigms of Pavlovian learning. *Psychological Bulletin, 114,* 90–99.

Bradbury, T. N., & Fincham, F. D. (1992). Attributions and behavior in marital interaction. *Journal of Personality and Social Psychology, 64,* 618–628.

Brockington, I. F. (1996). *Motherhood and mental health.* Oxford, UK: Oxford University Press.

Brodsky, B. S., & Stanley, B. (2008). Adverse childhood experiences and suicidal behavior. *Psychiatric Clinics of North America, 31,* 223–235.

Brown, G. K., Tenhave, T., Henriques, G. R., Xie, S. X., Hollander, J. E., & Beck, A. T. (2005). Cognitive therapy for the prevention of suicide attempts: A randomized controlled trial. *Journal of the American Medical Association, 294,* 563–570.

Brozovich, F., & Heimberg, R. G. (2008). An analysis of post-event processing in social anxiety disorder. *Clinical Psychology Review, 28,* 891–903.

Buckner, J. D., & Schmidt, N. B. (2009). A randomized pilot study of motivation enhancement therapy to increase utilization of cognitive-behavioral therapy for social anxiety. *Behaviour Research and Therapy, 47,* 710–715.

Burns, A., O'Mahen, H., Baxter, H., Bennert, K., Wiles, N., . . ., & Evans, J. (2013). A pilot randomised controlled trial of cognitive behavioural therapy for antenatal depression. *BMC Psychiatry, 13,* 33.

Burns, D. D. (1980). *Feeling good: The new mood therapy.* New York, NY: Avon Books.

Butler, A. C., Chapman, J. E., Forman, E. M., & Beck, A. T. (2006). The empirical status of cognitive-behavioral therapy: A review of meta-analyses. *Clinical Psychology Review, 26,* 17–31.

Buttner, M., O'Hara, M. W., & Watson, D. (2012). The structure of women's mood in the early postpartum. *Assessment, 19,* 247–256.

Castonguay, L. G., Constantino, M. J., & Grosse Holtforth, M. (2006). The working alliance: Where are we and where should we go? *Psychotherapy: Theory, Research, Practice, and Training, 43,* 271–279.

Castonguay, L. G., Goldfried, M. R., Wiser, S., Raue, P. J., & Hayes, A.M. (1996). Predicting the effect of cognitive therapy for depression: A study of unique and common factors. *Journal of Consulting and Clinical Psychology, 64,* 497–504.

Chambless, D. L., & Gracely, E. J. (1989). Fear or fear and the anxiety disorders. *Cognitive Therapy and Research, 13,* 9–20.

Chambless, D. L., & Ollendick, T. H. (2001). Empirically supported psychological interventions: Controversies and evidence. *Annual Review of Psychology, 52,* 685–716.

Chang, J. C., Cluss, P. A., Ranieri, L., Hawker, L., Buranosky, R., . . ., & Scholle, S. H. (2005). Health care interventions for intimate partner violence: What women want. *Women's Health Issues, 15,* 21–30.

Charbol, H., Teissedre, F., Saint-Jean, M., Teisseyre, N., Rogé, B., & Mullet, E. (2002). Prevention and treatment of postpartum depression: A controlled randomized study on women at risk. *Psychological Medicine, 32,* 1039–1047.

Cho, H. J., Kwon, J. J., & Lee, J. J. (2008). Antenatal cognitive-behavioral therapy for prevention of postpartum depression: A pilot study. *Yonsei Medical Journal, 49,* 553–562.

Clark, D. M., Salkovskis, P. M., Öst, L-G., Breitholtz, E., Koehler, K. A., . . ., & Gelder, M. (1997). Misinterpretation of body sensations in panic disorder. *Journal of Consulting and Clinical Psychology, 65,* 203–213.

Clark, R., Tluczek, A., & Brown, R. (2008). A mother-infant group model for postpartum depression. *Infant Mental Health Journal, 29,* 514–536.

Cohen, J. (1988). *Statistical power analysis for the behavioral sciences (2nd ed.).* Hillsdale, NJ: Erlbaum.

Cohen, L. S., Rosenbaum, J. F., & Heller, V. L. (1989). Panic attack-associated placental abruption: A case report. *Journal of Clinical Psychiatry, 50,* 266–267.

Cole, J. A., Ephoss, S. A., Cosmatos, I. S., & Walker, A.M. (2007). Paroxetine in the first trimester and the prevalence of congenital malformations. *Pharmacoepidemiology and Drug Safety, 16,* 1075–1085.

Cooper, P. J., Murray, L. M., & Romaniuk, H. (2003). Controlled trial of the short- and long-term effect of psychological treatment of post-partum depression. 1. Impact on maternal mood. *British Journal of Psychiatry, 182,* 412–419.

Cox, J. L., Holden, J. M., & Sagovsky, R. (1987). Detection of postnatal depression: Development of the 10-item Edinburgh Postnatal Depression Scale. *British Journal of Psychiatry, 150,* 782–786.

Craske, M. G., Kircanski, K., Zelikowsky, M., Mystkowski, J., Chowdhury, N., & Baker, A. (2008). Optimizing inhibitory learning during exposure therapy. *Behaviour Research and Therapy, 46,* 5–27.

Creedy, D. K., Shochet, I. M., & Horsfall, J. (2000). Childbirth and the development of acute trauma symptoms: Incidence and contributing factors. *Birth, 27,* 104–111.

Cuijpers, P., Brännmark, J. G., & van Straten, A. (2008). Psychological treatment of postpartum depression: A meta-analysis. *Journal of Clinical Psychology, 64*, 103–118.

Cutrona, C. E. (1984). Social support and stress in the transition to parenthood. *Journal of Abnormal Psychology, 93*, 378–390.

Czarnocka, J., & Slade, P. (2000). Prevalence and predictors of post-traumatic stress symptoms following childbirth. *British Journal of Clinical Psychology, 39*, 35–51.

DeRubeis, R. J., Brotman, M. A., & Gibbons, C. J. (2005). A conceptual and methodological analysis of the nonspecific argument. *Clinical Psychology: Science and Practice, 12*, 174–183.

DeRubeis, R. J., & Feeley, M. (1990). Determinants of change in cognitive therapy for depression. *Cognitive Therapy and Research, 14*, 469–482.

DeRubeis, R. J., Hollon, S. D., Amsterdam, J. D., Shelton, R. C., Young, P. R., . . ., & Gallop, R. (2005). Cognitive therapy vs medications in the treatment of moderate to severe depression. *Archives of General Psychiatry, 62*, 409–416.

Dimidjian, S., Hollon, S. D., Dobson, K. S., Schmaling, K. B., Kohlenberg, R. J., . . ., & Jacobson, N. S. (2006). Randomized trial of behavioral activation, cognitive therapy, and antidepressant medication in the acute treatment of adults with major depression. *Journal of Consulting and Clinical Psychology, 74*, 658–670.

Dobson, D., & Dobson, K. S. (2009). *Evidence-based practice of cognitive-behavioral therapy.* New York, NY: Guilford Press.

Doss, B. D., Rhoads, G. K., Stanley, S. M., & Markman, H. J. (2009). The effect of the transition to parenthood on relationship quality: An 8-year prospective study. *Journal of Personality and Social Psychology, 96*, 601–619.

Dugas, M. J., & Robichaud, M. (2007). *Cognitive-behavioral treatment for generalized anxiety disorder: From science to practice.* New York, NY: Routledge.

Dugas, M. J., Freeston, M. J., & Ladouceur, R. (1997). Intolerance of uncertainty and problem orientation in worry. *Cognitive Therapy and Research, 21*, 593–606.

Dugas, M. J., Gagnon, F., Ladouceur, R., & Freeston, M. H. (1998). Generalized anxiety disorder: A preliminary test of a conceptual model. *Behaviour Research and Therapy, 36*, 215–226.

Dugas, M. J., Brillon, P., Savard, P., Turcott, J., Gaudet, A., . . ., & Gervais, N. J. (2010). A randomized clinical trial of cognitive-behavioral therapy and applied relaxation for adults with generalized anxiety disorder. *Behavior Therapy, 41*, 46–58.

D'Zurilla, T. J., & Nezu, A.M. (2007). *Problem-solving therapy: A positive approach to clinical intervention (3rd ed.).* New York, NY: Spring Publishing Company.

El-Mohandes, A. A., Kiely, M., Joseph, J. G., Subramanian, S., Johnson, A. A., . . ., & El-Khorazaty, M. N. (2008). An intervention to improve postpartum outcomes in African-American mothers: A randomized controlled trial. *Obstetrics and Gynecology, 112*, 611–620.

Fairbrother, N., & Abramowitz, J. S. (2007). New parenthood as a risk factor for the development of obsessional problems. *Behaviour Research and Therapy, 45*, 2155–2163.

REFERENCES

Farmer, R. F., & Chapman, A. L. (2008). *Behavioral interventions in cognitive behavior therapy: Practical guidance for putting theory into action.* Washington, DC: APA Books.

Feeley, M., DeRubeis, R. J., & Gelfand, L. A. (1999). The temporal relation of adherence and alliance to symptom change in cognitive therapy for depression. *Journal of Consulting and Clinical Psychology, 67,* 578–582.

Field, T. (2010). Postpartum depression effects on early interactions, parenting, and safety practices: A review. *Infant Behavior and Development, 33,* 1–6.

Foa, E. B., & Kozak, M. J. (1986). Emotional processing of fear: Exposure to corrective information. *Psychological Bulletin, 99,* 20–35.

Foa, E. B., & McNally, R. J. (1996). Mechanisms of change in exposure therapy. In R. M. Rapee (Ed.), *Current controversies in the anxiety disorders* (pp. 329–343). New York, NY: Guilford Press.

Foa, E. B., Zoellner, L. A., Feeny, N. C., Hembree, E. A., & Alvarez-Conrad, J. (2002). Does imaginal exposure exacerbate PTSD symptoms? *Journal of Consulting and Clinical Psychology, 70,* 1022–1028.

Forty, L., Jones, L., Macgregor, S., Caesar, S., Cooper, C., & . . ., Jones, I. (2006). Familiaity of postpartum depression in unipolar disorder: Results of a family study. *American Journal of Psychiatry, 163,* 1549–1553.

Frisch, M. B. (2006). *Quality of life therapy: Applying a life satisfaction approach to positive psychology and cognitive therapy.* New York, NY: John Wiley & Sons.

Gavin, N. I., Gaynes, B. N., Lohr, K. N., Meltzer-Brody, S., Gartlehner, F., & Swinson, T. (2005). Perinatal depression: A systematic review of prevalence and incidence. *Obstetrics and Gynecology, 106,* 1071–1083.

Gilbert, P., & Leahy, R. L. (2007). Introduction and overview: Basic issues in the therapeutic relationship. In P. Gilbert & R. L. Leahy (Eds.), *The therapeutic relationship in the cognitive behavioral psychotherapies* (pp. 3–23). New York, NY: Routledge.

Gloaguen, V., Cotraumx, J., Cucherat, M., & Blackburn, I.-M. (1998). A meta-analysis of the effects of cognitive therapy in depressed patients. *Journal of Affective Disorders, 49,* 59–72.

Glover, V., & Kammerer, M. (2004). The biology and pathophysiology of peripartum psychiatric disorders. *Primary Psychiatry, 11,* 37–41.

Gold, K. J., Singh, V., Marcus, S. M., & Palladino, C. L. (2012). Mental health, substance use and intimate partner problems among pregnant and postpartum suicide victims in the National Violent Death Reporting System. *General Hospital Psychiatry, 34,* 139–145.

Goldstein, R. B., Black, D. W., Nasrallah, A., & Winokur, G. (1991). The prediction of suicide: Sensitivity, specificity, and predictive value of a multivariate model applied to suicide among 1906 patients with affective disorders. *Archives of General Psychiatry, 48,* 418–422.

Gottman, J., with Silver, N. (1994). *Why marriages succeed or fail: What you can learn from the breakthrough research to make your marriage last.* New York, NY: Simon & Schuster.

Grace, S. L., Evindar, A., & Stewart, D. E. (2003). The effect of postpartum depression on child cognitive development and behavior: A review and critical analysis of the literature. *Archives of Women's Mental Health, 6,* 263–274.

Grayson, J. B., Foa, E. B., & Steketee, G. (1982). Habituation during exposure treatment: Distraction vs. attention-focusing. *Behaviour Research and Therapy, 20,* 323–328.

Greenberg, L. S., McWilliams, N., & Wenzel, A. (2014). *Exploring three approaches to psychotherapy.* Washington, DC: APA Books.

Greil, A. L., Schmidt, L., & Peterson, B. D. (2015). Perinatal experiences associated with infertility. In A. Wenzel (Ed.), *The Oxford handbook of perinatal psychology.* New York, NY: Oxford University Press.

Griffiths, P., & Barker-Collo, S. (2008). Study of a group treatment program for postnatal adjustment difficulties. *Archives of Women's Mental Health, 11,* 33–41.

Grote, N. K., Bledsoe, S. E., Swartz, H. A., & Frank, E. (2004). Feasibility of providing culturally relevant, brief interpersonal psychotherapy for antenatal depression in an obstetrics clinic: A pilot study. *Research on Social Work Practice, 14,* 397–407.

Guler, O., Sahin, F. K., Emul, H. M., Ozbulut, O., Gecici, O., . . ., & Askin, R. (2008). The prevalence of panic disorder in pregnant women during the third trimester of pregnancy. *Comprehensive Psychiatry, 49,* 154–158.

Hagan, R., Evans, S. F., & Pope, S. (2004). Preventing postnatal depression in mothers of very preterm infants: A randomized controlled trial. *British Journal of Obstetrics and Gynaecology, 111,* 641–647.

Halbreich, U., & Karkun, S. (2006). Cross-cultural and social diversity of prevalence of postpartum depression and depressive symptoms. *Journal of Affective Disorders, 91,* 97–111.

Hale, T. W. (2008). *Medications and mother's milk (13th ed.).* Amarillo, TX: Hale Publishing.

Hanrahan, F., Field, A. P., Jones, F. W., & Davey, G. C. L. (2013). A meta-analysis of cognitive therapy for worry in generalized anxiety disorder. *Clinical Psychology Review, 33,* 120–132.

Hans, E., & Hiller, W. (2013a). Effectiveness of and dropout from outpatient cognitive behavioral therapy for adult unipolar depression: A meta-analysis of nonrandomized effectiveness studies. *Journal of Consulting and Clinical Psychology, 81,* 75–88.

Hans, E., & Hiller, W. (2013b). A meta-analysis of nonrandomized effectiveness studies on outpatient cognitive-behavioral therapy for adult anxiety disorders. *Clinical Psychology Review, 33,* 954–964.

Hardy, G., Cahill, J., & Barkham, M. (2007). Active ingredients of the therapeutic relationship that promote client change: A research perspective. In P. Gilbert & R. L. Leahy (Eds.), *The therapeutic relationship in the cognitive behavioral psychotherapies* (pp. 24–42). New York, NY: Routledge.

Harris, E. C., & Barraclough, B. (1994). Suicide as an outcome for medical disorders. *Medicine Baltimore, 73,* 281–396.

Harriss, L., & Hawton, K. (2005). Suicidal intent in deliberate self-harm and the risk of suicide: The predictive power of the Suicide Intent Scale. *Journal of Affective Disorders, 86,* 225–233.

Harriss, L., Hawton, K., & Zahl, D. (2005). Value of measuring suicidal intent in the assessment of people attending hospital following self-poisoning or self-injury. *British Journal of Psychiatry, 186,* 60–66.

Haugen, E. N. (2003). *Postpartum anxiety and depression: The contribution of social support.* Unpublished master's thesis, University of North Dakota, Grand Forks, ND.

Hauri, P., & Linde, S. (1996). *No more sleepless nights – Revised edition.* New York, NY: John Wiley & Sons.

Hendrick, V., Altshuler, L., & Strouse, T. (2000). Postpartum and nonpostpartum depression: Differences in presentation and response to pharmacologic treatment. *Depression and Anxiety, 11,* 66–72.

Heron, J., Robertson Blackmore, E., McGuinness, M., Craddock, N., & Jones, I. (2007). No 'latent period' in the onset of Bipolar Affective Puerperal Psychosis. *Archives of Women's Mental Health, 10,* 79–81.

Hewitt, P. L., Flett, G. L., Sherry, S. B., & Caelian, C. (2006). Trait perfectionism dimensions and suicidal behavior. In T. E. Ellis (Ed.), *Cognition and suicide* (pp. 215–235). Washington, DC: APA Books.

Hirsch, C., Jolley, S., & Williams, R. (2000). A study of outcome in a clinical psychology service and preliminary evaluation of cognitive-behavioral therapy in real practice. *Journal of Mental Health, 9,* 537–549.

Hofmann, S. G. (2004). Cognitive mediation of treatment change in social phobia. *Journal of Consulting and Clinical Psychology, 72,* 393–399.

Hofmann, S. G. (2012). *An introduction to modern CBT: Psychological solutions to mental health problems.* Malden, MA: Wiley-Blackwell.

Hofmann, S. G., & Smits, J. A. J. (2008). Cognitive-behavioral therapy for adult anxiety disorders: A meta-analysis of randomized placebo-controlled trials. *Journal of Clinical Psychiatry, 69,* 621–632.

Hollon, S. D. (2011). Cognitive and behavior therapy in the treatment and prevention of depression. *Depression and Anxiety, 28,* 263–266.

Hollon, S. D., Stewart, M. O., & Strunk, D. (2006). Enduring effects for cognitive behavior therapy in the treatment of depression and anxiety. *Annual Review of Psychology, 57,* 285–315.

Hollon, S. D., DeRubeis, R. J., Shelton, R. C., Amsterdam, J. D., Saloman, R. M., . . ., & Gallop, R. (2005). Prevention of relapse following cognitive therapy vs medications in moderate to severe depression. *Archives of General Psychiatry, 62,* 417–422.

Honey, K. L., Bennett, P., & Morgan, M. (2002). A brief psycho-educational group intervention for postnatal depression. *British Journal of Clinical Psychology, 41,* 405–409.

Horvath, A. O., & Greenberg, L. S. (1989). Development and validation of the Working Alliance Inventory. *Journal of Consulting and Clinical Psychology, 36,* 223–233.

Hughes, D., & Kleespies, P. (2001). Suicide in the medically ill. *Suicide and Life-Threatening Behavior, 31,* 48–59.

Jacobi, F., Wittchen, H-U., Hölting, C., Höfler, M., Pfister, H., . . ., & Lieb, R. (2004). Prevalence, co-morbidity, and correlates of mental disorders in the general population: Results of the German Health Interview and Examination Survey (GHS). *Psychological Medicine, 34,* 597–611.

Jacobson, N. S., Dobson, K. S., Truax, P. A., Addis, M. E., Koerner, K., . . ., & Prince, S. E. (1996). A component analysis of cognitive-behavioral treatment for depression. *Journal of Consulting and Clinical Psychology, 64,* 295–304.

Janseen, H. J., Cusinier, M. C., Hoogduin, K. A., & de Graauw, K. P. (1996). Controlled prospective study on the mental health of women following pregnancy loss. *American Journal of Psychiatry, 153,* 226–230.

Jesse, D. E., Blanchard, A., Bunch, S., Dolbier, C., Hodgson, J., & Swanson, M. S. (2010). A pilot study to reduce risk for antepartum depression among women in a public health prenatal clinic. *Issues in Mental Health Nursing, 31,* 355–364.

Joiner, T. E. (2005). *Why people die by suicide.* Cambridge, MA: Harvard University Press.

Joiner, T. E, Conwell, Y., Fitzpatrick, K. K., Witte, T. K., Schmidt, N. B., . . ., & Rudd, M. D. (2005). Four studies on how past and current suicidality relate even when "everything but the kitchen sink" is covaried. *Journal of Abnormal Psychology, 114,* 291–303.

Jones, I., & Craddock, N. (2001). Familiality of the puerperal trigger in bipolar disorder: results of a family study. *American Journal of Psychiatry, 158,* 913–917.

Kammerer, M., Adams, D., Casteleberg, B. B., & Glover, V. (2002). Pregnant women become insensitive to cold stress. *BMC Pregnancy Childbirth, 2,* 8.

Karekla, M., Forsyth, J, P., & Kelly, M. M. (2004). Emotional avoidance and panicogenic responding to a biological challenge procedure. *Behavior Therapy, 35,* 725–746.

Kazantzis, N., Whittington, C., & Dattilio, F. (2010). Meta-analysis of homework effects in cognitive and behavioral therapy: A replication and extension. *Clinical Psychology: Science and Practice, 17,* 144–156.

Kazdin, A. E. (2007). Mediators and mechanisms of change in psychotherapy research. *Annual Review of Clinical Psychology, 3,* 1–27.

Kleiman, K. K. (2009). *Therapy and the postpartum woman: Notes on healing postpartum depression for clinicians and the women who seek their help.* New York, NY: Routledge.

Kleiman, K. K., & Wenzel, A. (2011). *Dropping the baby down the stairs and other scary thoughts: Breaking the cycle of unwanted thoughts in motherhood.* New York, NY: Routledge.

Kleiman, K., with Wenzel, A. (2014). *Tokens of affection: Reclaiming your marriage after postpartum depression.* New York, NY: Routledge.

Klein, D. F., Skrobala, A.M., & Garfinkel, R. S. (1995). Preliminary look at the effects of pregnancy on panic disorder. *Anxiety, 1,* 227–232.

Kuyken, W., Padesky, C. A., & Dudley, R. (2009). *Collaborative case conceptualization: Working effectively with clients in cognitive-behavioral therapy.* New York, NY: Guilford Press.

Ladouceur, R., Talbot, F., & Dugas, M. J. (1997). Behavioral expressions of intolerance of uncertainty in worry: Experimental findings. *Behavior Modification, 21,* 355–371.

Lang, A. J., & Craske, M. G. (2000). Manipulations of exposure-based therapy to reduce the return of fear: An application. *Behaviour Research and Therapy, 38,* 1–12.

Lawrence, E., Nylen, K., & Cobb, R. J. (2007). Prenatal expectations and marital satisfaction over the transition to parenthood. *Journal of Family Psychology, 21,* 155–164.

Lawrence, E., Rothman, A. D., Cobb, R. J., Rothman, M. T., & Bradbury, T. N. (2008). Marital satisfaction across the transition to parenthood. *Journal of Family Psychology, 22,* 41–50.

Le, H.-N., Perry, D. F., & Stuart, E. A. (2011). Randomized controlled trial of a preventive intervention for perinatal depression in high-risk Latinas. *Journal of Consulting and Clinical Psychology, 79,* 135–141.

Leahy, R. L. (2001). *Overcoming resistance in cognitive therapy.* New York, NY: Guilford Press.

Lilienfeld, S. O., Ritschel, L. A., Lynn, S. J., Cautin, R. L., & Latzman, R. D. (2013). Why many clinical psychologists are resistant to evidence-based practice: Root causes and constructive remedies. *Clinical Psychology Review, 33,* 883–900.

Lilliecreutz, C., Josefsson, A., and Sydsjo, G. (2010). An open trial of cognitive behavioral therapy for blood- and injection phobia in pregnant women— a group intervention program. *Archives of Women's Mental Health, 13,* 259–265.

Linehan, M. M. (1993a). *Cognitive-behavioral therapy for borderline personality disorder.* New York, NY: Guilford Press.

Linehan, M. M. (1993b). *Skills training manual for borderline personality disorder.* New York, NY: Guilford Press.

Linehan, M. M., Goodstein, J. L., Nielsen, S. L., & Chiles, J. A. (1983). Reasons for staying alive when you are thinking of killing yourself: The Reasons for Living Inventory. *Journal of Consulting and Clinical Psychology, 51,* 276–286.

Lobel, M., Dunkel-Schetter, C., & Scrimshaw, S. C. M. (1992). Prenatal maternal stress and prematurity: A prospective study of socioeconomically disadvantaged women. *Health Psychology, 11,* 32–40.

Longmore, R. J., & Worrell, M. (2007). Do we need to challenge thoughts in cognitive behavioral therapy? *Clinical Psychology Review, 27,* 173–187.

Luty, S. E., Carter, J. D., McKenzie, J. M., Rae, A.M., Frampton, C. M. A., & . . ., Joyce, P. R. (2007). Randomised controlled trial of interpersonal psychotherapy and cognitive-behavioural therapy for depression. *The British Journal of Psychiatry, 190,* 496–502.

Lyons, S. (1998). A prospective study of post traumatic stress symptoms 1 month following childbirth in a group of 42 first-time mothers. *Journal of Reproductive and Infant Psychology, 16,* 91–105.

McMillan, D., Gilbody, S., Beresford, E., & Neilly, L. (2007). Can we predict suicide and non-fatal self-harm with the Beck Hopelessness Scale? A meta-analysis. *Psychological Medicine, 37,* 769–778.

McNally, R. M. (1989). Is anxiety sensitivity distinguishable from trait anxiety? A reply to Lilienfeld, Jacob, and Turner (1989). *Journal of Abnormal Psychology, 98,* 193–194.

MacPhillamy, D. J., & Lewinsohn, P. M. (1976). *Manual for the Pleasant Events Schedule.* Eugene, OR: University of Oregon.

Magee, W. J., Eaton, W. W., Wittchen, H.-U., McGonagle, K. A., & Kessler, R. C. (1996). Agoraphobia, simple phobia, and social phobia in the National Comorbidity Study. *Archives of General Psychiatry, 53,* 159–168.

Mann, J. J., Waternaux, C., Haas, G. L., & Malone, K. M. (1999). Toward a clinical model of suicidal behavior in psychiatric patients. *American Journal of Psychiatry, 156,* 181–189.

Martell, C. R., Addis, M. E., & Jacobson, N. S. (2001). *Depression in context: Strategies for guided action.* New York, NY: Norton.

Martin, D. J., Garske, J. P., & Davis, M. K. (2000). Relation of the therapeutic alliance with outcome and other variables: A meta-analytic review. *Journal of Consulting and Clinical Psychology, 68,* 438–450.

Martin, M., Hamilton, B., Sutton, P., Ventura, S. Menacker, F., Kirmeyer, S., & Mathews, T. J. (2009). *Births: Final data for 2006* Division of Vital Statistics, *National Vital Statistics Report, 57*(7). Retrieved from: http://www.cdc.gov/nchs/data/nvsr/nvsr57/nvsr57_07.pdf

Matthews, K. A., & Rodin, J. (1992). Pregnancy alters blood pressure responses to psychological and physical challenge. *Psychophysiology, 29,* 232–240.

Matthey, S., Barnett, B., Howie, P., & Kavanagh, D. J. (2003). Diagnosing postpartum depression in mothers and fathers: Whatever happened to anxiety? *Journal of Affective Disorders, 74,* 139–147.

Milgrom, J., Holt, C. J., Gemmill, A. W., Ericksen, J., Leigh, B., . . ., & Schembri, C. (2011). Treating postnatal depressive symptoms in primary care: A randomized controlled trial of GP management with and without adjunctive counselling. *BMC Psychiatry, 11,* 95.

Milgrom, J., Martin, P. R., & Negri, L. M. (1999). *Treating postnatal depression: A psychological approach for health care practitioners.* West Sussex, UK: John Wiley & Sons.

Milgrom, J., Negri, L. M., Gemmill, A. W., McNeil, M., & Martin, P. R. (2005). A randomized controlled trial of psychological interventions for postnatal depression. *British Journal of Clinical Psychology, 44,* 529–542.

Miller, W. R., & Rollnick, S. (2013). *Motivational interviewing: Helping people change (3rd ed.).* New York, NY: Guilford Press.

Misri, S., Reebye, P., Corral, M., & Milis, L. (2004). The use of paroxetine and cognitive-behavioral therapy in postpartum depression and anxiety: A randomized controlled trial. *Journal of Clinical Psychiatry, 65,* 1236–1241.

Mitte, K. (2005). A meta-analysis of the efficacy of psycho- and pharmacotherapy in panic disorder with and without agoraphobia. *Journal of Affective Disorders, 88,* 27–45.

Morrell, C. J., Slade, P., Warner, R., Paley, G., Dixon, S., . . ., & Nicholl, J. (2009). Clinical effectiveness of health visitor training in psychologically informed approaches for depression in postnatal women: Pragmatic cluster randomised trial in primary care. *British Medical Journal, 338,* 1–14.

Muñoz, R. F., Ghosh Ippen, C., Le, H.-L., Lieberman, A., Diaz, M., & La Plante, L. (2001). *The Mothers and Babies Course: A reality management approach.* San Francisco, CA: University of California, San Francisco.

Muñoz, R. F., Le, H.-L., Ippen, C. G., Diaz, M. A., Urizar Jr., G. G., . . ., & Lieberman, A. (2007). Prevention of postpartum depression in low-income women: Development of the Mamás y Bebés/Mothers and Babies Course. *Cognitive and Behavioral Practice, 14,* 70–83.

Murray, L., & Cooper, P. J. (2003). Intergenerational transmission of affective and cognitive processes associated with depression: Infancy and the pre-school years. In I. M. Goodyer (Ed.), *Unipolar depression: A lifetime perspective.* New York, NY: Oxford University Press.

Murray, L., Cooper, P. J., Wilson, A., & Romaniuk, H. (2003). Controlled trial of the short- and long-term effect of psychological treatment of post-partum depression. 2. Impact on the mother-child relationship and child outcome. *British Journal of Psychiatry, 182,* 420–427.

Murray, L., Arteche, A., Fearon, P., Halligan, S., Goodyer, I., & Cooper, P. (2011). Maternal postnatal depression in low-income women: Development of depression in offspring up to 16 years of age. *Journal of the American Academy of Child and Adolescent Psychiatry, 50,* 460–470.

Nardi, B., Laurenzi, S., Di Nicoló, M., & Bellantuono, C. (2012). Is the cognitive-behavioral therapy an effective intervention to prevent postnatal depression? A critical review. *International Journal of Psychiatry in Medicine, 43,* 211–225.

Navarro, P., García-Esteve, L., Ascaso, C., Aguado, J., Gelabert, E., & Martín-Santos, R. (2008). Non-psychotic psychiatric disorders after childbirth: Prevalence and comorbidity in a community sample. *Journal of Affective Disorders, 109,* 171–176.

Negron, R., Martin, A., Almog, M., Balbierz, A., & Howell, E. A. (2013). Social support during the postpartum period: Mothers' views in needs, expectations, and mobilization of support. *Maternal and Child Health Journal, 17,* 616–623.

Newman, C. F. (2007). The therapeutic relationship in cognitive therapy with difficult-to-engage clients. In P. Gilbert & R. L. Leahy (Eds.), *The therapeutic relationship in the cognitive behavioral psychotherapies* (pp. 166–184). New York, NY: Routledge.

Newman, M. G., & Borkovec, T. D. (1995). Cognitive-behavioral treatment of generalized anxiety disorder. *The Clinical Psychologist, 48,* 5–7.

Nock, M. K., Deming, C. A., Fullerton, C. S., Gilman, S. E., Goldenberg, M., . . ., & Ursano, R. J. (2013). Suicide among soldiers: A review of psychosocial risk and protective factors, *Psychiatry, 76,* 97–125.

Nolen-Hoeksema, S., Wisco, B. E., & Lyubomirsky, S. (2008). Rethinking rumination. *Perspectives on Psychological Science, 3,* 400–424.

Nonacs, R. M. (2005). Postpartum mood disorders. In L. S. Cohen & R. M. Nonacs (Eds.), *Mood and anxiety disorders during pregnancy and postpartum (Review of Psychiatry, Vol. 24, No. 4)* (pp. 77–103). Washington, DC: American Psychiatric Press.

Nonacs, R. M., Cohen, L. S., Viguera, A. C., & Mogielnicki, J. (2005). Diagnosis and treatment of mood and anxiety disorders in pregnancy. In L. S. Cohen & R. M. Nonacs (Eds.), *Mood and anxiety disorders during pregnancy and postpartum (Review of Psychiatry, Vol. 24, No. 4)* (pp. 17–51). Washington, DC: American Psychiatric Publishing.

Norcross, J. C., Krebs, P. M., & Prochaska, J. O. (2011). Stages of change. *Journal of Clinical Psychology: In Session, 67,* 143–154.

O'Hara, M. W., & McCabe, J. E. (2013). Postpartum depression: Current status and future directions. *Annual Review of Clinical Psychology, 9,* 379–407.

O'Hara, M. W., & Swain, A. M. (1996). Rates and risk of postpartum depression—a meta-analysis. *International Review of Psychiatry, 8,* 37–54.

O'Hara, M. W., Rehm, L. P., & Campbell, S. B. (1982). Predicting depressive symptomatology: Cognitive-behavioral models and postpartum depression. *Journal of Abnormal Psychology, 91,* 457–461.

O'Hara, M. W., Stuart, S., Gorman, L. L., & Wenzel, A. (2000). Efficacy of Interpersonal Psychotherapy for postpartum depression. *Archives of General Psychiatry, 57,* 1039–1045.

Olatunji, B. O., & Wolitzky-Taylor, K. B. (2009). Anxiety sensitivity and the anxiety disorders: A meta-analytic review and synthesis. *Psychological Bulletin, 135,* 974–999.

Olatunji, B. O., Deacon, B. J., & Abramowitz, J. S. (2009). The cruelest cure? Ethical issues in the implementation of exposure-based treatments. *Cognitive and Behavioral Practice, 16,* 172–180.

Olatunji, B. O., Davis, M. L., Powers, M. B., & Smits, J. A. J. (2013). Cognitive-behavioral therapy for obsessive-compulsive disorder: A meta-analysis of treatment outcome and moderators. *Journal of Psychiatric Research, 47,* 33–41.

O'Mahen, H., Fedock, G., Henshaw, E., Himle, J. A., Forman, J., & Flynn, H. A. (2012). Modifying CBT for perinatal depression: What do women want? A qualitative study. *Cognitive and Behavioral Practice, 19,* 359–371.

Oquendo, M. A., Bongiovi-Garcia, M. W., Galfalvy, H., Goldberg, P. H., Grunebaum, M. F., Burke, A. K., et al. (2007). Sex differences in clinical predictors of suicidal acts after major depression: A prospective study. *American Journal of Psychiatry, 164,* 134–141.

Pearlstein, T. B., Zlotnick, C., Battle, C. L., Stuart, S., O'Hara, M. W., . . . , & Howard, M. (2006). Patient choice of treatment for postpartum depression: A pilot study. *Archives of Women's Mental Health, 9,* 303–308.

Perlis, M. L., Jungquist, C., Smith, M. T., & Posner, D. (2005). *Cognitive behavioral treatment of insomnia: A session-by-session guide.* New York, NY: Springer.

Persons, J. B. (2008). *The case formulation approach to cognitive-behavior therapy.* New York, NY: Guilford Press.

Pinheiro, R. T., Da Silva, R. A., Magalhães, P. V., S., Horta, B. L., & Pinheiro, K. A. T. (2008). Two studies on suicidality in the postpartum. *Acta Psychiatrica Scandinavia, 118,* 160–163.

Powers, M. B., Sigmarsson, S. R., & Emmelkamp, P. M. G. (2008). A meta-analytic review of psychological treatments for social anxiety disorder. *International Journal of Cognitive Therapy, 1,* 94–113.

Prendergast, J., & Austin, M-P. (2001). Early childhood nurse-delivered cognitive behavioural counselling for post-natal depression. *Australian Psychiatry, 9,* 255–259.

Prochaska, J. O., & DiClemente, C. C. (1982). Transtheoretical therapy: Toward a more integrative model of change. *Psychotherapy, 19,* 276–288.

Prochaska, J. O., & DiClemente, C. C. (2005). The transtheoretical approach. In J. C. Norcross & M. R. Goldfried (Eds.), *Handbook of psychotherapy integration (2nd ed.)* (pp. 147–171). New York, NY: Oxford University Press.

Prochaska, J. O., DiClemente, C. C., & Norcross, J. C. (1992). In search of how people change: Applications to addictive behaviors. *American Psychologist, 47,* 1102–1114.

Rachman, S., & Hodgson, R. J. (1980). *Obsessions and compulsions.* Englewood Cliffs, NJ: Prentice-Hall.

Rahman, A., Malik, A., Sikander, S., Roberts, C., & Creed, F. (2008). Cognitive behaviour therapy-based intervention by community health workers for mothers with depression and their infants in rural Pakistan: A cluster-randomised controlled trial. *Lancet, 372,* 902–909.

Reinecke, M. A. (2006). Problem solving: A conceptual approach to suicidality and psychotherapy. In T. E. Ellis (Ed.), *Cognition and suicide: Theory, research, and therapy* (pp. 237–260). Washington, DC: APA Books.

Reiss, S., Peterson, R.A., Gursky, D.M., & McNally, R.J. (1986). Anxiety sensitivity, anxiety frequency, and the prediction of fearfulness. *Behavior Research and Therapy, 24,* 1–8.

Resick, P. A., & Schnicke, M. K. (1992). Cognitive processing therapy for sexual assault victims. *Journal of Consulting and Clinical Psychology, 60,* 748–756.

Robertson, E., Grace, S., Wallington, T., & Stewart, D. E. (2004). Antenatal risk factors for postpartum depression: A synthesis of recent literature. *General Hospital Psychiatry, 26,* 289–295.

Robertson Blackmore, E., Heron, J., & Jones, I. (2015). Severe psychopathology during pregnancy and the postpartum period. In A. Wenzel (Ed.), *The Oxford handbook of perinatal psychology.* New York, NY: Oxford University Press.

Ross, L. E., Sellers, E. M., Gilbert Evans, S. E., & Romach, M. K. (2004). Mood changes during pregnancy and the postpartum period: Development of a biopsychosocial model. *Acta Psychiatrica Scandinavia, 109,* 457–466.

Rothbaum, B. O., Foa, E. B., & Hembree, E. A. (2007). *Reclaiming your life from a traumatic experience: Workbook.* New York, NY: Oxford University Press.

Rudd, M. D., Joiner, T., & Rajab, M. H. (2001). *Treating suicidal behavior: An effective, time-limited approach.* New York, NY: Guilford.

Russell, E. J., Fawcett, J. M., & Mazmanian, (2013). Risk of obsessive-compulsive disorder in pregnant and postpartum women: A meta-analysis. *Journal of Clinical Psychiatry, 74,* 377–385.

Sackett, D. L., & Rosenberg, W. M. (1995). On the need for evidence-based medicine. *Journal of Public Health, 17,* 330–334.

Safran, J. D., Muran, J. C., & Eubanks-Carter, C. (2011). Repairing alliance ruptures. *Psychotherapy, 48,* 80–87.

Safran, J. D., Crocker, P., McMain, S., & Murray, P. (1990). The therapeutic alliance rupture as a therapy event for empirical investigation. *Psychotherapy, 27,* 154–165.

Samandari, G., Martin, M. L., Kupper, L. L., Schiro, S., Norwood, T., & Avery, M. (2011). Are pregnant and postpartum women at risk for violent death? Suicide and homicide findings from North Carolina. *Maternal and Child Health Journal, 15,* 660–669.

Sánchez-Meca, J., Rosa-Alcázar, A. I., Marín-Martínez, F., & Gómez-Conesa, A. (2010). Psychological treatment of panic disorder with or without agoraphobia: A meta-analysis. *Clinical Psychology Review, 30,* 37–50.

Schut, A. J., Castonguay, L. G., & Borkovec, T. D. (2001). Compulsive checking behaviors in generalized anxiety disorder. *Journal of Clinical Psychology, 57,* 705–715.

Segal, Z. V., Williams, J. M. G., & Teasdale, J. D. (2013). *Mindfulness-based cognitive therapy for depression (2nd ed.).* New York, NY: Guilford Press.

Sharma, V., & Sommerdyk, C. (2013). Are antidepressants effective in the treatment of postpartum depression? A systematic review. *Primary Care Companion CNS Disorders, 15,* e1–e7.

Shaw, R. J., Sweester, C. J., St. John, N., Lilo, E., Corcoran, J. B., . . ., & Horwitz, S. M. (2013). Prevention of postpartum traumatic stress in mothers with pre-term infants: Manual development and evaluation. *Issues in Mental Health Nursing, 34,* 578–586.

Siev, J., & Chambless, D. L. (2007). Specificity of treatment effects: Cognitive therapy and relaxation for generalized anxiety and panic disorders. *Journal of Consulting and Clinical Psychology, 75,* 513–522.

Silberman, S. A. (2008). *The insomnia workbook.* Oakland, CA: New Harbinger.

Sohr-Preston, S. L., & Scaramella, L. V. (2006). Implications of timing of mater-nal depressive symptoms for early cognitive and language development. *Clini-cal Child and Family Psychological Review, 9,* 65–83.

Spinelli, M. G., & Endicott, J. (2003). Controlled clinical trial of interpersonal psychotherapy versus parenting education program for depressed pregnant women. *American Journal of Psychiatry, 160,* 555–562.

Spring, B. (2007). Evidence-based practice in clinical psychology: What it is; why it matters; what you need to know. *Journal of Clinical Psychology, 63,* 611–631.

Stanley, B., & Brown, G. K. (2012). Safety planning intervention: A brief interven-tion to mitigate suicide risk. *Cognitive and Behavioral Practice, 19,* 256–264.

Stanley, C., Murray, L., & Stein, A. (2004). The effect of postnatal depression on mother-infant interaction, infant response to the Still Face perturbation, and performance on an Instrumental Learning Task. *Development and Psychopa-thology, 16,* 1–18.

Stewart, R. E., & Chambless, D. L. (2009). Cognitive-behavioral therapy for adult anxiety disorders in clinical practice: A meta-analysis of effectiveness studies. *Journal of Consulting and Clinical Psychology, 77,* 595–606.

Stirman, S. W., Buchhofer, R., McLaulin, J. B., Evans, A. C., & Beck, A. T. (2009). The Beck Initiative: A partnership to implement cognitive therapy in a com-munity behavioral health system. *Psychiatric Services, 60,* 1302–1304.

Strauss, J. L., Hayes, A. M., Johnson, S. L., Newman, C. F., Brown, G. K., . . ., & Beck, A. T. (2006). Early alliance, alliance ruptures, and symptom change in a non-randomized trial of cognitive therapy for avoidant and obsessive-compulsive personality disorders. *Journal of Consulting and Clinical Psychol-ogy, 74,* 337–345.

Swanson, M. S. (2010). A pilot study to reduce risk for antepartum depression among women in a public health prenatal clinic. *Issues in Mental Health Nursing, 31,* 355–364.

Tandon, S. D., Perry, D. F., Mendelson, T., Kemp, K., & Leis, J. A. (2011). Preventing perinatal depression in low-income home visiting clients: A ran-domized controlled trial. *Journal of Consulting and Clinical Psychology, 79,* 707–712.

Tang, T. Z., & DeRubeis, R. J. (1999). Sudden gains and critical sessions in cognitive-behavioral therapy for depression. *Journal of Consulting and Clini-cal Psychology, 67,* 894–904.

Tang, T. Z., Beberman, R., DeRubeis, R. J., & Pham, T. (2005). Cognitive changes, critical sessions, and sudden gains in cognitive-behavioral therapy for depression. *Journal of Consulting and Clinical Psychology, 73,* 168–172.

Tichenor, V., & Hill, C. E. (1989). A comparison of six measures of working alliance. *Psychotherapy: Theory, Research, Practice, and Training, 26,* 195–199.

Timpano, K. R., Abramowitz, J. S., Mahaffey, B. L., Mitchell, M. A., & Schmidt, N. B. (2011). Efficacy of a prevention program for postpartum obsessive-compulsive symptoms. *Journal of Psychiatric Research, 45,* 1511–1517.

Tracey, T. J., & Kokotovic, A.M. (1989). Factor structure of the Working Alliance Inventory. *Psychological Assessment, 1,* 207–210.

Van Orden, K. A., Lynam, M. E., Hollar, D., & Joiner, T. E., Jr. (2006). Perceived burdensomeness as an indicator of suicidal symptoms. *Cognitive Therapy and Research, 30,* 457–467.

Van Orden, K. A., Witte, T. K., Gordon, K. H., Bender, T. W., & Joiner, T. E. (2008). Suicidal desire and the capability for suicide: Tests of the interpersonal-psychological theory of suicidal behavior among adults. *Journal of Consulting and Clinical Psychology, 76,* 72–83.

Van Orden, K., Witte, T., James, L., Castro, Y., Gordon, K., . . ., & Joiner, T. E. (2008). Suicidal ideation in college students varies across semesters: The mediating role of belongingness. *Suicide & Life-Threatening Behavior, 38,* 427–435.

Wampold, B. E., Minami, T., Baskin, T. W., & Tierney, S. C. (2002). A meta-(re)analysis of the effects of cognitive therapy versus 'other therapies' for depression. *Journal of Affective Disorders, 68,* 159–165.

Warden, D., Trivedi, M. H., Wisniewski, S. R., Davis, L., Nierenberg, A. A., . . ., & Rush, A. J. (2007). Predictors of attrition during initial (citalopram) treatment for depression: A STAR*D report. *American Journal of Psychiatry, 164,* 1189–1197.

Webb, C. A., DeRubeis, R. J., Amsterdam, J. D., Shelton, R. C., Hollon, S. D., & Dimidjian, S. (2011). Two aspects of the therapeutic alliance: Differential relations with depressive symptom change. *Journal of Consulting and Clinical Psychology, 79,* 279–283.

Weck, F., Rudari, V., Hilling, C., Hautzinger, M., Heidenreich, T., . . ., & Stangier, U. (2013). Relapses in recurrent depression 1 year after maintenance cognitive-behavioral therapy: The role of therapist adherence, competence, and the therapeutic alliance. *Psychiatry Research, 210,* 140–145.

Wegner, D. M., Schneider, D. J., Carter, S., & White, T. (1987). Paradoxical effects of thought suppression. *Journal of Personality and Social Psychology, 53,* 5–13.

Weissman, M. M., Markowitz, J. C., & Klerman, G. L. (2000). *Comprehensive guide to interpersonal psychotherapy.* New York, NY: Basic Books.

Wenzel, A. (2011). *Anxiety in childbearing women: Diagnosis and treatment.* Washington, DC: APA Books.

Wenzel, A. (2013). *Strategic decision making in cognitive behavioral therapy.* Washington, DC: APA Books.

Wenzel, A. (2014a). Integrating psychotherapy and pharmacotherapy in perinatal psychiatric disorders. In S. M. Stahl & I. R. de Oliveira (Eds.), *Integrating psychotherapy and psychopharmacology: A handbook for clinicians* (pp. 224–241). New York, NY: Routledge.

Wenzel, A. (2014b). *Infertility, miscarriage, and neonatal loss: Finding perspective and creating meaning.* Washington, DC: APA Books (LifeTools Division).

Wenzel, A., & Stuart, S. (2011). Pharmacotherapy for postpartum anxiety. In A. Wenzel, *Anxiety in childbearing women: Diagnosis and treatment* (pp. 157–180). Washington, DC: APA Books.

Wenzel, A., Brown, G. K., & Beck, A. T. (2009). *Cognitive therapy for suicidal patients: Scientific and clinical applications.* Washington, DC: APA Books.

Wenzel, A., Brown, G. K., & Karlin, B. E. (2011). *Cognitive behavioral therapy for depressed Veterans and Military servicemembers: Therapist manual.* Washington, DC: U.S. Department of Veterans Affairs.

Wenzel, A., Haugen, E. N., Jackson, L. C., & Brendle, J. R. (2005). Anxiety disorders at eight weeks postpartum. *Journal of Anxiety Disorders, 19,* 295–311.

Westra, H. A. (2012). *Motivational interviewing in the treatment of anxiety.* New York, NY: Guilford Press.

Westra, H. A., & Dozois, D. J. A. (2006). Preparing clients for cognitive behavioral therapy? A randomized pilot study of motivational interviewing for anxiety. *Cognitive Therapy and Research, 30,* 481–498.

Westra, H. A., Arkowitz, H. A., & Dozois, D. J. A. (2009). Adding a motivational interviewing pretreatment to cognitive behavioral therapy for generalized anxiety disorder: A preliminary randomized controlled trial. *Journal of Anxiety Disorders, 23,* 1106–1117.

Winnicott, D. W. (1963). *The maturational processes and the facilitating environment.* London, UK: Hogarth Press and the Institute of Psychoanalysis.

World Health Organisation (2003). *Global strategy for infant and young child feeding.* Geneva, Switzerland: World Health Organisation.

Wright, J. H., Basco, M. R., & Thase, M. E. (2006). *Learning cognitive-behavior therapy: An illustrated guide.* Arlington, VA: American Psychiatric Publishing, Inc.

Yonkers, K. A., Wisner, K. L., Stewart, D. E., Oberlander, T. F., Dell, D. L., . . ., & Lockwood, C. (2009). The management of depression during pregnancy: A report from the American Psychiatric Association and the American College of Obstetricians and Gynecologists. *General Hospital Psychiatry, 31,* 403–413.

Young, M., Fogg, L., Scheftner, W., Fawcett, J., Akiskal, H., & Maser, J. (1996). Stable trait components of hopelessness: Baseline and sensitivity to depression. *Journal of Abnormal Psychology, 105,* 105–165.

Zajicek-Farber, M. (2009). Postnatal depression and infant health practices among high-risk women. *Journal of Child and Family Studies, 18,* 236–245.

Zayas, L. H., McKee, M. D., & Jankowski, K. R. B. (2004). Adapting psychosocial intervention research to urban primary care environments: A case example. *Annals of Family Medicine, 2,* 504–508.

INDEX

INDEX

relapse prevention 113, 188, 189–98, 201, 202
Relapse Prevention Plan 194–8; *see also* relapse prevention
relationships 179–87; development of new 186–7; family members 181–4, 197, 218; friendships 185–6, 197; mother-infant relationship 184–5; spouses or partners 6, 119, 179–81, 182, 209
resilience 23, 26
respect 57
response prevention 82, 147
restlessness 2
risk assessment for suicide 210–13
risk factors: perinatal distress 6–7, 22, 39; suicidal acts 210–12, 213
ritualistic behavior 141–2, 147, 150; *see also* obsessive compulsive disorder
role play 175, 176–7, 180, 185
Rollnick, S. 64–5
Rosenbaum, J. F. 148–149
Ross, L. E. 14–15, 17
routine care/usual care 34, 40–1, 43, 45, 203, 204–5
rumination 16, 26, 116, 167, 179
ruptures in therapeutic relationship 51, 53–6

Safety Plans 214–16
safety signals 146–7
Safran, J. D. 53
scary thoughts 16–17, 61–2, 209
self, sense of 1
self-blame 46
self-care 1, 4, 82, 83, 123–8, 129–30, 209
self-confidence 164, 187
self-criticism 28, 49, 103
self-efficacy 129, 145
self-esteem 6, 26, 112, 130
self-fulfilling prophesies 128
self-harm 210
self-monitoring form 141–2, 149, 150
self-soothing 128, 214
session structure 69–80, 83–4
shaping 182
Sharma, V. 207
Shaw, R. J. 46
Sigmarsson, S. R. 37
single parenthood 7

situation: cognitive behavioral model 20, 22, 25; thought records 98–100
situational anxiety 26, 27
sleep disturbance 2, 32, 61, 114, 123, 126–7; *see also* insomnia
sleep hygiene 82, 124–7, 194
Smits, J. A. J. 36
social anxiety: avoidance 136; case examples 27, 199; efficacy of CBT 37, 38; estimated social cost 217; exposure 137, 138, 139, 142–3; new relationships 186; prevalence 5; symptoms and diagnosis 3
social support 42, 169–70, 202; group approaches 41, 204; lack of 6, 17; new relationships 186–7; as protective factor against suicide 211, 213, 216
socioeconomic status (SES) 7, 17
Socratic questioning 9, 44
Sommerdyk, C. 207
Spinelli, M. G. 9
spirituality 211, 213
spouses or partners 6, 119, 179–81, 182, 209
stages of change model 63, 67, 69
stimulus control 126
stonewalling 180
Strauss, J. L. 53
strengths: case examples 27, 28, 30, 31; cognitive case conceptualization 23, 24; motivational interviewing 64; recognition of 32
stress: case examples 32; cognitive behavioral model 20; diathesis-stress approach 17–18, 21; physiological responses to 148; *see also* life stress
Stuart, E. A. 41–2, 43
Subjective Units of Discomfort (SUDs) 142–3, 144, 145, 151, 154
suicidal ideation 2, 193, 210–16
summarizing 51, 65, 70, 77–8
support 61, 63; Relapse Prevention Plan 196; therapeutic relationship 49, 56, 208; *see also* social support
Sydsjo, G. 45, 148

Tandon, S. D. 42
tapering of sessions 198–9, 201
technology 103, 134
therapeutic alliance 48–9, 50–1, 204

246